MILLICAN DALTON

MILLICAN DALTON

A SEARCH FOR ROMANCE & FREEDOM

by

M. D. ENTWISTLE

MOUNTAINMERE RESEARCH
RISHTON - BLACKBURN - ENGLAND

Published by
Mountainmere Research
69 Harwood Road, Rishton, Blackburn,
Lancashire, England BB1 4DH
info@mountainmere.co.uk

Second Edition
Published January 2022
The right of M. D. Entwistle

British Library Cataloguing in Publication Data
A catalogue record for this book is available from the British Library

ISBN-13
978-0-9547213-2-9

This book is dedicated to Dad,
who first introduced me
to the story of Millican Dalton

HAPPY THE MAN

Happy the man, and happy he alone,
He who can call today his own:
He who, secure within, can say,
Tomorrow do thy worst, for I have lived today.
Be fair or foul or rain or shine
The joys I have possessed, in spite of fate, are mine.
Not Heaven itself upon the past has power,
But what has been, has been, and I have had my hour.

JOHN DRYDEN

CONTENTS

PREFACE

The first question I asked upon hearing of a character who quit employment to live life in a cave was "Why?" A short paragraph with accompanying sketch pointed out to me in A. Wainwright's *Pictorial Guide to The North Western Fells* initially brought this subject to my attention; it was small in detail but huge in appeal. Millican Dalton's free choice to become a mountaineering guide and live in tents, caves and huts, and his extraordinary life in general seemed to be quite incomprehensible. Why would someone make such a decision? Why did he dislike conventional living? What urged him to seek a lifetime amongst Mother Nature?

In my mind it would be a safe bet to assume that the majority of the working population would like to follow in Dalton's footsteps—to quit work for good to pursue their own dreams. I am one of those people and his tale was something of an inspiration.

My purpose in writing this book was the result of a search for answers and a desire to learn more. After a preliminary inspection of this character it became apparent that very little was actually known. I harvested only limited and vague information from books and magazines with much of it containing anomalies, contradicting statements and deviations from the truth. I was therefore in more or less the same position as when I started—none the better for my discoveries. If I was to find out more, the only way forward was to research the man myself. Having ample spare time, knowledge of researching and a serious determination to unearth the truth, I proceeded to collate information through a systematic approach.

The material in this book comes from a wide variety of sources. Various institutions had to be visited around the country, such as county record offices, museums and libraries. Valuable and indispensable anecdotes were obtained through interviews with those who knew him in one capacity or another and from scores of letters, emails and telephone conversations.

An undertaking of this nature was not an easy task and many stumbling blocks were encountered en route. Sources of information proved difficult to locate; many existed but tracing them was a different matter. Some people were more than forthcoming with information; others were not. The spelling of his name, which should be straightforward, was most problematic, with spelling mistakes, especially from transcription, ranging from Millicent, Milligan, Milean to the most lackadaisical William, leading to identification difficulties. However, these complications simply formed part of the investigation. As information became fruitful, a fascinating story began to unfold, which, to me, was completely encapsulating. When I began my research I had no intensions of writing a book, but as I garnered a tale together I knew I was on the trail of a great story and the completion of the project was simply a matter of course. A book was merely an afterthought.

Millican Dalton: A Search for Romance and Freedom has been well received, featuring on the lecture circuit, radio and television. It has hit a chord with many other like-minded individuals who related to Dalton's ideals and upon reading this book—one couple created an environmentally conscious luggage brand, musicians waxed lyrically, and an actor produced a one-man play. In the years since the first edition was published in 2004 I managed to unearth more information and photographs, which now form part of this second edition.

Whilst this book is a biography it is not intended to be a distinguished piece of literature or a complete history. To write a comprehensive biography on such a subject would be nigh on impossible. Some of the better known biographical subjects leave easily accessible memoirs, diaries, letters and other personal effects which simplify the research process enabling a quick, detailed picture to be built. This was not the case with Dalton; no memoirs, no diaries. Nonetheless, by researching as widely as possible I hope to have portrayed an accurate and interesting picture. It was my intention to give the reader an insight into the life of a remarkable solitaire, his way of thinking and his daily experiences. This book forms a link between the past and present, and serves as a reminder to all who are engrossed in busy modern-day life, the importance of simple living and the real reasons for life—not the pursuance of material items, but of genuine happiness. I believed it was essential to preserve such an inspirational true-life story for future generations, as with the passage of time, the passing of people and the destruction of written information, the facts can be lost forever.

Consequently this is the story of Millican Dalton, Professor of Adventure.

M. D. Entwistle

Updated January 2022

INTRODUCTION

The solitude of the hills and mountains, and the beauty of the streams and patchwork fields of Borrowdale in the English Lake District have attracted many eccentric characters over the centuries, and, for some, the chance to stay and create a new life was too good of an opportunity to miss.

Amongst these incomers were a small minority who chose to lead a lifestyle so far removed from what is considered ordinary they have earned themselves the title of hermit. Unimpressed by the conventional life journey expected of them, they refused to walk the treadmill of ambition, greed, jealousy and materialism that keeps the rest of us inline with the wishes of our administrators, deciding instead to shape their own destiny in a way most of us would struggle to imagine. Unhappy with the burden of modern living and disillusioned conformity, they threw away everything to live amongst Nature in caves, tents and huts, with only life's necessities.

Most have been eclipsed by history, but for others their labours have made an everlasting impression, and they are still acknowledged to the present date. Indeed, Keswickians, for example, have been well primed over the years by the likes of the seventh century priest and confessor St. Herbert, the Hermit of Derwentwater (d.687); the nineteenth century Scottish wandering artist and phrenologist George Smith, the Skiddaw Hermit (1827-1876); and in the first half of the twentieth century by the last of the Borrowdale Hermits—the Victorian adventurer, and erstwhile insurance clerk, Mr. Millican Dalton (1867-1947).

He did what most bored City clerks only dream of, and quit his job with a vengeance for a life in the open air, and never looked back. Redefining the concept of home, from that point forward the ground became his bedroom and a campfire his kitchen. In the beginning he lived in various parts of the Essex countryside, and in later years at Marlow Bottom, Buckinghamshire, spending each summer for nearly fifty years in the Borrowdale Valley.

Millican brings the perceived image of the Lakeland hermit into real life terms because, until recent years, he was still well remembered by so many in Keswick area and beyond. The vegetarian, teetotal, socialist, philosopher and vehement supporter of world peace gained a reputation as an early "Dealer in Adventures," and was a teacher and mentor in the fledgling outdoor pursuits industry. His multi-activity adventure holidays were revolutionary, and his whimsical tours around the mountains of the British Isles and Europe, and his experimentation with lightweight camping equipment mean his name is now synonymous with the great outdoors. Latterly his idiosyncrasies, in particular his radical troglodytic existence in a Borrowdale 'Cave Hotel,' have led many, understandably, to mistake his life as a grand parody.

Unlike the average hermit he was an integral part of the local community who were sympathetic towards his cause, having no apparent objections to his seemingly rebellious, feral, rent free residence down the valley. He stood on his own, but far from antisocial, there were many who visited his hermitage beneath the cliffs of Castle Crag, especially amongst the young summer tourists who climbed the fells and pitched their camps near him. In them he had a ready made audience to which he could proclaim his philosophies. A man truly ahead of his time, he promoted equal opportunities and sustainability long before the terms were coined, and was an advocate of self-development and the development of others.

Millican Dalton: A Search for Romance & Freedom is a collection of facts and personal memories, some written verbatim, others photographed, which offer a glimpse into the peculiar world of a Lakeland legend. Read the stories, and as you ponder the many photographs: look at the faces; appreciate the simplicity; consider the era; absorb the surroundings; place yourself in the picture, and the combination will take you on your own escapade with Millican Dalton.

R. H. Mayson

MR. MILLICAN DALTON

CHAPTER ONE

THE EARLY YEARS

L ife is a journey, but who knows where it will end? Is our destiny predetermined by the Universe or can it be challenged? Millican Dalton elected to find out and a bold decision at the age of 36 to turn his back on a future of comfort and ease changed the course of his life forever; an incessant search for romance and freedom, thrills and adventure, ending a world away from his orthodox beginnings in Nenthead.

Nenthead village, one of England's highest, lay historically in a high remote area of southeast Cumberland surrounded by the rugged Pennine landscape, situated adjacent to the borders of Durham and Northumberland. The discovery of vast quantities of lead and zinc, which could be viably mined, resulted in the London Lead Company (LCC), also known as The Quaker Company, purchasing much of the land around Nenthead. They subsequently expanded an original smelt mill and mine, making it one of the first purpose built industrial villages in Britain.

Whilst the high open moorland may be a thing of beauty it made life hard for the early inhabitants. With a latitude of 55ºN and an altitude of 1434 feet Nenthead yields one of nation's snowiest and coldest climates with an annual average temperature of 6.5ºC. Nonetheless, the LLC played a major role in the development of the village and the surrounding area, providing high standards of education and social welfare. Nenthead was basically born through the necessity of homes for mine employees; jobs were plentiful and the population boomed. Practically all those who lived in or around Nenthead worked for the LCC.

William Dalton, a Quaker, was one such employee who worked as a smelt mill agent and lived on the outskirts of the village at Foulard with his wife Frances. She was part of the Millican family from Alston and stayed at home to raise their seven children—five boys and two girls. As was the norm the wife's maiden name was used as a child's forename and so, unsurprisingly, the second youngest child was named Millican Dalton.

Millican Dalton was born on 20 April 1867 in the family home at Foulard. He was actually the second child to bear the name, but the first, Lucy Millican Dalton, died at the age of two and a half in 1860. The eldest brothers, William Tinniswood Dalton (b.1854), John James Dalton (b.1856) and Joseph Crosby Dalton (b.1858) had reached their teens by the time Millican was born and already living away from home at boarding school. Elizabeth Crosby Dalton (b.1865) and Henry George Dalton (b.1868) completed the family.

Further bad fortune struck the family when Millican was only seven. In 1874, whilst working away from home, William Dalton died of heart disease, aged 47, at The Grove in Ilkley, Yorkshire, where he had been seriously ill for two weeks. His body was subsequently returned home and interred in Alston Cemetery. Frances, now widowed with three children to raise, fortunately had the help of family and friends, and an annuity paid to widows of LLC employees eased financial worries. Additional help was received from her father, Tinniswood Millican, who for many years was Resident Manager of the LLC and responsible for lead mining operations in Weardale (Stanhope and Romaldkirk), Dufton and Alston Moor. Evidently he was a wealthy and influential man, highly esteemed and well known for his business capabilities.

To ensure the success of their strict non-denomination education system the LLC required all children to receive schooling from the age of six. Accordingly all the Dalton children attended Nenthead Grammar School until the age of 11 or 12 and then boarded at Brookfield School, also known as Friends' School, Wigton, Cumberland. Pupils were nominated by a Quaker overseer and paid £16 each per annum. School records, currently held at Carlisle Records Office, indicate that none of the children were Quakers or even members of the local Quaker Monthly Meeting. However, William Dalton was a Quaker and on these grounds admission was preliminary granted. According to reports forwarded to Brookfield School, Millican had made 'very good progress in reading, writing and arithmetic' and based on this he was accepted as a pupil on 15 January 1878.

The Brookfield education was intensive and the teachings rather more advanced than at Nenthead School. Subjects studied as part of the curriculum ranged from ornithology, entomology, meteorology, gardening, astronomy, chemistry and human physiology to French and Latin. Each day was lived in strict accordance with the school rules and was twelve hours long. Commencing at 7:00 a.m., pupils rose an hour earlier and were expected to be prepared for a day in fear of the Lord.

Millican soon showed an interest in the activities of the school and became a member of the Band of Hope on 24 April 1878. This was a temperance organisation for working class children, who, along with their teachers, had a common goal to remain habitual abstainers from intoxicating liquors. Membership was through written application with a signed pledge: 'I agree to abstain from intoxicating liquors as beverages.' Efforts by all members helped educate public opinion so that the evils of the 'demon drink' could be diminished and finally abolished. Music played an important role with competitions held between different Band of Hope choirs. Meetings, conducted once a term, composed of lectures and guidance concerning the problems associated with alcohol. As a reward, days out such as visits to the seaside were arranged on a regular basis. Furthermore to his membership of the Band of Hope was his election as curator of the Cabinet Class (a collection of curiosities ranging from an Oriole's nest to roman pottery). It was Millican's responsibility to maintain and catalogue the growing collection of artefacts donated by various members of the community.

From around the mid-1870s the lead industry had fallen into decline due to cheap imports and over the next decade levels of unemployment rose. Population figures for Nenthead plunged by a fifth after scores of families emigrated to the Americas and Australia in search of work. Indeed, Millican's eldest brother, William Tinniswood Dalton, was one such migrant who had moved to London in 1871 where he articled as an architect, before emigrating to Canada in 1880. There he established himself as a prolific architect, designing scores of Vancouver's buildings, and a pioneer mountaineer among the high peaks of British Columbia. Later he would make the first assent of Mount Garibaldi and have Mount Tinniswood named in his honour.

With Nenthead's socio-economic problems in mind, Frances contemplated a move south to North London. Several years prior, in the summer of 1873, Millican's aunt, uncle and cousins had already made the move settling at 92 Bishopsgate Street, Middlesex, to manage a carpet warehouse. A decision was made for her when Tinniswood Millican died at home in West Nenthead House on 2 April 1879. Since William had also died and with unemployment rising there was nothing to keep the family in the region. The children, all well educated, would be limited for employment at their level, and with extended family already living in the city, it therefore seemed a logical destination.

Soon after Tinniswood Millican's death, Frances, Joseph and Elizabeth, along with aunt Isabella F. Burns, James L. Burns and 14-year-old servant girl Annie Thomson also from Nenthead, moved into number 3 Brownswood Road, Middlesex. Funding a move to the capital was not too much of a problem. Frances still received an annuity from the LLC, which, with income from her ample inheritance and board and lodgings from the others, was sufficient for her needs. Although the family had moved, Millican and Henry remained at Brookfield school where they studied until 22 December 1880 before leaving to live in London full-time and continue with their education.

Frances had made a wise decision to move, and the need to migrate south for a better future had been justified, but nevertheless proved to be a huge culture shock to all concerned. For years they had benefited from copious amounts of fresh air, big skies and rolling countryside, but suddenly found themselves in a whole new world of madding crowds and the misery of the dreaded London smog. Over the years smog related deaths rose remorselessly with the worst tragedy experienced in 1880 when two thousand people died in one week. It was a major scourge of Victorian London and left many with debilitating respiratory diseases.

Not totally happy with their new surroundings, the Daltons soon decided to move again and in a bid to find a cleaner, more attractive area to live opted for a home in Highams Park, Chingford, Essex. It was on Castle Avenue near the junction with The Avenue; it was larger than Brownswood Road, had the benefit of a garden, and was reasonably distant from the city. The Victorian house, named 'Hillside,' had architectural character and featured a turret on the corner. This is where Millican had his room.

By now the brothers had become more daring and increasingly adventurous, having grown out of their usual playtime habits. Upon acquiring a length of genuine Alpine rope, Millican began looking for ways in which it could be utilised. Eventually he found that the usual descent from his room to the garden was rather too conventional so he constructed a rope ladder, secured it out of the window and used it in preference to the stairs. As a treat for his brothers, Millican would sometimes let Joseph and Henry make the defiant journey downwards.

Neighbours also found themselves drawn into the vertical manoeuvres emanating from his bedroom window. Willing boys, hauled from the ground to the dizzying heights of the turret in Alpine fashion, were directed to paddle with their arms in order to avoid colliding with the glazed kitchen roof and to continue until they reached the sanctuary of the attic window two stories above the ground. His 'tuition' was also passed onto friends Jack and Mary, and neighbours Dorothy and brother, and although their average age was only seven they quickly learnt to climb trees. On one occasion pseudo 'Uncle Millican' had them sat astride the branch of an old elm tree when their horrified mothers returned shrieking "Like so many birds on a bough!"

In future years Millican became particularly enthusiastic about tree climbing or "boling" with the added safety of the climbing rope. This involved traversing and ascending large oak or beech trees—or any tree with a coarse bark. Substantial trunks offered cracks, chimneys, cols and face climbs and provided excellent substitutes to rock faces. The brothers' spirit of adventure, although in its infancy, then progressed onto recreational camping, which had recently been invented. After obtaining a tent, the intrepid brothers ventured on weekend camping expeditions to nearby Epping Forest, the playground of East London, where hour upon hour was spent in the woodlands improving their camping, campcraft and tree climbing skills.

On one of these expeditions Henry challenged Millican to a fire lighting contest. It was a damp and cold winters day in the thick of the forest, and snow on the ground increased the difficulty of the task, as the wood was wet. Nevertheless, Millican took up the offer and agreed that no artificial means other than matches should be used. As a wind-up, Henry secretly produced some firelighters from inside his coat, which enabled his fire to instantly catch hold. Millican, who was initially amazed, soon discovered the fraudulent act and was not too pleased. On another occasion when offered a thin slice of white Windsor soap masquerading as 'cheese' between two crackers his remarks were unrepeatable. It was perfectly clear at this stage that a sense of humour was not one of Millican's strengths.

After years of childhood fun and adventure, and with their extended education coming to an end, adulthood beckoned. Facing the prospect of work, Millican first sought employment in the heart of the City of London.

The Victorian City of London, unequivocally the world's financial powerhouse, was an immensely complex sphere of banks; stockbrokers and jobbers; insurance brokers and agents; shipbrokers; merchants and dealers in every currency and commodity imaginable. Gainful employment was difficult to obtain, and the only way within the City was through influence. Nepotism ruled and new recruits were generally hired through recommendation.

Consequently, it was through Joseph, who was already working in the mundane world of insurance, that Millican managed to obtain an apprenticeship with the Union Assurance Society (Fire and Life) in their Chief Office at 81 Cornhill, EC. An apprenticeship was seen as the precursor to a career which held out the promise of occupational mobility and improved status—though the status had waned from fifty years prior and wages were poor.

Insurance clerks may have been among the highest remunerated groups in the City's clerk class, but its members were notoriously overworked and underpaid compared to other sectors in the community. Many did not consider pen-drivers, with their inky fingers and shiny trouser seats, as real men, and although being a clerk was a good job for the time, manual workers, who generally earned more than the better educated clerks, looked down on them with pity—after all, for their efforts they had all the drudgery but received few of the rewards of commercial enterprise. Indeed, a large portion of their wages was spent on keeping up appearances—a white shirt with stiff collar and tie; a black jacket and waistcoat; a bowler hat—the prerequisite for any City position.

Upon completing his apprenticeship at the Union, Millican eventually progressed up to the unenviable position of Fire Insurance Clerk. Henry, incidentally, followed his elder brothers into the low-paid fire insurance sector. Nonetheless, the Daltons were not a family without means which, combined with their wages, allowed for a better than average way of life, and sufficient money was available to fund the much enjoyed camping expeditions which had become a major element of their lives.

On reaching the age of twenty, Millican, accompanied by brothers and friends, took full advantage of their spending power and roamed further afield to camp in the wilds of the Lake District, Scotland and Wales—the destinations of choice for Victorian explorers. It was a natural progression opening the door to a world of novel adventures.

Astronomical Report (Read 4. II. 1880.)

We have not had many opportunities of making astronomical observations but we had a view of the sun yesterday & saw 5 sunspots as far as we could make out 2 large & 3 small ones. A sunspot is composed of 3 parts the nucleus which is very dark in the centre, the umbra outside this rather lighter & the penumbra outside of all lighter still & the whole spot floats in the photosphere or bright surface of the sun.

Signed
M. Dalton

Millican Dalton

BROOKFIELD SCHOOLWORK 1880

M. D. Entwistle

FOULARD (LEFT), 3 BROWNSWOOD ROAD (RIGHT)

CHAPTER TWO

TRAMPING AND CAMPING

Victorian camping pioneers existed in an era before workers were entitled to holidays. It was only after the 1871 Bank Holiday Act enshrined in law that Easter Monday, Whit Monday, the first Monday in August and 26 December (if a weekday) should be official holidays, that the common worker was able to enjoy a long weekend to do as they pleased. Even then, paid holidays did not materialise until the Holidays with Pay Act 1938. Life was pretty grim for most. Poverty was widespread and money was hard to come by, meaning that only a lucky few had the disposable income to spend on the luxury of a holiday, especially away from home. Tramping and camping was a pastime predominantly reserved for English middle-class professionals and those born with a euphemistic silver spoon in their mouth.

However, in the last decades of Queen Victoria's reign British society transformed irrevocably; it was an era of remarkable change, particularly in the realm of outdoor pursuits. Without doubt, the instigator was the great expansion of the railways in the late 1860s which brought easy access to the countryside within reach of the masses; previously an area only accessible by several days travel by horse or on foot. The safety bicycle with pneumatic tyres then arrived in the 1880s offering a safe and practical alternative to the penny-farthing. Advances in photographic techniques from William Henry Fox Talbot's paper-based positive-negative system of photography in the late 1830s towards Frederick Scott Archer's wet collodion process on glass-plate negatives in the early 1850s had also helped popularise the outdoor scene by bringing sharp, detailed images of outdoor life to the attention of a flabbergasted public.

Around this period the 'Open-Air Life' gained momentum from what was a relatively sedate emergence into something more mainstream. Nature Lore, Woodcraft, camping, and mountaineering in Britain had become increasingly merged with largely leftwing principles that anticipated the dawn of a 'New Age' of human collaboration, social justice, health and world peace.

The heritage of Woodcraft owed a good portion of its existence to the late Victorians and their visions of 'Back-to-the-Land' that impelled a melting pot of men and women towards another movement, the 'Simple Life.' This urge was driven not only by freedom of choice, but also by religion, political reform, economics, revolution, and health reform. An eclectic mix of dress reformers, food reformers, occultists, homeopaths, animal rights activists, pantheists, feminists, socialists, liberals, anarchists, land reformers and nationalists formed the beginnings of a group that has been termed the 'Illuminated Underground' or 'Romantic Radicals.'

Romantic imagery of the 'Open-Air Life'—colourful depictions of tramping tours, rafting holidays, gipsy caravanning, and extravagant picnics—vaunted by famed authors including, but not limited to, Robert Louis Stevenson, George Borrow, Jerome K. Jerome and Kenneth Grahame, and the deeper philosophical works of leading transcendentalists Henry Thoreau and Walt Whitman, drew larger numbers towards the perceived romanticism of vagabond and gipsy life.

Romantic myths surrounding vagabonds and gypsies, who were at that time, in all reality disdained social outcasts, created a paradoxical image of wanderlust and, ironically, they became characters to be secretly envied or perhaps openly admired, leading to the concept of the 'Wanderer.' Not bound to the occasional days outing, weekend trip or rare week's holiday, they were free souls, able roam the 'open road' at their leisure; to enjoy the simple pleasures of life and revel in the delights of Mother Nature having preserved the freedoms that modern society had rejected in the their quest for betterment. A bohemian rouge for all things gipsy had been born.

These monumental changes to society formed the ingredients for a revolution in the outdoors. Millican and company subscribed to these notions and participated in nearly every aspect of this revolution. On their camping trips, rather than carry equipment in rucksacks upon their backs, which would have been impossible, they loaded vast weights of blankets, heavy canvas tents and photographic equipment onto their bicycles; the use of a bicycle for the transportation of equipment being their equivalent of a porter's trolley. This proved awkward though as the excessive amounts of gear prevented the bicycles from being ridden and consequently they had to be pushed to their destination. On nearing their proposed camp, more often than not in fading daylight, a last push would be made up tracks like Sty Head Pass; an activity at that time known as "pass storming." They would finally pitch their tents in total darkness, most of the time not knowing their exact position. Understandably, jaunts of this nature took significant planning and packing, and proved to be rather laborious.

For years the Dalton brothers struggled with transporting large amounts of heavy equipment in this manner, but during the late 1880s Millican and his inseparable brother, Henry, began tinkering with gear in a bid to make transportation and handling in general more bearable. Their pioneering developments made real progression upon learning of Thomas Hiram Holding's research into lightweight camping, whose vast knowledge of camping skills was derived from an epic 1200 mile crossing of the American prairies in 1853 by waggon train with his parents at the age of nine. In 1877 he then made a journey through the Highlands of Scotland where he camped and cruised the lochs in a canoe, which was the first mode of transport for the early recreational camper. Holding was, in fact, the father of modern recreational camping. Prior to recreational camping, tents had been reserved for the likes of gypsies, vagabonds and the military. Holding, a tailor, had gathered with friends in the rear of his shop on Maddox Street, London, where they discussed ideas on reducing weight. Eventually after in-depth analysis of individual items of kit, an outfit weighing a mere ten pounds was developed; this could be carried in the poaching pocket of a Norfolk jacket. Considering the limitations of available materials, this was a remarkable feat. It was during these experiments that Holding invented the first portable tent.

The design and manufacture of lightweight equipment was all well and good for localised camping, but it still needed transporting to holiday in distant parts of the country. Holding, therefore, unsurprisingly, also became the father of lightweight cycle-camping. A chance conversation with a friend had led Holding to design suitable lightweight kit for cycling and, along with three friends embarked on a cycling-camping expedition in Ireland. He later wrote a book on the subject titled *Cycle and Camp in Connemara* (Warde Locke 1898). Thirteen readers of this book, who remain unknown, showed their interest and immediately contacted Holding. As a result the Association of Cycle Campers (ACC) was formed in 1901, thought to be the first camping club in the world and now known as the Camping and Caravanning Club. The first meet, in the Club's foundation year, composed of just six members, including Holding. These stalwarts cycled from London, Bath and Birmingham with their specially devised lightweight kit and camped in Ickleton Road, on the outskirts of Wantage, Oxfordshire.

Lightweight cycle-camping as a pastime boomed following its inception after rousing a great deal of interest within the outdoor fraternity by providing the ability to carry smaller loads quicker and easier over greater distances. Dalton, though no stranger to camping with bicycles, was an early adopter of lightweight cycle-camping using his own improvised gear having dispensed with his hitherto heavy packs—lightweight tents, cooking utensils, food and clothing could be loaded onto his bike and, although generally ridden, still had to be pushed to their destination on many occasions due to the sheer weight of the photographic equipment, but nevertheless allowed superior control. Their cameras, whose wood and brass construction, combined with glass-plate negatives and a sturdy tripod essential to hold the camera steady for the long exposures required, made them extremely heavy and cumbersome. Despite their weight, a camera was considered an essential item of kit enabling the brothers, but especially Henry, to photographically record every trip with assiduous zeal.

Subsequently, Millican became a member of the ACC and joined at some point between the Club formation and 1907. The nature of his relationship with Holding is unclear, but they undoubtedly knew each other on a personal basis as their paths crossed many times. It is generally assumed in some circles that Millican Dalton helped in the creation of the Club. Supporting this claim was the *Essex Review* 1948 which clearly stated his involvement. Nonetheless, material held in the archives of the Camping and Caravanning Club shows no such participation, although as these archives remain incomplete his part played in the Club's orchestration cannot be categorically ruled out. Also contrary to belief, again according to archived material, he was never Club President and very unlikely to have been a District President. Captain Robert Falcon-Scott, RN, who was to later become known as 'Scott of the Antarctic,' was, however, Club President and headed the organisation from 1909 until his tragic death on the Ross Ice Shelf, Antartica in 1912.

With the dawn of the 'Golden Age' of British rock climbing, a new sport was spawned after Eton-educated Walter Parry Haskett-Smith made his historic, lone, maiden assent of Napes Needle in 1886 and raised his standard by tying a handkerchief to its summit and left it there "fluttering in the breeze." Becoming aware of this and of other great climbing feats, the Dalton brothers, ever keen for new experiences, set out in the late 1880s in the footsteps of legendary names such as J. W. Robinson, William Cecil Slingsby, Owen Glynn Jones and, of course, Haskett-Smith. Years of tree climbing had set the scene for rock climbing to which they soon became empowered, finding the associated exercise, scenery and exposure exhilarating.

Though the great outdoors in general had become increasingly accessible, rock climbing was the latest pursuit which drew a distinct line between the haves and have-nots. It was, in all essence, a pastime for the wealthy, or at least a sport for those of affluence; a realm only open to those who could afford the expensive thick tweed jackets, boots, alpenstock or axe and Alpine rope essential for this most dangerous activity.

Already familiar with the Lake District, in particular the Borrowdale Valley, the brothers searched for their own piece of rock and began to combine cycle-camping with rock climbing; the all important climbing gear was easily carried on their bikes. With free time restricted by work patterns and the inconvenience of travel from the South, public holidays provided the only sufficient opportunity for extended excursions.

Scafell Pike was considered the ideal mountain to pitch camp under, with Wasdale the prime base for many Easter, Whitsuntide and Christmas trips. Wasdale, the so-called "Swiss Alps of England," afforded a training ground for aspiring Alpinists because of its close proximity to the large crags and high fells and was a honeypot for British climbers.

One such Easter camping expedition was described by Mr. G. P. A. Richards, who worked with Millican in the same office, during a lecture at the Collegiate Schoolroom, Potters Road, Barnet for the New Barnet Mutual Improvement Society on 10 November 1890. There he read an essay entitled *Tramping and Camping in the English Lakeland*, illustrated by a number of lantern slides.

Magic lantern slides brought the world to life in pictures and took photographic displays to the next level. Their large scale projected images provided spectacular entertainment and education becoming one of the most popular types of public entertainment until cinema took centerstage. This was one of the main reasons adventurous travellers struggled with cumbersome cameras; it allowed them to document their expeditions to far-flung destinations around the British Isles and distant lands overseas; their photographs then became popular subjects for lantern slideshows in which they could exhibit their achievements to an innocent, paying audience. With a plethora of high quality anecdotes and photographs in their possession, taken on their own adventures, the friends had decided to turn showmen and thought of this as a good opportunity to promote the great outdoors from their perspective, and, to an extent, promote themselves (their magic lantern shows were to continue for several decades; and a very small selection are described hereon).

The *Barnet Press* 15 November 1890 published a report of Richards lecture:

> After a few remarks by the Chairman, the Rev. G. E. Gardner, the essayist explained that he formed one of an adventurous party, who, during the Easter of 1889, explored the rugged wilds of Westmorland and Cumberland, and aided by a number of lantern slides, produced from the photographs taken by the amateur photographers Messrs M. and H. Dalton, who formed part of that, as of every other holiday, proceeded to read his paper. The start from London Euston was made under most unpropitious auspices, so far as weather was concerned, but when Lakeside station, Windermere was reached, the weather was delightful, and the ride on the steam yacht from end to end of Windermere was fully appreciated.
>
> From Waterhead, Ambleside, where the steamer was left, the explorers went on to Rydal where the tent was pitched, this operation taking about fifteen minutes, the rest of the day being spent examining the beauties of this delightful district—Rydal

Falls, the River Rothay, Rydal Water, etcetera, of which some excellent photos were obtained, and then repose was sought and found.

The events of the next fortnight were then both verbally and visually brought under the notice of the audience, who were introduced to mountain, stream, lake and waterfall, with a rapidity that left little time for breath, and which roused in those who were so fortunate as to have personal acquaintances with the district, a vista of remembrances and a strong desire to resist the senses, and as for those who have never seen the places described so vividly, they must indeed long for the time when they too could bid adieu to Barnet, and for a season revel in the enchanted land brought under their notices. Of the lakes, the essayist gave the palm of beauty to Ullswater, with its Three Reaches; but could not assign to any one fall, or force, the superiority. Many were visited, but all seemed to suffer from a lack of water, Lodore, immortalised by Southey, being in particular a mere chasm, filled with rocks riled up in every conceivable shape, but leaving the water to be discovered only by much search.

The adventures met with by the party were numerous and, in many instances, amusing; at one spot where the tent had been pitched owing to darkness coming on, it was found that the water was mostly composed of insects, and only half a mugful obtainable at a time; however, this, insects and all, was soon converted into cocoa, and the campers settled down to an evening meal, forming an object of interest to a party of country folk, who volunteered, with much delight, the information that a dead sheep had been lying in the stream forming the water supply for more than a week. A midnight tramp across Stake Pass was graphically portrayed, the tent being pitched at the top, at 2:30 a.m., and the door left open to enable anyone who was awake at the time to see the sunrise. Only one claimed to have done this, the others not waking before 8:00 a.m., and even he admitted that he might have made a mistake when it was found that a natural phenomenon must have occurred to have witnessed the uprising of the monarch of the day—the tent door having been facing due-west.

An ascent of Helvellyn naturally formed one of the many excursions taken; it was made up the Grisedale Pass and along the Swirral Edge, and from this mountain one of the finest views was obtained, though somewhat obscured by mist. Striding Edge, the scene of the death of Charles Gough, was pointed out, and the audience were reminded that both Scott and Wordsworth have made memorable the fidelity of the ill-fated traveller's. dog.

The essayist, in closing, drew attention to the fact that, unlike an ordinary trip to some seaside resort, the impressions received in a tour to Lakeland are not dissipated away in a month or so of the return, but ever remain fresh upon the memory, ready to be revived by anything calling up the associations connected with it.

Proving successful, and satisfied with the attentiveness of the audience, the friends took their show on the road with a series of winter lectures based on the same theme. A performance at the Toynbee Hall, Whitechapel 24 February 1891 for the Toynbee Camera Club was warmly received as reported by *Photography: The Journal of the Amateur, The Professional & The Trade*:

> Henry Dalton read a very interesting paper entitled *Camping and Tramping in English Lakeland*, an account of a holiday spent in that district, and illustrated with some sixty views taken during the tour.
>
> A description of camp luggage and photo apparatus, and the best way to carry same was given. There is very little difficulty in obtaining suitable camping ground, and very beautiful pictures of places quite away from the route of the usual tourist were shown. Mr. M. Dalton very kindly worked the lantern.

Demand continued and twelve months later the friends returned to the Barnet Mutual Improvement Society for another lecture on 7 March 1892. A report in the *Barnet Press* 12 March 1892 further publicised their exploits:

> The remembrances of the previous paper by Mr. G. P. A. Richards no doubt contributed to the large audience which assembled to hear his essay on *Camp life in North Wales*, and there was no doubt that everyone went away delighted with Mr. Richard's contribution to the many excellent papers delivered that session; this was due not only to the bright, interesting account of a holiday spent in a novel fashion, but also to the photographic souvenirs of the tour reproduced with the aid of the magic lantern by Messrs. M. and H. Dalton.
>
> Starting from Euston, North Wales was speedily brought before the audience by the essayist, and scene after scene came forward with startling rapidity, each being illustrative of some place visited, or some frolic indulged in "far from the madding crowd." At Llandudno Junction the railway officials relaxed their usual severity, and upon being asked the next train to Betws-y-Coed, made a mysterious reference to Betsy Jones; this was a joke and was solved upon arrival at Betws-y-Coed by the discovery that the population of that village consisted almost entirely of persons rejoicing in that surname, the only exceptions bearing that of Evans.

Some miles away from Betws-y-Coed a suitable camping ground was found, supplied with the essentials of camp life—viz., wood and water—well sheltered and commanding a good view of the Llugwy Valley. From the headquarters various excursions were planned and successfully carried out, under all conditions of weather, gloriously fine days, and days of soaking rain, and nights generally spent in soothing and deep slumber, but, one occasion at least, employed in waiting for the hurricane outside the canvas walls to blow the whole colony down the mountainside; this event happily did not take place, and the campers were able to resume their excursions to such places at the Swallow Falls, Fairy Glen, Conwy Falls, and Capel Curig.

The miniature Ffestiniog Railway was used to convey the campers to Trawsfynydd, the place selected for the next camp from which the Dolgellau district and Cader Idris were visited, and the tour terminated in a most fitting fashion by the ascent of Snowdon, when the clerk of the weather was in his kindest mood, and allowed the party the pleasure of gazing on hundreds of square miles of land and sea.

The essay was listened to with much attention, and repeated laughter showed that the numerous jokes with which the essay was interpreted, had told, while the charming views were so well shown by the Messrs. Dalton were greatly appreciated.

Magic lantern shows, whilst attracting reasonable sized crowds, still only offered a limited audience. To supplement them Millican, aiming to enlighten the wider public, took up his pen to write an article for the *Penrith Observer* 12 January 1897 regarding another expedition; this time involving a brush with death.

THE PERILS OF WINTER MOUNTAINEERING

My account of an incident, a narrow escape on the Pillar Mountain, which occurred recently, may be of interest. Three of us were enjoying a winter camp during the Christmas holidays, at the foot of Wastwater. On Sunday, the 27 December 1896, we climbed by the way of Red Pike and Windy Gap to the top of the Pillar Fell. From the cairn we were descending the ridge leading to the Pillar Rock, with the intention of scaling the latter, by routes different from those followed by us on previous occasions.

Snow lay in patches down the ridge, and we enjoyed two or three short "glissading" by the way. At one point the ridge was entirely covered with the snow, which also lined two gullies branching down east and west of the Pillar. Both of these gullies are very steep, and terminate, like most of those of the Ennerdale side of the mountain, in vertical precipices. I, a little in advance of the others, slid cautiously down the snow ridge, and towards the west gully, halting perhaps thirty yards down. My brother, Mr. H. G. Dalton, followed next, and stopped a yard or two above me. We were studying what could be seen of Pillar whilst waiting for the third man, Mr. E. A. Pollard, when we heard a shout of glee from him as he caught sight of the tempting slope. "This is all right," said he, and stooped down in the style know to sliders as "little man." Almost before the words were out of his mouth, however, he lost his balance and sat right down and finally fell full length on his back. We two onlookers reared with laughter at the sudden termination of Pollard's jubilation. But we soon saw it was no laughing matter. The last two attitudes had increased his pace materially and he travelled with force against a couple of jutting rocks. These did not stop him, but slowed him round nearly broadside on, in which position he came down slightly to our left. My brother had in the meantime jumped into the track, and was fortunately able to bring him to a standstill; whilst I, wishing to have some share in the rescue, collared the alpenstock dropped by my brother in his haste, as it was commencing a journey down the gully.

"Are you much hurt?" was our first query; and we were greatly relieved to hear the reply, "No, except for a bit of a bruise on my shin," rubbing the injured member, as he spoke, "but I thought I was a 'goner' that time. I'd quite lost all hope of stopping myself." And indeed a look round convinced us all that, had Pollard not been pulled up by my brother, he must have shot over a sort of nutmeg grater of stones sticking through the snow and thence inevitably right down the gully and over the waterfall at its feet.

After the occurrence we crossed the ridge and descended the other gully as far as its junction with Walker's Gully, where a similar accident (but with a fatal termination) happened some years ago. Just as we arrived there, however, mist began drifting past us, discharging odd snowflakes as it went; and a glance at our watches showed that darkness must soon be upon us. We were therefore reluctantly compelled to forego the chief object of the ascent.

Retracing our steps to the cairn, we were met near the top by a regular blizzard of hard snowflakes, which peppered our faces like shot, several times forcing us to stoop, propped by our alpenstocks, to avoid being blown bodily down the slope. Notwithstanding this disagreeable accompaniment the walk through the mist and gathering darkness along to Black Sail Pass would alone have well repaid us for the exertion of the climb. On our left was a magnificent series of precipitous crags projecting eastward, enclosing deep gullies, the upper lips of the latter being fringed

27

with horseshoe perpendicular inner edges would have furnished fine climbing practice had time permitted.

Next inline was Henry Dalton who wrote an article for *Camping* regarding an expedition to the Isle of Skye undertaken in 1898:

"Well," said The Wanderer, as he stroked his flowing red moustache, "there's provisions for a fortnight—four packing cases full of food, and at Oban we will lay in some coals and firing!"

"Have you got the oatcakes and onions?" asked The Climber.

"Yes," responded The Wanderer. "And the biscuits and coffee, the tea and sugar, the Swiss milk and rice, prunes, nuts!"

"Stop!" said The Climber; "enough!"

This was the prelude to the excursion to the Coolin Hills, the wildest corner of Skye.

It was June, and after a night under canvas above Oban, we boarded the Highland Chieftain in the early morning, and swung off for Ardnamurchan Point and for Loch Scavaig, which runs deeply into the Coolin Hills.

The day was not amiss, nor yet particularly fine, so that as we came near the great crags of Gars Bheinn, with its mad torrent leaping down, it was by no means certain what lay in store for us. There were three of us, hardy mountain climbers and campers, already picturesque, and accompanied by a gipsy tent, a contrivance of wooden rungs and red blankets, under which we were to take refuge.

As we went into the landing-boat among the usual tourist crowd that walks the half-mile to the foot of Coruisk (and ever afterwards says it has seen The Coolins), curious eyes swept us, and their owners wondered what mischief was brewing.

The mischief was that we, the Wanderer, the Climber, and the Precocious Boy, were on foot for a camp at the head of Loch Coruisk.

As the tourists returned to the MacBrayne steamer, the three adventurers were hiding away certain stores among the heathery ground, and extracting from the packing cases necessities for a frugal existence until they could return for more stores. No more steamers might come for a fortnight.

The scene gradually resumed its quietude of desolation; the afternoon was wearing on, and the mists which had wrapped the great peaks of the Coolins had rolled upwards and off. Scarcely a tree was in sight, and the only track in all that stretch of rock and heather was the short footpath from the shoe of Scavaig to the foot of Coruisk. Coruisk is a freshwater loch, about three miles in length, which, from a point about half a mile from the rough Scavaig shore, cuts right into the semi-circle of the outer Coolins, and in all the Highlands there is no wilder spot. Not a hut, not a sheep, not a tree of any size shows in that great glen. Sometimes the great crags hang gloomily over the water, sometimes they break into glens of desolation, and away from Coruisk fleets the bouldered torrent that carries its surplus waters to the sea-loch of Scavaig.

Presently this stream had to be crossed. Stockings were off, and boots put on bare feet, so that we could safely cross the slippery boulders. Then three figures slowly worked round the great ribs of rock and the gigantic boulders, and up and down the heathered mounds. The weights were heavy enough; tent baggage, ice axes, climbing ropes, provisions. One of the trio found he was carrying nearly seventy lbs. Under the cliffs of Sgùrr Dubh the three struggled. Why had they come to do such labour? they asked in their hearts. At last the baggage was thrown down upon a little shore where the mountain-stream joined the lake and the only dry and unrocky place in all that valley. Old driftwood, the remains of climbers huts, was gathered, and smoke of a fire rose in the air. The gipsy tent, too, arose with its red cover; we were at home once more, for every camp is a home. At leisure we noticed the little roses which grew among the sand of the shore of the lake. Now and again a great bird, buzzard or eagle, swept across the hollow glen, travelling from Sgùrr nan Eag to Bidein, or from Ghreadaidh to Dubh. What an atmosphere in those names! Alasdair, Sgumain, Mhic Choinnich, Sgùrr nan Gillean! We felt like prehistoric men or Norse freebooters visiting these solitudes for the first time. At the foot of the loch we had noticed a rather dilapidated boat, oarless, forsaken, once the property of some adventurous sportsman, no doubt.

Someone suggested the capture of this vessel, and so next day we gathered from the debris of the wooden huts suitable strips of planking, and next evening saw us, a veritable Swiss Family Robinson, with packing cases, aboard the risky boat, paddling from the gunwale edge, guided by a long plank at rear, and slowly overhauling the grey surface of the lake.

About mile up we found a low island, one big bed of white and blue hyacinths, and almost covered with the eggs of sea-birds, which rose in alarmed flocks as we landed.

The peaks at the head of the glen, though perhaps four miles away, revealed every seam and gully.

Then came the days of climbing those rude and rough surfaces.

As we waken up in the gipsy tent, we feel the sun warming the air, and there is a sound of humming flies and bees, and the quiet trickling voice of the stream running into the loch; now and again the noise of the morning wind stirring the heather is also heard. Bending to miss the cross ribs of the tent framework, we push out and stand on the little piece of flat land at the head of Coruisk. It is a sensation worth the labour of heavy loads and long journeys. The camp looks up the glen, and over the whole scene there lies a mystery and strangeness beyond all description. Stark and grey the peaks of Alasdair and Ghreadaidh rise from the grey-brown walls of rock that hem in the three-mile glen, and on each flank of the pathless boggy hollow rise crags that put to test the mountain craft of the climber. There is a persistent song from a little bird that flits from rock to rock; he cannot understand the wisp of the smoke which is arising from below the camp tripod, nor those bare white figures that splash in the shallower part of the loch. His ancestors have told him nothing of those restless white bodies which emerge and handle a towel on the sandy shore, while another figure, covered with some kind of raiment, which is not feathers, busies itself with various shining things on the turf. All this time the great hills at the head of the glen have not moved; they have not moved for a million years. Only at unreckonable moments they shiver, and a great crag falls to pieces, and the black gullies resound with the clatter of falling rocks. Today we are to climb up on the shoulders of those gods of the mountains, and, yes, sit on their very foreheads. We shall struggle up those chasms, worn with the coursing of their tears. Perhaps they have self-pity, in that being so old and so cumbersome they cannot leap in the glorious midsummer sun.

We wander in and out of the bogs and up and up the slopes of the hills, till we are confronted by the gaunt precipices of the Coolins. Sometimes, after arduous scrambles, rope-girt, we find ourselves thrust back upon the unsteady scree, to begin again; sometimes we enter gullies, water-pooled, where a dragon must have lurked in bygone days. At times we have to climb accumulations of snow which have escaped the eye of the hot sun. As we come up, one of us touches a great boulder that is waiting his time to jump down the crags; with a roar and a crash he bounds out, and as he goes divides his forces. We are so small on those grey slabs that he does not see us. At last we stand on the ridge, but it is scarcely safe to stand.

On the ridge of Ghreadaidh absentminded admiration of the wildness of the hills is dangerous; there is no grass on which to lie, only narrow razor edge of stone pointing to the sky, and precipices everywhere. Today it is blue weather, and the clouds lie tired upon the sea that stretches to some small rocks upon the horizon. These are the Hebrides. Nearer, Rum, Muck and Eigg dream in strange volcanic shapes on the sea. Once we were not so fortunate on Ghreadaidh or were we more fortunate? As we climbed from Glen Brittle and reached the saddle, Coruisk lay gloomy, with clouds smoking up the flanking crags. A dull and dreadful light lay on the loch, and as we surmounted the ridge, thunder-peals played upon the corries. Suddenly the storm leaped upon us, and all the bare rock crannies of Mhadaidh ran with white snakes of streamlets. The mist enclosed us, and then was flung to the very zenith, and strange grey towers, whose bases were still storm-swept, lifted their heads like phantastic dreams around us. The ridge was swept by a sleety rain, and we felt the moisture soaking every part of the interior of our clothing. A rucksack rolled and slipped over the edge of the ridge, and leaped a thousand feet sheerly into space; it is there, still in some inaccessible ghyll, or wedged on some dizzy rock platform.

Eleven o'clock at night, and it is still light; it seems a pity to enter the gipsy tent, but tomorrow is a new day, and then we intend to picnic by Loch Scavaig. There are no possible visitors within five hours scrambling of that strange shore. The old boat will carry us down Coruisk.

Lectures and newspaper articles illustrating the friends excursions, all portrayed as daring escapades in the wilds of wherever, captured the flavour of the day, but lurking beneath the entertainment and educational aspect lay a degree of bravado used to help bolster a growing reputation among the outdoor fraternity and beyond. These were the foundations on which Millican learnt to court publicity; the start of a marriage that would last a lifetime.

Over time he became so engrossed in the outdoor scene that work began to interfere with leisure. Walking and climbing the mountains, fells and dales, and his deep appreciation of the countryside had established a firm bond with the natural world. Aware that leisure pursuits gave him the ability for appropriate self-expression and a feeling of complete happiness he developed an urge to live life in the open-air. As a result, moulded by Nature and fuelled on adventure, he contemplated the idea of becoming a mountaineering guide.

H. G. Dalton

"MILLICAN - GRASMERE 1888"

R. H. Mayson

PIONEERING MOUNTAINEER

CHAPTER THREE

VOCATIONAL RETHINK

Eventually the Daltons moved as a family unit from Highams Park to 99 Osbaldeston Road, Stoke Newington; a more than savvy option for Joseph and Millican who only paid their mother 12/6 per year and 6/- per week rent respectively—they certainly lived a charmed life still having the assistance of a servant. Staying in the neighbourhood until some point around 1897 their spirited Cumberland mother then acquired a property at Elm Villas, 226 Hale End Road, Hale End, Woodford Green, Essex for £366.

Prior to 1901 Joseph had married and bought a house on the same road at number 149 Hale End Road. He, unlike his brothers, had progressed on from the world of insurance and was now Examiner of Stamps at the British Government's prestigious India Office, Whitehall—though drastic changes were on the horizon for Millican who was seriously struggling with the concept of employment.

Records within the Union Assurance Society archives show that life within 81 Cornhill was not too far removed from the offices of today, with workplace politics an everyday occurrence. Perennial petty arguments over open windows, the amount of fuel on the stove, office moves, or pens being taken from desks; and complaints about the lift, or the size of cups of tea at the Aerated Bread Company became more than monotonous.

The Union was a cliquey male only environment, whose staff had worked and socialised together for decades. Colleagues became like family, and many family members worked there, which fermented an office full of coded 'in-jokes' and banter.

Despite the pay gap with other sectors, this was a group of middle or lower middle class workers with a relatively good quality of life. Their physical environment within the Union was pretty comfortable, but there can be no pretence that the work was interesting, and the tedium at times increasingly unbearable. In these wretched offices boredom ruled. The inky drudgery of endless insurance policies and stacks of ledgers, crossing t's and dotting i's all day long, made the work repetitive and mind-numbingly dull, leaving clerks exhausted by the end of the day, tired of, not with, their work.

The late nineteenth century may have seen the invention of the career ladder—a psychological tool used by management—offering the possibility of promotion to make workers happier, improve their status, and to some degree deliver an emotional boost, but Millican had no interest of climbing the heights ruled by societies gauge or in toeing the corporate line any longer.

Millican was far from happy at the Union and had not been employed all that long when he realised working life was his prison. Set against the burden of employment and weariness of discontent he had succumbed to ennui and despair and felt an overwhelming sense of restriction, like a caged wild animal. He wanted to be free and live a more adventurous and varied life for the magic of the fells had drawn him into a world of risky enjoyments and bold escapades, where he could celebrate the unexpected and the eccentric. The deciding trigger for change was Henry David Thoreau's book, *Walden; or, Life in the Woods* (1854). Upon reading this and absorbing Thoreau's doctrine, Millican finalised plans to live as a free range human and to embark on a voyage of social experimentation and independence.

The animal roared and from this point forward Millican would gamble everything in order to treat his life as a chemical experiment. Setting the wheels in motion at the start of February 1899 he set out in search of his own ideal corner of England in which to live. His first step was to place classified advertisements in the press—a pivotal period that would transform the rest of his life.

UPTON PARK AND DAGENHAM GAZETTE
4 FEBRUARY 1899

LAND, COTTAGE, ORCHARD—Wanted, to RENT or PURCHASE, PLOT,
in retired situation; with or without cottage (any state of repair) and orchard:
within 20 miles of London; Essex preferred.
Dalton, Elm-Villas, Hale-End, Woodford Green, Essex.

BARKING, EAST HAM & ILFORD ADVERTISER
14 JUNE 1902

ORCHARD wanted; in good bearing, in neighbourhood of London.
Also Plot of Land,
1/2 to 2 acres; in retired situation; not more than 25 miles out.
Dalton, Elm-Villas, Hale-End, Essex.

Initially, in order to overcome his unhappiness, whilst the search for land continued, he escaped the chaos of the City, to some extent, by acquiring a plot in the rural farming community of Thornwood, North Weald, Essex. Dalton's plot, referred to as "Esperança," a Portuguese name meaning hope, was a permanent base on which he made home—nothing more than a primitive portable tent, with a ground sheet, blankets, and a few useful cooking utensils—amongst extensive hectares of farmland sometime between 1899 and 1901. Other residents of Thornwood made up the small community; immediately adjacent was shipping clerk and climbing companion, Ernest Pollard, who had also chosen a life under canvas; whilst the Flemings, Neales and Foresters made bricks and mortar homes their preference.

Short-term happiness was found, however the twenty mile commute into the City and the continual boredom of daily working life still proved too much. Consequently a philosophy, using *Walden* as a foundation, was developed in which he firmly believed—a philosophy that would enable him to live life exactly how he wanted.

The foundation of his theory of life, as will become clear, was centred on romance, freedom, self-reliance and escapism, bringing together a collection of progressive beliefs including pacifism, vegetarianism, teetotalism; and socialism, especially its principles of equality and social justice.

This *was* Millican Dalton, and on these principles he stood firm. Without any concerns of selfishness or self-importance, the basis of his philosophy predominantly revolved around himself; a non-conformation with societies expectations was number one priority. Lifestyle, pastimes and ideals, chosen carefully to work in perfect harmony, all formed part of a determination to shape a better future with the sole purpose of preventing a return of that feeling of restraint.

Energised with this newfound, life changing philosophy and guided by desire he pursued his dreams of freedom wholeheartedly. Realising that a self-sufficient existence was achievable funded by means of a small, private income, it was without hesitation that Dalton executed his exit strategy and in 1903 exchanged convention for self-fulfilment. Abandoning the regularity of a normal workday routine he headed into the great outdoors—not just for the weekend, for the summer holidays, or even a year—but for a lifetime. "I felt stifled," he said, "day after day I went to the office at the same time. But this was not the life for me. I gave up my job in the commercial world and set out to seek romance and freedom."

Successfully accomplishing his first goal, upon resigning from his job at the Union Assurance Society he remained on his plot of land and soon became accustomed to his newfound freedom and was basically thankful for the opportunity to live in the outdoors as a way of life, and to wake each morning to a day he could call his own.

Characteristics of romance, the imaginative projection of the real world, include an examination of personality and the potential of the mind, a focus on one's passions and creative spirit at the cost of rules and protocol; and a greater appreciation of the beauties of Nature. Through adopting these notions and looking at life in a different perspective—basically through rose tinted spectacles—life in general could be carefree and more enjoyable, even downbeat situations could be perceived as idealistic. Clarifying the benefits of camping in a future *Fell and Rock Climbing Club Journal* (1913, titled *A Camping Holiday*) he wrote:

> Camping provides the completest possible change from ordinary civilised town existence; and, being the healthiest kind of life, as well as the jolliest and most unconventional, is the best antidote to the rush and stress of city work. The open-air life has been found by experience to be a cure, not a cause, of rheumatism, as it is likewise for consumption and neurasthenia.
>
> Among the many advantages camping has over house or hotel, the chief is that one is in the open-air in view of the ever-varying aspects of mountain, lake and river, from getting up to bedtime. Camping also combines perfectly with other open-air sports and pursuits—such as rowing, mountaineering, fishing, swimming, painting, botanising, and the study of wildlife.

Millican's article is of significant interest and provides a firsthand insight into what factor health may have possibly played in his decision to quit work. As stated, he considered the outdoor life to be a cure and not a reason for rheumatism, consumption and neurasthenia. Did he experience the cures himself, or was he relating to a family member or friend? Considering that, when the article was written, Dalton had lived outdoors for almost a decade, it could be supposed that he was in fact referring to his own vast wealth of experience. It is possible then, with the impression that he gives, a degree of ill health, perhaps acquired whilst living in the thick of the London smog, contributed to his alternative lifestyle.

Did he really suffer from rheumatism and did the exercise of 'open-air sports' ease the pain? Was Millican Dalton seeking the 'open-air life' as a treatment for consumption, better known as tuberculosis? Consumption plagued thousands of Londoners for which Victorian doctors commonly prescribed fresh air. To what extent, if any, did he suffer neurosis? Was his self-help approach and his 'antidote to the rush and stress of city work' intended to cure the problem? Symptoms of neurosis, amongst others, include mild depression and a difficulty in relating to the immediate environment, but without loss of reality and repression. As repression prevents adequate self-expression it would also provide an explanation to why he wanted to search for freedom.

That, of course, is all conjecture, but whatever the truth behind these health issues his direction in life had taken a drastic turn. Not only was his camp noticeably fresher than his previous southern residences, it also provided a vital antidote to the symptoms of conventional modern-day living.

By 1906, at the latest, Millican made another move, presumably after finding a more suitable plot of land, fourteen miles southeast to Billericay. At this stage the district was totally rural and Billericay still had the mentality of a small East Anglian country town, the type that if a stranger walked into a shop all conversations would stop and heads turn to stare. Although awakened somewhat by the arrival of the railway the town remained a backwater deep in pastoral Essex, snuggled among well wooded countryside, farmland and sleepy rural roads yet still only twenty miles from central London. It was a great Plotland area, much of it owned by the wealthy Petre family.

Plotlands, an English phenomenon, owed their existence to the agricultural decline of the 1870s when cheap imports from British colonies and the Americas bankrupted farms which in turn led them to sell off their land cheaply in small plots; offering a perfect opportunity for Londoners looking to flee the cramped conditions of the inner city.

It was here that Millican joined a Simple Life commune consisting of around twenty smallholdings insipidly known as "The Camp," located between Buckwyns and Buttsbury, at the end of a rutted black cinder track running from Perry Street. The Camp, or as one visitor referred to it: "the camp of the open-air cranks," was a nonconformist community of people sharing similar beliefs and values—home to the likes of Gilbert Williams, Secretary of the Essex Socialist Federation, and home colonist S. C. Potter, who championed Socialism and Anarchism with Independent Labour Party and Social Democratic Party comrades around the country.

Buckwyns, as with all Plotlands, evolved outside the conventional planning system and the self-built settlement was tolerated by the local council. Due to the lack of planning restrictions Buckwyns took on a character of its own, and as many could not afford housing anyway, simply made home in tents, old caravans or rustic shacks built from discarded materials—all without water and sanitation.

Millican chose to erect a tent on his acre of freehold land; it had freedom and space; and was very idyllic with a real sense of rural life. Befitting his frugal approach to living was the small-time cultivation of a fruit and vegetable garden allowing for a virtually free source of food; the warmer Essex climate providing ideal husbandry conditions, yielding ample harvests of freshly grown crops.

Yet amid the residents were an element who took this standard of living to the extremes and not long after Millican's arrival the Billericay Rural District Council issued closing orders against a number of Simple Life huts in its district as being "unfit tor habitation." The huts in question were constructed of "old boxes and mud, and in some of them rabbits and chickens were running around on the bare ground."

Family and friends, given no say in the matter, had no choice but to accept and appreciate his simple living, high thinking, down-to-earth and straightforward philosophy of life, although many thought he was somewhat unconventional. With work a distant memory, sufficient time was available to concentrate on the important issues in life such as self-expression, holidays, outdoor pursuits and above all the establishment of his guiding business.

H. G. Dalton

"THE ENGLISH THOREAU"

Aviva Group Archive

UNION ASSURANCE SOCIETY, 81 CORNHILL

CHAPTER FOUR

PROFESSOR OF ADVENTURE

Unsurprisingly, Millican's ambitions had altered vastly from his hopes whilst still a scholar. Long gone was any ambition to be successful in the commercial world—that was left to other members of his family, who where, evidently, very successful in their chosen careers. Instead his dream of working as a mountaineering guide started to materialise.

Publicity was achieved by marketing campaigns that employed the power of media. Classified adverts in target newspapers, considerably cheaper than display advertising, promoted his holidays both locally and nationally. The choice of target newspapers throughout his new career give the impression that his services were routinely aimed at a leftwing audience. One of Millican's opening advertisements featured in *The Clarion*, fondly referred to by its readership as "*The Perisher.*" This was a weekly illustrated journal of social reform; its political articles and editorials aimed to "make Socialists" by explaining the principles of Socialism "in the simplest and best language at our command." Regarded as one of the most influential Socialist newspapers ever published in Britain, it was responsible for creating thousands of Socialists and inspiring a whole movement—the Clarion Movement.

THE CLARION
11 MAY 1906
ENGLISH LAKELAND

Cheap Camping Holidays arranged.

WALKING, BOATING, MOUNTAIN CLIMBING, and NIGHT MARCHING.

Fortnightly from June 16 to August 12.

Fourteen days' tour as above £3 5s., exclusive of rail to camp, about £2 extra.

Personally guided by M. DALTON, Mountaineer,

c/o "Clarion," 72, Fleet Street, London.

Another early advertisement appeared in *Fabian News*, the organ of the evolutionary socialist Fabian Society. This was a free, monthly, private circular distributed to its members, and whilst not intended for the general public, copies were available to non-members on payment of an annual subscription.

FABIAN NEWS
FEBRUARY 1907

The Simple Life can be enjoyed in a Tent at Billericay
Camping Holidays—Tours in the English Lake District, etc.
Boating, Mountaineering, Adventures, etc. £4 5s. for 14 days.
Particulars of M. Dalton, Buckwyns, Billericay, Essex.

Whether or not Millican Dalton was a full member, single group member or simply a subscriber to the Fabian Society is uncertain, but he most definitely identified as a Fabian in some capacity as his name appears in the Society's Executive Committee Meeting Minutes in which they chronicled correspondences on 27 February 1893 from 'M. Dalton, Teetotal Fabians' and then again on 12 January 1894 'Millican Dalton: Sending annual donation of £4, and advice Re: Christian World. Reply we don't think it wise to include ourselves.'

The 1880s had witnessed an uprising in Socialist activity in Britain with the Fabian Society, founded 1884, rooted firmly at its core. Not long after its formation, the original founders were quickly joined by George Bernard Shaw, who, along with some of the most prominent radical leftwing thinkers of the late Victorian era, quickly rose to the leadership and were instrumental in its continued development. Their goal was to bring about a complete restructure of society by means of intellectual debate and parliamentary processes. Propaganda included lectures, publications and demonstrations; though they stood firmly against revolutionary tactics, unlike the communist Marxist parties who adopted violence to overthrow capitalism.

Instead the Fabians adopted a process of slow, bloodless "intellectual gorilla warfare" by infiltrating other organisations including the press, universities, local government, political parties and Trade Unions to spread their democratic socialistic ideals and create changes to society from within. Its 'Basis and Rules' was to 'aim at the reorganisation of society by the emancipation of Land and Industrial Capital from individual and class ownership.' The British Labour Party then grew from the Fabian Society. There can be no doubt about Millican Dalton's political stance.

Millican's initial advertisements were nothing out of the ordinary, but he swiftly masterminded a radical approach. Engaging an unprecedented, authoritative marketing strategy (never before seen to promote outdoor pursuits) using highly dramatic terms to describe his range of activities, coupled with an equally impressive title, added an exceptional degree of excitement to his holiday programme, conjuring up sensationalistic images of pure escapism in the minds of prospective clients.

He began promoting himself as Millican Dalton: Dealer in Adventures, Conductor of Tourist and Camping Parties—the sobriquet said it all.

Affordability was the key. The proposition of cheap holidays attracted custom from a wider client base, but still offered the prospect of a decent income, and in all reality a mountain guide could often make enough in two months to sustain them for the rest of the year, which was perhaps handy as he only intended on working for a few weeks each season.

Whilst the majority of ordinary citizens were content getting their thrills from dodging motor omnibuses and the latest films in the cinema palaces, there were those who were tired of ordinary Wakes Week seaside holidays with their donkey rides, Punch and Judy shows, striped deck chairs, dripping ice-cream cones, and strolls along the prom; and others who were simply desperate to escape the stiff formality of routine home duties. They might not have known exactly what they wanted, but nevertheless sought something different and a whole new world away from their humdrum daily lives. Millican Dalton was the catalyst, purveying alternative holidays that sparked their imagination, encouraging others to leave normality completely behind, if only temporarily.

Word of his new profession quickly spread and within no time he was guiding thrill-seeking groups on trips to Ireland, Wales, Scotland, the English Lake District and the River Thames; and for those with deeper pockets guided holidays to Austria and Switzerland.

Dalton made the point: "I would like to tell of many wild expeditions—in Scotland, a three days 'trek' across Rannoch Moor, bivouacking in the open without a tent, passing thro' the dark defile of the Pass of Glencoe at midnight. 'Over the sea to Skye,' we pitched our tent in the savage solitude of Loch Coruisk, walled in by the Cuillin Hills, whose rugged ridges provide the finest rock climbing in Britain; of Kenmare Estuary and Killarney; of Christmas and Easter camps by Scafell; and of camps in Switzerland at the foot of the mighty Matterhorn."

When in England's Lakeland he chose to operate in the north of the District, the Borrowdale Valley acting as the hub from which the locally known Borrowdale Hermit ran his business throughout the summer months. For many seasons at the start of his guiding career, Millican pitched his tent and made camp at High Lodore above the Borrowdale Hotel on a grassy slope beneath the shadow of Comb Crags. This camp was the principle base for his camping tours and used by arrangement with Mrs. Jane Wilson of High Lodore Farm.

High Lodore provided everything he could wish for—mountains and crags, lakes and rivers, and a close proximity to Mother Nature. Dalton wrote about this camp in his article *A Camping Holiday*:

One of my favourite camps is a steep fell side in Borrowdale, commanding a perfect view of a perfect lake, Derwentwater, framed by mountains on each side, with the purple bulk of Skiddaw in the distance; and I have watched many gorgeous sunsets from that spot, as we cooked over a wood fire and dined in the open. On one such occasion we reclined in our red blankets, gazing on the ever changing tints of the sky, yellow, orange, crimson, pink and grey, merging into the blue, purple and violet of the hills—all these colours duplicated in the lake beneath.

Common assumptions propound Millican Dalton as the first Lakeland guide, but, on the contrary, by no means was he the first mountaineering guide in the Lake District or elsewhere for that matter. Historically local shepherds had acted as guides to the first walkers well before he was born. They had excellent knowledge of the mountains and knew of routes up rock faces prior to the advent of recreational rock climbing.

As time elapsed witnessing the decline of traditional Lakeland industries and the increase in tourism, it was realised that, with so many new faces visiting the region, the principle hotels should provide guiding services for their guests. In effect the outdoor scene had become so popular that up to the end of the nineteenth century fell guides were as well recognised in the Lakes as in Switzerland—although the numbers were somewhat less. Guides proved a major benefit to those guests who had insufficient confidence to enter the hills on their own.

One such guide emerged in Wasdale sometime around 1908. Literature from the Wastwater Hotel read: 'A first class Dauphine guide and climber has been engaged, who will conduct climbers on the various climbs in the district at a moderate charge.' His name was Josef Gaspard, a resident guide employed by the season by John Ritson Whiting, who remained a regular at the hotel until the commencement of World War I.

Gaspard was by all accounts a competent climber, but failed to pioneer any routes as he tended to be busy teaching novices and did not generally venture onto the more difficult rock. Boisterous games in the hotel's billiard room—billiard fives and the traverse of the room using the walls and tables—provided entertainment in the evenings, but Gaspard never joined in with the other climbers or "Tigers." They sniggered at the idea of a guide and considered Gaspard more of a servant; after all he cleaned the guests boots that totalled over forty pairs on most occasions. Even before Gaspard's arrival the hotel had hired guides for decades. The hotel brochure for 1869 stated 'Post Horses, Mountain Ponies, Wheeled Carriages, Boats, Guides, Post boys, Boatmen &c. always in readiness.' In reality, early guides acted both as a porter and someone who could point out the right fell, leaving the rest to the "Gentleman Adventurer."

Promotion of Millican's services was not restricted to press advertisements. Valuable publicity was also achieved through word of mouth; trade shows and exhibitions; newspaper and magazine articles; and lectures. Posters placed in shop windows around Keswick—in Maysons' and Abrahams' photographic studios, and in Arden's bookshop, for example—publicised 'Camping Holidays, Mountain Rapid Shooting, Rafting, Hairbreadth Escapes.'

Elsewhere strategically sited placards publicised the favoured phrase: 'Camping and Tramping in the English Lakes.' A close friend and climbing partner, Ralph H. Mayson, whose family owned the aforementioned photographic business on Lake Road, produced a series of picture postcards, which Dalton signed and gave admirers; some including his address doubled as business cards. It was an ideal partnership; Mayson had a deep affinity of photography and Dalton enjoyed striking a pose and made a magnificent subject, becoming the centrepiece of his artistry on many occasions. Besides advertising his services, the Lake Road emporium sold the series of postcards; more than affordable and a favourite holiday souvenir among Victorian and Edwardian tourists. Mayson, who rarely left Lakeland, referred to him as "a true gentleman of the hills," which was probably one of the reasons he became something of a favourite amongst the ladies, though the real reason goes much deeper than that.

Although having made the choice to quit work as an employee, at some point in 1907 or 1908 he decided to accept the position of Secretary for the Co-operative Holidays Association (CHA) at the recently established Newlands Mill Guest House. There he was employed for a season or two as one of the many 'helpers who will promote the intellectual and social interests of the party with which they are associated,' however, he soon, unexpectedly, found himself out of a job.

Additional to the necessary administration duties associated with the position of Secretary, he was also expected to take guests on compulsory rambles covering ten to fifteen miles per day and speak on the natural and social history of the locality. Millican, it seems, had his own agenda, and landed himself in trouble with the management after introducing his group to the joys of rock climbing. Discarding the fact that he was working as a volunteer, these actions were seen as far too dangerous for novices and his innocent initiative earned him the sack. Never one to be disheartened, the unsuccessful stint at the CHA was put down to experience and so he concentrated on his own guiding business.

As briefly mentioned, during the nineteenth century the region's economy had shifted from one dependent on hill farming, manufacturing and mining to an economy increasingly centred on tourism—but it was Millican's intervention that initiated the evolution of the Lake District from a tourist destination for relaxation, contemplation and spiritual breaks into a large scale adventure playground.

Necessitated by this increase in tourist trade was the formation of a work programme that was generally drawn up at the beginning of the year, and was a fusion of structured programs and unstructured spontaneous experiences "arranged by circumstance" as he put it. Dates in the programme could be reserved by individuals, groups or for Club meets. Each year's programme followed the same format so that winters could be spent at 'home' in the south of England, the summer months guiding in the Lake District, several weeks distributed between trips to the Alps for the Alpine season and other parts of the British Isles, and the remaining months following his own adventures. A camping programme from 1913 read:

CAMPING TOURS
Through Lovely Scenery

ADVENTURES - NIGHT RAMBLES - BOATING
RAPID SHOOTING - BATHING - MOUNTAINEERING

Why not have your own real adventures and thrilling experiences, under safe leadership, and study Nature firsthand, instead of merely in books? Camping is a complete change from ordinary existence, and is undoubtedly the freest and healthiest mode of life, the fear of rheumatism is quite baseless, due precautions being taken. Among the many advantages over hotel or lodgings, the chief is perhaps that one is in the open-air in view of the ever varying aspects of the scenery, from getting up to bedtime—and even all night at times.

Select small camping parties (limited to 20) will be personally conducted by

MILLICAN DALTON
(Otherwise known as Robinson Crusoe, Buffalo Bill,
Peter Pan, Sinbad the Sailor, the Wizard of the North, & Co.)
An expert mountaineer and camper well acquainted with the various districts.

ENGLISH LAKE DISTRICT

JUNE 22 - AUGUST 30

SEPTEMBER 27 - OCTOBER 11, 1913

PROGRAM

The address of the camp is:—C/o M. Dalton, High Lodore Farm, Keswick.

SAT— From Keswick Station, coach or walk four miles to the farm.

SUN— Quiet day about camp.

MON— Lodore Falls (pleasant scramble), Watendlath, Borrowdale, Bowder Stone.

TUE— Boating on Derwentwater; Shooting the Rapids; Bivouac on island.

WED— Sunrise Breakfast; Mountain ascent Scafell; Rock-climbing if desired; supper on mountainside.

THR— Lazy day about camp.

FRI— Honister Pass, Buttermere and Crummock Lakes, Scale Force.

SAT— Helvellyn and Ullswater can be visited independently.

SUN— Walk round Derwentwater, by Castle Hill, Friar's Crag, Portinscale, Brandlehow; or quiet day.

MON— Mountain ascent—Great Gable—by most interesting route, passing the Needle and noted rock-climbs, which can be done if desired. Supper out.

TUE— Rafting on the Lake, bathing, picnicking.

WED— Greenup, Easedale, Grasmere, and Rydal. Bivouac overnight in open, or in cave if wet.

THR— Windermere can be visited independently, before returning, via Dunmail Raise, Thirlmere, Harrop Fell and Watendlath to Camp.

FRI— Row round Derwentwater.

Special MOUNTAINEERING weeks will also be arranged, Sept. 27-Oct. 11.

Mountaineering is the best form of exercise; it uses all muscles, develops surefootedness, nerve and self-reliance, in an exhilarating atmosphere, amid scenes of grandeur not otherwise accessible. All the climbs are well known, and selections can be made to suit novices or experts. Climbing in the British Isles is perfectly safe under experienced guidance.

The Program is subject to modification by weather, etc, and is of course typical. It will be seasoned to taste with further real adventures and experiences such as the following:—

- Fording a Rapid River.
- Shooting the Rapids.
- A Dinner of the Savage Club on a Desert Island (temperature permitting).
- A Sinbad the Sailor Act (write for photo card of this, price 2 1/2d).
- Exploration of a Cave.
- Lost in the Mountain Mist.
- A Thunderstorm on the Mountains (weather permitting).
- Dangling over the Precipice.
- Astride the Razor Ridge (photo).
- Ascent of the Needle, Great Gable (photo).
- Climbing a Chimney (photo).
- Varied Hairbreadth Escapes (arranged by circumstances).
- Midnight row on Derwentwater, and Bivouac on island (photo).
- A Sunrise Breakfast by the Lake.

TERMS.

The full tour including two weeks' camping, boating, mountaineering and meals £3
Camping, meals and walking excursions only, per day, 4/-, per week 25/-
N.B.—The 14-day return fare from London is additional 27/-
Less than 3 in a tent and more 'luxury' if desired, extra.

The food provided is simple but good and in quantity to cope with the camp appetite. The cooking is part of the gipsy experience and campers are expected to assist in rotation. This does not prevent anyone going excursions, but it can be escaped if desired by payment of 1/- per week. VEGETARIANS are properly provided for.

Ladies are welcome to the camp. There is nothing new in ladies camping, the custom being at least 10,000 years old. One camping club almost contains 100 ladies.

EASTER.

A Mountaineering party will be arranged, the scenery and conditions at this time being similar, tho' on a small scale, to the Swiss Alps. Camp will be pitched at the foot of Scafell in the best climbing centre.

Cost inclusive of 12 mile drive from and to Seascale Stations, for the 4 days 35/-
Omitting the drives 25/-
Return rail from Euston 25/3

WHITSUN HOLIDAYS.
UP THE RIVER
Maidenhead to Sonning.

The combination of Rowing and Camping allows one to view the river under varying aspects from dawn to dusk. A party will travel from Paddington to Maidenhead on Whit-Saturday afternoon, row up past the beautiful woods of Cliveden to Cookham and camp in a beautiful situation by a good bathing-pool—Thence by Marlow and Hurley to Henley, and pitch on a wooded island below Sonning—Monday back to Maidenhead, and London. A feature of this trip is the navigation of weir whirlpools and their rapid currents.

Charge including rail return fare, boat hire, all meals, lock fees and accommodation in the tents, 25/-

Friday evening to Tuesday morning 7/6 extra.
Week, Oxford and back 53/-
Ladies, 2/4 reduction.

* * * * *

Disclosure of Millican's programme found its way into the press the following year, and so began the long succession of references to his eccentric escapades; refreshing feel-good articles that are always of interest to the public at large breaking up the doom and gloom of daily reporting.

Year after year for almost half century, Dalton retreated to the south of England for its milder winters, returning to Borrowdale the following year with the bluebells and swallows where he would then stay till the end of summer. On his reappearance he would create quite a stir. Local children would run around excitedly, repeatedly shouting "Millican Dalton's back! Millican Dalton's Back!…" To them he was like a movie star and regarded as a celebrity. For friends his reappearance meant the chance of more adventures and days on the fells, and for tourists the opportunity to be guided by the man who was developing a reputation as a leading light.

49

Conceived by many as an all round expert, his wide ranging and mastered skills eventually earned him an impressive accolade, a name which he was very fond. "Among my friends I am known as the Professor of Adventure and during the summer months I conduct parties on expeditions" said Dalton.

No hanging over cliffs, I say,
No desert isles, no wrecks at sea—
One hairbreadth risk per holiday
Is quite enough for me.

Each year I hazard all with fate
(One little slip, and I am done);
My danger is, I ought to state,
A monetary one.

I go away resolved to learn
The rules by thrifty souls applied;
Inevitably I return
Broke to the cheerless wide.

Each day I watch my balance grow
Fine by degrees and smaller still;
Then comes the culmination blow;
Mine host his little bill.

O' tell me not of those who frisk
On brink of cliff or raging foam—
It's nothing to the hairbreadth risk
I run off walking home!

R. H. Mayson

THE HIGH LODORE CAMP

R. H. Mayson

POOR BELAYING TECHNIQUE OR PUBLICITY SHOT?

R. H. Mayson

PROMOTIONAL POSTCARD

R. H. Mayson

PROFESSOR OF ADVENTURE

53

R. H. *Mayson*

"HAIRBREADTH ? ESCAPES"

R. H. Mayson

"CLIMB = 8000 FEET"

H. G. Dalton

KEEPING WARM AROUND THE CAMPFIRE

H. G. Dalton

MILLICAN MAKES CAMP

CHAPTER FIVE

ACTIVITY HOLIDAYS FOR ALL

P roviding a wide, unparalleled range of activities distinguished Dalton from other guides of the day who simply promoted mountain guiding services. His trailblazing multi-activity holidays, undoubtedly the first in Britain, included the usual hiking and climbing, but also integrated expert recreational tuition in camping and outdoor cuisine, rapid shooting, rafting, canoeing and sailing—and geology, botany, debate, philosophy and self-development from an educational perspective.

From a welfare perspective he would advise clients on the correct choice of clothing and footwear for the varying weather conditions so they could enjoy their time outdoors in comfort; a wet, cold or overheating soul would have been put off for life otherwise, as any initiate suffering discomfort on their first camping trip will equate.

Domestic trips ranged from the gabbro rocks of the Cuillin Hills to the iconic shores of Loch Lomond and all the way to Cornwall where the weathered golden granite cliffs meet the deep blue-green Atlantic waves, but it was in the Lakes that Dalton taught the majority of his clients the skills and safety aspects of rock climbing, introducing many first timers to the most exhilarating of sports. Novice climbers, generally taken on the Districts easier routes, enjoyed jaunts to Pillar Rock's New West, Central Jordan and Pendlebury Traverse; to Napes Needle on Great Gable and Dove's Nest in Combe Ghyll, for example.

Lamentably, rock climbing was subject to climatic change, but never one to be deterred by bad weather, the excitement continued whatever the sky could unleash with his clients shown the unexpected benefits of heavy rain. There is, of course, a silver lining to any situation and northern Lakeland, harbouring England's wettest spot, provided ideal wet weather conditions for ghyll scrambling in Lodore Falls, Borrowdale or Stanley Ghyll in Eskdale whilst in spate.

Indeed by many he became known as the "Skipper" for his high regard for water sports; he was as well renowned for sailing as he was for climbing. Rowing and sailing, rather genteel pastimes, could be replaced by the high adrenaline buzz of mountain rapid shooting if faster action was required. This was more often than not undertaken on the three mile northerly course of the River Derwent which connects Derwentwater with its twin lake, Bassenthwaite, because according to Dalton: "Shooting the numerous rapids in its course, and getting the boat back again upstream, provides as exciting and novel a sport as to be had anywhere in the British Isles." Indicating the exclusivity of his holidays he added, "Our camp crews are the only passengers up that river." And if his crews acted as the only passengers on the river, then they were probably the only people rafting on the lake. In the summer of 1912 Dalton and several of his party played potted "Peter Pan" on Derwentwater. Explaining the construction of the raft Dalton wrote: "I discovered some felled trees lying in a wood on the shore; some of them were 35 feet long, and took five men to shift into the water. We lashed seven of these trunks securely together with an Alpine rope, and found the raft would carry a crew of five. We used branches as paddles, and went a long way out from the shore. I also rigged up a Scotch plaid as a sail."

This eclectic blend of outdoor recreation and education, now known, unsurprisingly, as Outdoor Education, was also in complete contrast to holidays offered by the CHA and the scores of competitors promoting outdoor breaks. Crucially, several decades passed before other organisations, for instance the Youth Hostel Association, Outward Bound, the Brathay Trust and Local Authorities, were established and had the inclination to enter the fray; and almost 100 years before the establishment of the English Outdoor Council.

First hand accounts of the various activities undertaken on Millican's adventure holidays and their fundamental qualities exist courtesy of his article *A Camping Holiday* and a submission titled *A Gipsy Holiday* written by W. G. Hanson for *The Boy's Own Paper* published 24 December 1910, both referring to the same holiday in the summer of 1908. Hanson wrote (unfortunately paraphrased for copyright purposes):

> I needed a holiday that would offer a whole new perspective to my everyday existence. My goal? To return into the fold of Mother Nature's bosom, to savage myself for a week at least, and to command the life of a vagrant. The problem? I had no prior experience of camping out, and none of my friends could offer advice.
>
> Then I thought of the English Thoreau; the associate of the Simple Life— Millican Dalton—who for ten months of the year is to be found relishing life in a gipsy tent at Billericay, in Essex, where, on a whim, he fulfils the role of Robinson Crusoe. The other two months for several years past have been spent in the English Lake District; his charming appearance never ceasing to rouse the inquisitiveness of

the conforming tourist particularly around the towns of Ambleside and Keswick. Tall, liberated, sporting, weathered by wind and sun, as unconventional in his dress as in his customs, he could be easily described in the same romantic sentence as Mr. Maurice Hewlett's Jack Senhouse.

I first met his acquaintance at the Newlands Vale Guest House where for two weeks in the month of August he acts as guide, philosopher, and friend to the patrons of the Co-operative Holidays Association; but to understand him fully one must savour his daily routine in the camp he pitches in alternate weeks near the riverside hamlet of Grange-in-Borrowdale, and on the pebbled south shore of Rydal Mere beneath Loughrigg Fell, two miles from Ambleside. He had sent to me a programme which specified night-rambles, mountain ascents, rock-climbing, boating, bathing, cycling, and photography. I was prepared for all, bar the rock-climbing. Despite a note on his handbill that rock-climbing is the finest form of physical application, and that the carefully chosen and well renowned climbs when guided by an expert are completely safe, and although I was fully aware that Millican was considered an expert climber by those in the Lake District, I hesitated a little. However I was reassured by his script in which he said: "Any active walker can become a crag-climber, if he likes, with practice. Nerve grows with experience, and sufficient muscle can also be developed. Besides, skill saves a lot of muscle. The ordinary rock-climbs are not so tiring as might be supposed; there are so many rests while waiting for the other men on the rope to climb."

On Saturday 8 August 1908 I arrived in Keswick, and, following the directions sent, left the Station and headed into the bustling town towards the market square and Moot Hall, and along the Borrowdale Road past Abrahams' photographic studios, onwards to his awaiting gipsy camp. Someone once said that it takes a Londoner to make a gipsy; it is probably true that the town-bred are most suited to benefit from the joys of camp life. Although on the road bound for Borrowdale but a few minutes, gone was the life of the urban starting point, which had long receded from memory; the dark satanic mills, bellowing chimneys and their dark acrid smoke, the hustle and bustle of the streets, and the fret and impatience of which is inherent to all town life I thankfully vacated.

Before stretched the open road, a passageway to freedom—steep banked hedgerows on both sides with treasures of fern and flower and native woodlands— breaks in which disclose sudden vistas of immense beauty; peeps of high fell and rugged crag; wispy waterfalls; lake and idyllic islands; and sparse uplands. The Borrowdale Road is one of the finest and loveliest in England; a road no varying weather can mar; almost more beautiful on sully and stormy days than in blazing sunshine, and at its best when the rain gives over, the clouds break, and the sun shines through causing me to purposefully advanced at a pace which must have made Time shudder with envy.

There was nothing objectionable to break the stillness save my own voice, now attuned to holiday joy; the ring of boots on gravel; the breaking of waves on the lakeshore; and the bleat of startled Herdwicks'. As luck had it there were no hustling motors or charabanc traffic to harrow their way amid a cloud of unstirred dust upsetting the silence.

A coach with a black and white pony between the shafts and a ragged Patterdale Terrier on the seat beside the driver; a stray cyclist repairing a puncture by the roadside; a pedestrian or two; and a few ruddy-faced children playing in the woods around Calf Close Bay were all I came across.

Later that evening I reached High Lodore Farm, perched beneath Shepherd's Crag, and the site of our camp which was to be pitched in an adjacent field. After unpacking the farm cart on which the camping equipment had been transported from Rydal, the first task was the erection of the tents, two for the men at the bottom of the sloping field and one for the young women at the top. Yes, you may be surprised, but there were four ladies among us, three of whom, after seven days in camp at Rydal, had walked over the fells from Grasmere by means of Easdale Tarn, Sergeant Man and High Raise to Borrowdale. The male contingent totalled seven men, including Millican and his younger brother Henry. All three tents were identical being A-shaped with two vertical poles at opposite ends, and stood about five feet six inches high and six feet six inches square, each large enough to house four people. Squat tents of this design have many advantages over the Army bell-tent, principally their ability to resist bad weather much better, and their manufacture from stout calico by far the best material to withstand Lake District wet and gales. Every camper had two red blankets, and of course each tent was provided with a waterproof ground-sheet. After the tents had been erected, and the camp established, a wood fire was lit.

We sat in a circle around the campfire and a holly branch tripod with soot-blackened pot placed over the red-hot coals, after which our evening meal was cooked and shared, and then we retired to our tents for the night in eager anticipation of pending escapades.

The weather clerk looked down on us with great sympathy and of the week that ensued we only had one squally night, when, however, we panicked and thought the tents would be snatched by the high winds swirling around the valley and whisked away into Derwentwater; but, heartened by our conductor, my fellow novices and I took it philosophically so we turned over and went back to sleep. It was a new experience, and one we had all purposefully sought out.

A cold, wet ghyll-scramble up the thunderous Falls of Lodore, and a picnic at Watendlath by the Devil's Punchbowl, and a return trip down the old packhorse track to Rosthwaite and Grange-in-Borrowdale decorated with its twin-arched bridge formed the principle features of the first days expedition.

Then there was a days boating on Derwentwater and the River Derwent, including the shooting of the rapids near Portinscale, and on our return another picnic luncheon on the northern shore of St. Herbert's Island, with a magnificent sunset thrown in—no restaurant can equal the open air on a fine summer day for a spot for dining. On the following day an ascent of 3210 feet to the summit of Scafell Pike, the rocky roof of England, and rock-climbing up the famous Kern Knotts Chimney on Great Gable, with supper on the mountainside by the magnificent waterfall of Taylor Ghyll Force plunging down through a wood of firs, and a descent of the Sty Head Pass at midnight guided only by help of the moon's rays and the faint distant lights of Stan Edmundson's Farm at Seathwaite.

Each morning as we finished breakfast our host would sling a climbing rope across his broad shoulders, and look intently across the lake leaning on his iron-shod alpenstock, handmade by a blacksmith in Chamonix by the way, patient yet eager for us to muster.

Thursday, being what our conductor called an "off" morning, gave us the chance to entertain ourselves, so some, little inclined for exertion, spent a lazy day about camp, or photographing the natural beauties of Borrowdale with which the valley abounds; others, seeking further thrills, went off for more rock-climbing whilst the finite opportunity availed, among them Millican's cousin, Tom Rennison, who on that day daringly climbed the Napes Needle on Great Gable alone without rope or companion. That was Millican Dalton's first classic climb. "I did it alone and without an axe," he said, "but that was a feat which I would not repeat alone now I have had more experience," and he solemnly rebuked the younger man for his rashness.

Then, that same evening, we sat round the campfire, discussing a multitude of topics, but chiefly of climbing and camping, extracting from our leader stories his most unusual and out-of-the-way camping experience in the Isle of Skye a decade before.

"It was quite an expedition," said Millican, "as we were pitched five miles from the nearest house, and we had to take coal, firewood, and provisions for a fortnight by steamer from Oban and to erect a gipsy tent, as the ordinary tents could not stand the fury of the Atlantic gales. The climbing was known to very few at that time, and the climbs, being usually more vertical than the English climbs, were looked upon as more dangerous, but the handholds are more plentiful to make up."

Kicking the logs on the fire, he sent a starburst of orange sparks high into the atmosphere, and stared into the flames, momentarily spellbound in deep thought. Then he plunged into a dramatic performance of his hairbreadth escapes and epic adventures in the back of beyond, and at midnight there was still a lingering afterglow when the full moon slowly rose behind the three little tents, flooding the valleys, crags and Fells of Borrowdale with its celestial glow.

"Wouldn't it be nice on the lake to-night?" said one of the girls.

"Yes! Shall we go?" replied Millican, adding "so four of us commandeered a boat, and rowed the two miles down the winding Derwent, and onto the open lake. Broken silver edged clouds drifted across the moon, and as we pulled lazily along, misty, wispy vapours rose from the surface of the water, veiling and unveiling the surrounding wall of mountains. Landing on one of the wooded islands, we made a big blazing fire of sticks, boiled water in an oatcake tin, put in some slabs of chocolate which one man happened to have in his pocket, dug out some old Swiss-milk tins for drinking vessels, and with some oatcake, had a light impromptu "supper of the Savage Club," and talked of past adventures. Re-embarking, the star-spangled sky was perfectly clear, with faint indications of the approaching dawn. It was four o'clock when we got back to camp, quite ready for the sleep deferred."

The next day we walked to Seatoller and through the shadows of Honister Pass to the green fields and gleaming waters of Buttermere Vale and back; and on Saturday morning we were up before four o'clock and round by Manesty Park to see a most welcoming sunrise; after which we lit a fire and breakfasted beside Myrtle Bay, the impromptu meal being followed by an exhibition of skill on the part of our host in the navigation of a hastily improvised raft constructed of the stems and branches of the trees that grew by the lakeside. After this mirth-provoking exhibition we walked through the sylvan splendour of Brandlehow Woods, and climbed the beautiful, smooth, twin-haunched banks of Catbells to take a last view of the landscape we were about to leave. We looked around in all directions and said farewell to the enchanting combination of hill, lake, wood and dale, and made our reluctant descent towards High Lodore for the final time.

After lunch our party decamped and the cart packed ready for our conductor's return to Rydal and the new week's tours. Proceeding homeward bound, we all left in opposite directions, our paths never to cross again, but frequent reminiscence of our most pleasurable and vigour-bestowing summer holiday will materialise in the thoughts of those who were honoured to revel in a week's hospitality provided by Mr. Millican Dalton, Prince of Good Fellows, and hasten their longing for another gipsy holiday.

One of the female adventurers described her experience as the jolliest, wildest week of her life, whilst another was compelled to record his memories in the form of this short poem:

Sing hey for the joys of a Simple Life
In a waterproof tent near Lodore;
With a heart that rejoices in soft woodland voices,
Or vibrates to the torrent's roar!

Hurrah for a night on the cold, hard earth—
A ground-sheet to save you rheumatics;
And some stuff (meant to eat) left to tickle your feet
And cause, in the night, acrobatics!

What can equal the joys of the cooking that you
Have taken a personal share in?
For it's few, you'll agree, can get grass with their tea
Or attempt other mixtures as darin'.

So here's to the song of the Woodland Life,
The zest of the quest for your forage;
Let the cynics prate still of the joys of the grill,
But give me some rain in my porridge!

You care not a jot for conventional rules—
Don't use china—it can t stand the racket!
Take your egg in your hand (for egg-cups are banned),
And pour out the salt from the packet.

So hey for the joys of the Camper's Life,
Unfettered 'neath skies boundless freedom;
Where the murmuring rills sing the song of the hills
And you don't wear much clothes—you don't need 'em!

Another participant on one of his courses, 'Signet,' commented:

"Of course, to undertake a holiday of this description means that you must give up any 'encumbrances,' and social pleasures are at a discount. However, if health is worth more than fortune; if the possibility of knowing the most beautiful country better than any guide book can portray; if the abolition of any restrictions on time or plans—if any of these things is accounted really worthwhile, then the example of Mr. Millican Dalton, of Billericay, can be safely followed, with the knowledge that supreme satisfaction will follow a short period of acclimatisation, and that you may possibly alter a great part of your future life."[1]

The public exhibitions also continued and 11 March 1910 witnessed a novel experiment, lauded by the *North London Tribune* as a form of entertainment for those in search of a change from the usual stereotyped lantern lecture. *Camping Adventures in British Wilds* was the subject of the charming lecture given by Mr. Henry Dalton and, as they were described, a strong troupe of his friends, at the South Place Institute, Finsbury, home to the world's oldest free-thought organisation.

Illustrated by limelight pictures and tableaux, the lecture was of special interest to holiday campers, Scouts, and, indeed, all who lived in the open air. The camping experiences narrated by Henry related chiefly to the English Lake District, which he specially recommended to holidaymakers who had decided to join or to form a camping party. Speaking from a twenty-three years' experience of camping, he said:

My brother Millican, my friends and myself have been so fortunate to have had only three weeks' wet weather, and only once did we have the disagreeable experience of a stream running through the camp. Sometimes, when the wind was very high, there was a difficulty with regard to the tent, and I remember hearing of a camping-out party whose tent was blown over a wall. According to our own experiences, campers do not go in for botany or any similar pursuits. Referring to our own party, it is our custom, after we have become used to this way of spending a holiday, to camp out for a week in one spot, and then remove to another. This removal is accomplished with the assistance of bicycles, on which the tents and other equipment are placed, and the heaviest part of my own luggage being the photographic apparatus. I consider that the finest photographs are secured at early morning, and somewhat late in the evening, as some beautiful light effects are then obtained.

There is no need for campers to fear that their property will be stolen by tramps or other wanderers. I only recollected two cases of petty theft, and in one of these the thieves were railway navvies, who were, however, caught in the act. It is usual for those who have had some years' experience of camping to sleep in the open whenever the nights are fine, the tents being only used for sleeping purposes in bad weather.

I recall how on one occasion a rat ate a number of eggs which had been placed outside the tent, and we have suffered from thieving dogs, who were particularly fond of butter, and one of these canine robbers once bolted with a canister of butter which he had much difficulty in breaking open.

In the country districts extraordinary things are said about our party. We have been asked "Are you going to Klondyke or the North Pole," and a question sometimes addressed to us is "Where is the bear?"—always accompanied by laughter—while some of the country people think we belong to a circus.

How to light a camp fire is a question that is very often put. "Easiest thing in the world" would probably be the retort of anyone who hasn't tried it. Let him try—if you are not in hurry. I advise the camper to look for elder, larch or pine, as being the best woods for the purpose. Do not use rotten wood. This has lost its spirit, the gas which really makes a fire burn. Avoid, too, waterlogged wood; it will only char or smoke vilely. Do not light a fire in a hole or against a wall. There is an old Irish saying that: "no two people ever yet made a fire without quarrelling," and that is good advice to keep in mind when the risk arises.

The lecture was illustrated by numerous lantern slide views of picturesque Lakeland, Skye, and Killarney, these being shown by Millican. The pictures also showed members of the party ascending the precipitous heights which abound these delightful districts.

After an interval for refreshments some living tableaux vivants, illustrative of camp life under canvas, were shown. The live figures being represented by the Messrs. C. L. Howse, A. G. Everett, E. H. Stirling, L. de Gackowski, Madge Smyth, and Mr. James Evans, during which the audience saw the actual process of pitching a tent in the midst of realistic mountain scenery, the lighting of a fire, the cooking and eating of a meal, and the preparations for turning in for the night. Finally, there was a wrestling bout, the Daltons of course natives of Cumberland; the competitors replete with traditional costume of long johns and embroidered white vests, and black velvet centre pieces worn over the top. The match was decided by the best of three falls, the winner throwing his opponent twice in succession.

There is a fine line between being adventurous and dangerous, but it is enough to create excitement bordering on fear and an uncertainty that Millican capitalised on to add exhilaration to his expeditions, and 'hairbreadth escapes,' as far as others were concerned, occurred on practically every expedition. An account of such an escape was published in the first newsletter of the Northumberland Mountaineering Club dated December 1948. R. K. Vinycomb recalled an adventure to a gully on Scafell during rough weather at an Easter weekend camp in Wasdale around 1912.

After stopping to eat lunch the large party gathered at the start of Deep Ghyll and roped themselves together. Upon the discovery of a peregrines' nest and supposedly due to the curious "peregrin-ations" they jestingly christened the route "Peregrines Gully." Rather than carry their rucksacks they decided to leave them in the little cave that remained unblocked by twenty-five feet of snow.

Passing over a lengthy snow slope, the party was then faced with the challenge of a substantial ice bulge at the top of the next pitch and was overcome by cutting steps with their axes. With half the party having safely negotiated the frozen obstacle, weather conditions took a turn for the worse when a serious blizzard advanced. The "Skipper" decided to lead his party off by the West Wall Traverse, but to make the situation worse the route was blanketed with thick, mirrored ice and gave all cause for concern. With no pause in the whiteout it took the group until midnight to reach camp and George's farm lodgings where they devoured a well-deserved meal of ham and eggs. Once settled for the night all were relieved and happy to have survived, yet experienced, a hairbreadth escape.

Importantly, all guiding was carried out with the addition of a philosophy that was well and truly being lived out. However, Dalton did not stop with his creation of activity holidays; he had bigger plans than that and experimented with new attitudes and challenged conventional wisdom with his introduction of mixed-sex camping parties.

Antiquated perceptions judged outdoor adventure as an extreme pastime, a masculine club open only to the hardiest grizzled explorers. As a result outdoor pursuits and sports in general were routinely considered unfeminine. Millican's groundbreaking activities were seen as highly controversial and guardians of tradition values and common decency believed such activities would encourage loose behaviour—but he was ready to break with tradition and cast off the impediments to personal freedoms, acknowledging that the outdoors and Nature were free to be enjoyed by all.

Common sense prevailed and the mixed-sex group trips continued. 'The charms of camping are well known and keenly appreciated by a growing number of holidaymakers of both sexes,' wrote Dalton. Times were changing and women had already begun to seek liberation and interests free from gender-imposed roles. They sought to empower themselves through their own involvement in outdoor recreation, and this option was facilitated further by Millican Dalton who helped pave the way for positive changes through his progressive thinking, which reduced the gender gap in the great outdoors.

As a social reformer who became well known in the social movement, he would ask female rock climbing novices "Skirt detachable? Take it off!" He offered women breeches to cast off their cumbersome, heavy, ankle length skirts and petticoats designed to avert blushes, so they could feel the rope and move freely as males.

Millican commented on this subject in *The Daily News and Leader*, Saturday 20 June 1914, in an article under the heading *Cycling Notes*:

You may be interested to know that in the Lake District last year there were at least 50 ladies of my personal acquaintance who discarded the skirt even on the valley roads as well as on the crags. For serious rock climbing a skirt is quite impossible, and even on easy climbs it is an element of danger, being apt to dislodge stones on the following climbers. On the simple ground of propriety, a slight consideration of the conditions will show that for any sort of climbing proper feminine costume is really very improper.

To me it has always appeared quite irrational and stupid for a woman to handicap herself needlessly by unsuitable dress in any active sport. I wonder how your prehistoric Taunton correspondent would fancy himself on a cycle in a skirt and corset! He is, of course, ignorant of the fact that Chinese women have worn trousers for thousands of years, and do still—I recently observed one of them in the busy Commercial Road, E., quite unconcerned and almost unnoticed.

Few of the feminine members of my Lakeland holiday camps wear a skirt at all during the while of their stay, either walking or cycling, unless they go into the neighbouring town of Keswick.

Regardless, even the wearing of breeches by women was condemned as immoral. At first the appearance of women in such attire attracted considerable attention amongst sensation mongers, and it took some years for the novelty to wear off.

Millican's contribution towards gender equality through the championing of women's rights should not be discounted, after all this was an era in which women still did not have the basic right to vote.

VOTES FOR WOMEN
12 JULY 1912
Camping in English Lake District for both sexes;
climbing and boating; inclusive terms, 25s. to 30s. weekly.
Write for programme—Dalton, The Camp, Grange, Keswick.

THE SUFFRAGETTE
25 JULY 1913
ADVENTURES FOR WOMEN!
Camping Holidays, Mountaineering, Rapid-shooting, etc.,
25s. to 30s. weekly; for both sexes.
Particulars of DALTON, Post Office, Grange, Keswick.

In addition to the distinct educational and physical benefits of outdoor pursuits, Millican also espoused self-development and the development of others. As a mentor he actively encouraged his clients to take risks and enjoy the thrills associated with hazardous outdoor activities. The potential risks and consequences involved in these activities, and the individual's influence on the outcome promoted personal development. His character-building holidays promoted self-awareness and identity; boosted feelings of well-being and self confidence; developed talents and potential; and enhanced clients lives by helping them fulfil their dreams.

To augment his income, particularly during the winter months, Millican, now a well-seasoned camper, began producing custom camping equipment that was sold by recommendation. Innovative designs, influenced by his own experiences, was purposely of a lightweight concept long before it was commercially available. At first, manufacture was by hand, but the acquisition of a hand-operated Singer sewing machine sped up the process and within no time he was producing scores of tents, sleeping bags and unframed rucksacks.

Designs varied from wall tents and bell tents to tepees and bivouacs. In order to ensure the tents remained lightweight, yet waterproof and durable, their manufacture benefited from a fine Egyptian cotton with a tight weave, which during wet weather would soak up moisture, swell and become waterproof keeping the interior dry, working in the same principle as the more modern branded material known as Ventile. Waterproof groundsheets, supplied to keep the bedding dry, fit the footprint of the tent and pockets running the full length of the flysheet allowed for storage of miscellaneous items. Impressively, even by todays standards, a two-man tent weighed in at less than three and half pounds! Early one-piece tent poles, too long to be carried on a rucksack, were used in the same way as an alpenstock. Evolved designs featured two-piece brass-jointed bamboo tent poles and pegs cut from holly trees, notched to hold the guy lines. Decorations in the form of the heraldic 'eagle displayed' adorned the outside of some tents; the exact symbology of these being unknown.

Gipsy or bender tents, simple shelters made using hazel or willow withies, were also manufactured. The withies, pushed into the ground then bent and woven together forming a strong dome shape, then found themselves covered with cotton blankets or tarpaulin. These geodesic dome tents, with their covers weighted down with stones, could easily withstand intense winds.

For bedding, woollen Jaeger blankets found themselves transformed into sleeping bags with the addition of a zip. An unusual design feature was the ability for the bag's occupants to stand and walk, and detachable hoods, replaceable when necessary, increased comfort and warmth.

Rucksacks, made to order, could be bought in a variety of sizes, with or without pockets. Advertisements specified 'Handicraft by a years user—Millican Dalton. Art green Willesden or brown proofed canvas, light, durable; broad, stiff web shoulder straps, adjustable, unhooking; with pole sling. Much superior to factory made: less bulky that Norwegian, third of the weight and half the cost.'

Not only was his equipment available for sale, it could also be hired, proving to be an invaluable service to the public, in particular to the working classes, and consequently the possibility of camping became within reach of the masses regardless of their social status.

Lightweight camping continued to be a passion and something he spent much time contemplating. Millican was well known to be very pleased with his achievements in significantly reducing weight into more transportable loads and much humour was had regarding his obsession with weight. Typically when camping in Wasdale he would purchase 1/2d. sheets of stamps from the visiting postman which allowed him to send anything from a postcard to a parcel. On one occasion his purchase was greeted with the sarcastic comments "Yes, but think of all the extra weight you are carrying!" Despite his lightweight camping equipment, climbing gear remained heavy and it was not uncommon for 200 lb. loads to be pushed to extraordinary places such as the strategic mountain pass crossroads at Esk Hause!

As regards Esk Hause, W. T. Palmer, author, journalist and fellow rock climbing enthusiast, witnessed Millican on the pass one wet and misty afternoon hunting for "a foolish virgin or other truant from his party." Palmer happily offered assistance, but Millican, well aware of the most likely outcome refused and said he assumed the lady would have wandered down to Brotherilkeld in Eskdale and was probably having afternoon tea at the Woolpack Hotel as they spoke. Millican was indeed correct as most lost souls on Esk Hause unintentionally end up at the Woolpack. As Palmer stated, it is common for parties wishing to visit the Woolpack to descend from Sty Head, but rare for a party making a visit the Woolpack to wander up to Sty Head; but, of course, most experienced ramblers are aware of the rough ground beleaguering upper Eskdale.

H. G. Dalton

MILLICAN'S PARTY WALKS THROUGH GLENCOE

Millican Dalton

1913 PROGRAM

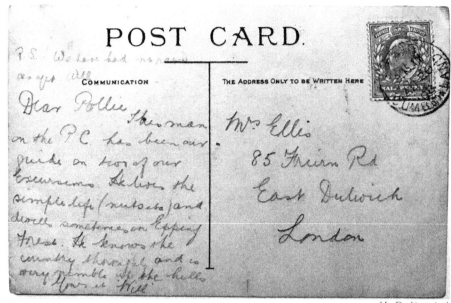

M. D. Entwistle

"THIS MAN ON THE PC HAS BEEN OUR GUIDE"

M. D. Entwistle

"WENT CAMPING ON THE RIVER THAMES WITH HIM"

H. G. Dalton

RELAXING ON THE SHORES OF LOCH LOMOND

G. C. Potts

"ABOVE TAYLOR GHYLL FORCE" - 29 SEPTEMBER 1920

G. C. Potts

"THE ROCK ARÊTE, TAYLOR GHYLL" - 29 SEPTEMBER 1920

G. C. Potts

"ON HARTER FELL" - SEPTEMBER 1917

R. H. Mayson

SCRAPBOOK CUT-OUT

T. J. Rennison

"A SINBAD THE SAILOR ACT"

T. J. Rennison

"THE SKIPPER"

T. J. Rennison

PLAYING POTTED PETER PAN ON DERWENTWATER

CHAPTER SIX

WIZARD OF THE NORTH

Millican's change in lifestyle brought with it a whole new freedom of choice and the opportunity to dress as he wished, not forgetting that Victorian fashion was of a conservative nature. The prosaic male look in general was desperately lacking in creativity, and the military-style uniformity had built a society of men who were happy to see others dressed the same, as opposed to seeing those who craved individuality. Cue Millican Dalton.

Early in his new life he clothed himself in traditional shirts and knickerbockers. This soon changed and his appearance became most distinctive, differing greatly from that of the day, making him instantly recognisable—his histrionic style, according to one commentator: "defined him by some as possibly one of the most singular men this country contained."[2]

People who saw him spoke of similar descriptions. One commented "at first sight a battered Scout hat gave the impression that he was one of that numerous fraternity, but a second glance made it quite clear that no Scout would be content to pass through this country in such a weird costume"[3]; others thought he looked like a veteran of the Boer War, Robin Hood or Robinson Crusoe. Resulting from his unorthodox appearance were many nicknames ranging from Rob Roy and the Goblin to Peter Pan and the Wizard of the North, to name but a few. Distinguished not just in clothing but also in stature, he stood clear of the crowd and was head and shoulders above most, well over six feet tall —"he walked with a long, lithe step, covering a great piece of ground with a stride that seemed to be effortless."[4]

To compensate for life on a minimal income, he adopted cost cutting exercises and began designing and manufacturing his own clothes with the use of his trusty sewing machine. Fashion reforming designs were simple yet strong and efficient, though clearly not desirable to others. For one reason or another the clothes never seemed to be finished and never hemmed, the edges simply turned up and left to fray. Thrifty and alert, he lived off his wits and would keep a keen eye open for discarded fabrics with which he could manufacture clothing or camping equipment—canvas, sail cloth, oil skins, string and rope.

A Tyrolean theme, inspired by trips to the Alps, was the basis for his designs creating an outlandish image to complement his carefully crafted marketing strategy; a brand, whether intentional or not, had been established. Upon his head sat not a Scout's hat, but a large Tyrolean felt fedora that became his trademark. Worn religiously, it was clipped up at the side and decorated with a heron or pheasants feather. On one occasion the brim of the hat was held in place with what looked like a huge ruby, but on closer inspection turned out to be nothing more than a red glass jewelled reflector from his bicycle! Accessorising was visibly essential, so a sprig of heather sometimes complimented the ornamental feather.

The uncomfortable, stiff, starched collar, and three piece black suit had long since gone the way of the dodo; and instead the rest of his attire consisted of a well worn loose fitting shirt, a rough old khaki or dull olive green jacket and brown shorts. The shorts, worn every single day—without fail—had been made from a pair of corduroy trousers cut down to the shin, the lower part then rolled up his sinewy legs to the thigh, exposing a pair of much discoloured and chapped knees; his knees so tanned, often described as copper-coloured, that it was difficult to distinguish them from his shorts. When climbing the shorts would be ingeniously unrolled to protect the knees from abrasion, the remainder of his legs being wrapped in army-surplus puttees; long strips of cloth, spiralled tightly around the leg from ankle to knee to provide support and additional protection.

Dalton had always laid claim to be the inventor of shorts as opposed to the commonly perceived Robert Baden-Powell, hero of the defence of Mafeking and founder of the Boy Scout movement. It was certainly a bold claim to make, but in reality neither was responsible for such an invention. Uniforms of the South African Constabulary and Army consisted of shorts well before Millican Dalton or Baden-Powell thought of them. Shorts at that time had not become a familiar fashion concept and only worn in hot climates principally by soldiers; long trousers or knickerbockers were all the rage. Interestingly though, it is true to some extent that both men had an involvement in the introduction of short trousers.

When Baden-Powell sent a letter to the parents of boys inviting them to the first Scout camp on Brownsea Island 25 July 1907 he used the word 'shorts' in the camp kit list. Existing photos of the Brownsea Island camp, however, show none of the pioneering Boy Scouts in shorts. Baden-Powell used the term 'shorts' again in the first part of *Scouting For Boys* (1908) as part of the 'ideal Scout uniform.' Therefore it is possible that Baden-Powell introduced shorts as a fashion concept for young people and by including them as part of Scout uniform they became popular garments. Fashion, so it would appear to the observer, was not on Dalton's agenda, but he did promote the wearing of shorts to his clients, and so, perhaps, it could be claimed that he introduced shorts as functional sportswear for both sexes.

It may seem a strange concept, but adult males did not really wear shorts prior to the mid-1920s, and even then it took the Men's Dress Reform Party, founded in 1929, to press for change by making shorts a key health feature in their manifesto. The *Tailor & Cutter* journal considered it 'odd' for middle-aged men and elderly gentlemen to be dressed like boys and the National Federation of Merchant Tailors labelled the MDRP 'dress quacks' who were 'monkeying' with men's attire.

A touch of colour was added to his otherwise ascetic clothing with the aid of a red woollen Scotch plaid; this had multiple uses. Primarily it was draped over his shoulders and used as a shawl, enveloping every part of him when it rained; when cold weather approached and temperatures dropped it served as a blanket to supplement his sleeping arrangements; on other occasions acting as an improvised sail for his rafts. Friends and family had also adopted the use of plaid wraps, as did many others. It was a common item judged indispensable for mountain safety by alpinists and pedestrian tourers due to its adaptability, lightweight nature and ability to keep the wearer warm when wet; a potential lifesaver if caught out in the mountains.

On his feet he wore handmade leather boots finished with clinkers and three headed Tricouni nails, generally without stockings or socks; although a comfort item to most, socks were detested and avoided whenever possible. Around camp life was free, easy, careless and more often than not bootless, preferring to walk around barefoot. Elsewhere, lightweight moccasins or sandals; an item considered peculiar to the realm of cranks; became a more comfortable option and worn in preference to the heavy, sturdy nailed boots. On the rare occasions that socks were worn, 'foot cloths'—pieces of cloth covering the heel and sole of the foot—prevented premature wear and the need for darning repairs.

His dress was the same year in and year out, varied only by coloured rags tied around his ankles when rough ground compelled the use of boots; they kept out the scree. A leather belt and handmade rucksack upon the back complimented his hallmark outfit. He was born to meet fate, and needed no valet.

Dalton was a smoker, a chain smoker to be precise and never seemed to appear without an unfiltered, high-tar Wills's 'Wild Woodbine,' which he kept in a small tin box. All strenuous activities were undertaken with a "gasper" in his mouth, and, pausing frequently to light another, would consume each and every smoke as though inhaling oxygen. Whether a genuine lover of smoking or nicotine dependant, after starting he was unable to quit; evidently a cigarette was needed before he could function properly as they helped build up steam!

As a rather strange spectacle for some guests, Dalton frequented the public bar of the Borrowdale Hotel once or twice a week to buy Woodbines in packs of five. Dressed in his shabby Tyrolean gear and contrasting greatly with the hotel's plush interior, he intrigued the residents who looked on with great interest but never scorn. He never loitered and rarely talked or mixed with the hotel guests, probably because his clients were made to wait outside whist he made his purchase. Yellow tar stained fingers and whiskers showed that he enjoyed plenty of Woodbines: "I hadn't better say anything about the tobacco habit. It's a bad habit, isn't it? But we must have some creature comfort. And cigarette smoking is difficult to get rid of. Perhaps I do smoke rather too many cigarettes," confessed Millican.

His smoke stained beard, an abundance of magnificent, manly, Victorian-style facial hair that had turned grey early in life, was generally sported in the form of an unkempt goatee beard, but this was reduced to a moustache should the occasion necessitate.

Sat below the hat were twinkling, shrewd, bright blue eyes contrasting with his permanently copper-coloured tanned face, which some say looked like wrinkled leather. Whether the glow to his skin was acquired through endless time spent outdoors, or through a lack of soap and water, general cleanliness was not a priority and not always practical. A culmination of smells from body odours, wood smoke, tobacco and general outdoor living was, apparently, quite repulsive and good advice was to stand well upwind! His nephew, Nick Dalton, said: "I cannot recall ever seeing my uncle wash, though I suppose he must have done from time to time."

Regardless of the lack of hygiene, camping outdoors did not mean that all home comforts had to be neglected. As a matter of fact, he refused to rough it and was adept at achieving comfort wherever possible. Sleeping arrangements, although Spartan, made for a satisfying nights sleep. His mattress was a springy bed of dry bracken upon which he slept rolled up in the "wondrous comfort" of an eiderdown quilt and in the colder months a long burning fire kept temperatures around the immediate area above freezing.

In fact he was a little too accustomed to sleeping in the outdoors, and this became more than obvious during a visit to an aunt's house. Arrangements had been made to spend the night with the family and, having made up his bed, his aunt thought he would be comfortable, but could not believe her eyes after Millican complained that the bed was too soft and dragged the bedding onto the floor forthwith where he spent the night.

Millican courted jests, somewhat understandably, with his homely appearance and often became a subject for mockery amongst a minority of individuals who sneered at his ragged handmade clothes. Undoubtedly aware that his self-styled Tyrolean image singled him out, he smilingly acknowledged the interest betrayed by glances, seemingly unconcerned with other's attitudes. Whether or not some thought he looked strange, his notorious appearance made him one of the "outstanding sights" of Keswick. All forms of publicity, as any marketeer will agree, are classed as an asset, and as a result his image was used to promote the 'Keswick Boot,' as sold by boot maker Frederick Birkett of 2 St. John Street, Keswick, who sold 'Boots and shoes, specially suitable for the district, made to measure on the premises.'

Reflecting his curious outward appearance was his curious inner self. Dalton was a charismatic and instantly likeable person whose honesty, natural modesty, and unselfish nature made him many friends, though it must be admitted that there were others who disliked him and thought of him as an oddity. As a man of education and culture, he possessed excellent communication skills that enabled dealings with people from all walks of life. Highly intelligent, adaptable and very opinionated he could hold a conversation on a vast range of subjects. Although choosing to reject City life and step away from conventional society, he upheld the right to speak out, never hesitating to voice his opinions on issues that stirred strong emotions within; politics and social injustice bring prime examples. Skeptical of the motives behind unproven scientific theories, he adopted an anti-science stance happily trusting his own judgement. However, the unusual, confident and sometimes forceful expression of his views, both oral and written, sometimes raised eyebrows or prompted ridicule.

Funding this frugal existence was purely through Millican's own means, but nevertheless, handling money on a day-to-day basis was generally deemed unacceptable as it meant enduring the problems associated with it; greed and capitalism forming no part of his philosophy. For reasons obvious to all, dealing with money for food and provisions was unavoidable, but that, apparently, was his limit. In later years he never looked to turn a profit, and frequently refused payment for his services in the form of cash, but would gladly accept gestures of appreciation in the guise of cigarettes, food or newspapers. "In long association, I never knew him charge anything for his services beyond a trifle for camping expenses" wrote friend Mabel M. Barker. At one point, to the astonishment of the Post Office, he even refused payments of interest on his savings because they contradicted his socialist ideals. Here was a man who stood by his principles. He was determined not to be a capitalist.

Maintaining a positive attitude enabled Millican to always see the advantage of getting up and doing something regardless of what the day brought with it. Lakeland mists never daunted him, in all weathers, come rain or shine, sun or snow, he was out walking, climbing or cycling. There was always purpose in his face, a wealth of fell-lore in his keen eyes, something determined and invincible throughout his aspect. In his presence people felt a thrill such as comes to one with the cry of the hounds or at the challenge of a man's eyes when he gallops past on his steed towards a high fence; it was a call to action; an absolute necessity to do or die.

This go-getting attitude did not, however, mean that he hurried. On the contrary, the clock had no hands; life was taken at a laid-back pace and he was never known to rush, always content to do things in his own time. Hour after hour was spent leisurely examining his surroundings. Particular enjoyment was found exploring hill and dale with a rucksack packed with supplies, stopping to brew whenever and wherever he felt the urge. Indeed remnants of his fires dotted the landscape, most of which were lit simply to make a pot of coffee.

R. H. Mayson

THE KESWICK BOOT

Carlisle Library

CORNER OF ST. JOHN'S STREET AND STATION STREET

FRCC Collection

THE INVENTOR OF SHORTS?

H.G. Dale

"EASTER 1913"

Archives

"MILLICAN DALTON, ESQ."

CHAPTER SEVEN

DIETARY VALUES

Campcraft, the art of outdoor living, was an indispensable skill studied as part of Dalton's curriculum, forming a fundamental element of all camping holidays. He possessed years of knowledge and through carefully explained lessons, the novice could learn the expertise of the professional camper. Students studied the purpose of camping; the choicest locations to camp and the vital positioning of tent or bivouac; the principles of sanitation; equipment inventories; and the creation of bedding and fireplaces. With a hands-on approach to teaching, the construction and lighting of fires, their management, and development for either warmth or cooking became crystal clear. Comprehensive explanation on the correct choice of fuel, from kindling to logs, was ensued by enlightenment in the production of outdoor fare and the adaptation of recipes for use on an open fire. Through years of practice he had become a campfire expert. Knowing that larch, juniper, yew and holly burnt the best and longest; his fires efficient, yet effective.

Cooking over real flames, a contrivance from the dawn of man, was considered the only way to prepare food and nothing was substitute for a good old-fashioned wood fire. Apparently a gift of a portable Primus stove by an unknown woman, though accepted in good grace, proved to be rather unwelcome, as being from the old school of thought no way was this sufficiently traditional or satisfying enough to be utilised. Without any further consideration the comparatively clean, kerosene burning stove was demoted to the corner of the tent where it was knocked around for weeks before being discarded.

Every person taught by Dalton soon became acutely aware of his dietetic ideals; he would tell them "I use only the barest necessities of life and am a vegetarian," and on other occasions would cite "I'm a vegetarian and live mainly on wholemeal bread I bake myself." Millican had made the decision to become a vegetarian at the age of 33. From what is known he never publicly explained the reasons behind his vegetarian beliefs, but they most likely relate to the food reform concepts of the Simple Lifer. Food reform in that period invariably meant vegetarianism; it was not a new phenomenon, but it was still stigmatised, and much discussion had in regard to the upholders character and as to whether the diet could sustain a hard-working person—exactly the same discussion which takes place today. Although strictly abiding to these beliefs he was never heard pontificating the virtues of a non-flesh diet and remained dispassionate.

Millican was a follower of the "Wallacite" sect of vegetarians. The majority of noble vegetarians were known as "Wallaceites" or devotees of the system of food-reform introduced by Mr. Joseph Wallace and advocated by his wife Mrs. Leigh Hunt Wallace who was a member of the Vegetarian Federal Union from 1889-1911 and a leading figure in late nineteenth century vegetarianism. As a "Wallacite" he only ate pure, wholesome ingredients, guaranteed to be free from deleterious substances or adulterants; for instance yeast (a ferment, the product of brewery vats, not expelled from the loaf by baking), cheap fats, chemicals, artificial colouring matter and mineral salts.

Baking homemade wholemeal bread to the recipe of Mrs. Wallace, forming the cornerstone of his diet, was a technique which had been mastered, a skill made all the more impressive as it was done without the aid of a conventional oven, and it was obvious that campfire cuisine was a specialty. In addition to bread, he also baked rudimentary oatcakes, scones and the occasional 'fancy' cake as a treat for guests, again made to a "Wallacite" recipe.

He really did use only the barest of necessities and told one visitor to his camp "Use is everything. We dress too much, we eat too much, almost everything we do is too much. Put a man to it, and see what he can put up with. The Chinese live on rice, so why can't we live on bread?" Well aware that a billion people live on rice alone with no nutritional deficiencies he was right to surmise that the ingredients in his bread could maintain a healthy body; his mix was heavy, coarse textured, unrefined bread, packed with goodness and flavour; highly fibrous, high in proteins, carbohydrates and iron and fundamentally filling—it certainly was a meal in itself; but make no mistake, Dalton did not live on bread alone, but still avoided all luxuries—well, bar two.

Benefiting from of a vast knowledge of wild edibles provided a free supply of food to supplement his vegetarian diet. He knew where to look depending on the season, what to pick, and what to avoid. The lushness of the Borrowdale Valley produced copious amounts of fruits, nuts and edible plants. Hazel nuts, which grew near the River Derwent were, according to Millican, some of the best he had ever tasted, apparently being at their best quality in autumn. Berries, including damsons, raspberries, blackberries and bleaberries, growing wild along the lanes, on lakesides, riversides, hillsides and on the valley floors were all put to use. Sometimes the addition of nuts and berries to the bread dough further increased its taste and nutritional value.

More than proficient at catering for large groups of people, much pleasure was had in acting as host; always happy to cater for friends, clients or even strangers to whom he offered his routine menus. The result of his culinary efforts was plain and simple, altering little except for seasonal variations, but he produced tasty and nourishing food, or in the words of one diner "satisfactory and succulent." However, not everyone could stomach the modest catering, proving too unpalatable for some would-be diners due to unintentional ingredients—ash, cinders and insects—which somehow found their way into the billycan. This was a true eye-opener for many first time campers new to camp cuisine, who were only familiar with homemade food.

Of course not all foodstuffs could be foraged from the land and so shopping trips were still a necessity. When resident in the Lake District, trips to Keswick or Plaskett's Store in Rosthwaite were made on his trusty bicycle. Supplies including oats, wholemeal flour and coffee, commonly listed for purchase, were obtained from J. S. Allinson's, grocer and provision dealer, 25 Main Street, Keswick, who offered 'Everything of the best at the lowest prices.' As a rule he only bought raw ingredients from which he could make his own meals, proving to be the most cost efficient and healthiest method. In contrast, whilst based at his southern residence, he continued to fulfil the role of smallholder.

Recognising the value of food and the need for a well-fuelled body and hearty appetite, he commented "After you have been on the fells all day you can eat anything that is plain and wholesome though, of course, you can eat a whole lot of it." However, it was not just essential to feed after a day on the fells, but just as important before the days activities began. After all 'you are what you eat' and if an energetic day was to be had, a good start was in order. Every day commenced with breakfast and generally consisted of what Millican referred to as "parched oats"—dry fried oat flakes, roasted in a pan. The roasting, traditionally a Dalesman technique, added some flavour to the normally bland taste. "For breakfast I have porridge," he said, "I put the meal into a frying pan and partly roast it before I add the boiling water. I am a bit of a sweet tooth and I serve it with syrup."

During the day Brazil nuts, conveniently stored in his pocked, provided a simple snack whilst out and about, especially when climbing to help maintain high energy levels. Evening meals of bread, more often than not accompanied by boiled vegetables, concluded the days intake.

He was a Godfather of Green long before the buzzwords 'sustainability' and 'carbon neutral' were even conceived; and an early adopter of the Three R's—Reduce, reuse and recycle—without the need for government intervention or words of wisdom from environmentalists. An early adopter of creative upcycling, it was found that, as a matter of course, he could supply himself with all the kitchen equipment needed from Grange tip—or any tip for that matter. Grange tip, on the opposite side of the River Derwent to Cummacatta Wood, was a happy hunting ground for Dalton proving that one man's rubbish is indeed another man's treasure. Ever alert for things for free, such treasure was salvaged and put to all sorts of uses. Discarded food tins and pots, to which wire handles had been added, provided cooking vessels of differing sizes. Gadgets of all descriptions, devised with the help of a vivid imagination, assisted in the preparation and cooking of food. Rustic instruments such as tongs, sculpted from suitable lengths of wire, saved burnt fingers. Reclaimed barrels and empty bottles made the imperative transportation and storage of water easy.

Fresh water, a plentiful commodity in the Lakes, was, surprisingly, not always that easy to find. As the story goes, on a scorching day during the height of summer, Dalton and a friend, a school teacher, found that their water bottles had run dry whilst climbing on Scafell, on the rocky upper slopes of which there is no water. In desperate need of refreshment, they began to hunt for a draught of water to cool their parched throats. Although close to the wettest spot in the country they were distant from all visible watercourses and no water was to be found anywhere, even though the previous week had witnessed torrential rain. The friend was close to giving up the search, but Dalton was not beaten, shouting "Come on. I know where there is water!" Leading the way to a nearby weather station, he opened the door, withdrew the rainwater gauge, and without delay the thirsty duo quickly emptied the receptacle of its handsome volume of water. "I always wonder what the keeper said on his next visit," said the schoolteacher "when he found that one place on Scafell had been free from rain during an unprecedented week." Diluting the legend, friend, the Rev. George Chapman Potts, eventually set the record straight "As for the Scafell rain gauge, what actually happened was that at the earliest opportunity the exact amount of water drunk was carefully placed in a bottle from a spring above the col between Lingmell and the Pikes, and put back in the rain gauge. So probably nothing amiss was ever noticed."

From the age of eleven Millican was well aware of the problems associated with alcohol and by all accounts maintained his pledge with the Band of Hope, even in adult life. In preference to alcohol was a heavy consumption of very strong, black coffee that was, after smoking, Millican's only other luxury. "The only recipe for making good coffee is to use plenty of it. I never boil the coffee. I bring it three times to the boil, but never boil it. That's a drink fit for a connoisseur. I can drink coffee all the day long," explained Dalton. Once more syrup was used as a sweetener; he did not hold back and added so much it was said a teaspoon could be stood up in his brew! Becoming rather famous for his addiction to coffee, his adoration for brewing-up was referred to as his "ruling passion." During times of inclement weather cup after cup would be knocked back in anticipation of a settled spell. Freshly baked bread and brewed coffee flooded his camps with a delicious urbane aroma.

Millican's vices rarely, if ever, strayed from coffee or Woodbines, but, surprisingly, the apparent unfaltering abstention from alcohol was said to have hit a stumbling block when Dalton was in Keswick with Ralph H. Mayson, Bill Ireland and a Mr. Barron. Whether through his own choice or by trickery, Dalton succumbed to the intoxicating effects of drink in the bar of the Royal Oak Hotel on Station Street. This fermented much joy among the friends, and after the session the merry group staggered to Mayson's Emporium on Lake Road, where it was suggested Dalton should have his portrait taken to capture the drunken moment.

With the exception of alcohol the consumption of this sufficiently varied, vegetarian diet satisfied all food classes. It was a nourishing, vitamin enriched and high fibre diet. Assured that his diet and the outdoor life increased resistance to illness , Millican said, "I never have a cold."

Millican Dalton may have been an outlier, but he was in fact influenced, to some degree, by lifelong mentor and close friend Reginald Ernest Way. They had met through chance in 1912 when Millican was climbing trees in Epping Forest, prompting Way to strike up conversation.

R. Ernest Way, N.D., was a pioneer naturopath and well-known writer on health, who lived in the exclusive Park District of Glasgow at 3 Woodlands Terrace. Way was the first qualified practitioner in Glasgow and the west of Scotland after graduating at the Edinburgh School of Natural Therapeutics, a practising member of the National Cure Association, and naturopath to the Scottish Society for the Prevention of Vivisection. A dedicated subscriber to the Nature Cure School, he mentored Millican on the subjects of 'natural healing, health fads, fallacies, and facts,' 'winter colds and constipation,' 'manipulative treatment,' 'education for natural health,' 'diet as a basis of health,' and 'nudism and health.'

Both men had fostered a deep mutual respect for one another. Certainly, Way looked upon Millican as a brother keeping a sentimental treasure trove of correspondences and promotional material in a wooden trunk. Amongst his collection of memorabilia was 9.5 mm cine film footage of Dalton rock climbing naked, but it is said that the quality of the film was poor and rather over-exposed!

Considered an integral part of the Way family, in Dalton's later years he stayed with Ernest, his wife Marjory and their son, Kenneth, in Scotland at their property near

Lochlomondside for most of many winters during the 1940s—always pitching a tent in their garden—and was looked upon by Ken as a second father. Marjory, or "Peggy" as Millican referred to her, not wanting to see him go without, took him under her wing, knitting him the woollen socks which helped keep the scree out of his boots, that he reluctantly wore at her insistence. Though, with all due respect, Millican had already dealt with more pain than a little scree in his boots.

H. G. Dalton

"LUNCH TIME"

93

G. C. Potts

"CAMP NEAR DOVE NEST" - MILLICAN WITH ERIC BOWSER & FRIEND

G. C. Potts

MILLICAN MAKES REFRESHMENTS

H. G. Dalton

MANAGING THE FIRE

H. G. Dalton

BREW TIME

CHAPTER EIGHT

DEATH ON GREAT GABLE

British rock climbing had enjoyed a great deal of success since Haskett-Smith's first ascent of Napes Needle with many breakthroughs and spectacular achievements witnessed—though a disastrous accident one blustery Monday morning on 21 September 1903 was to signal an end to the carefree years of the sports 'Golden Age.'

The accident, dubbed "the worst in the annals of British mountain-climbing," left the climbing fraternity reeling after Richard W. Broadrick, Henry L. Jupp, Stanley Risdale and Algernon E. W. Garrett died whilst attempting to climb the treacherous north-facing Scafell Pinnacle, the hardest route on the mountain. Broadrick "exhausted," had exchanged places with Garrett who subsequently lost his footing, then fell, and, tied to all of his companions by an Alpine rope, dragged them 200 feet to the bottom of Deep Ghyll where they all perished. It marked a grim milestone as the first deaths of a group of roped climbers in England and left some of the Lakeland crags robed in everlasting mourning. Indeed, it was a tragedy which took the sport many years to overcome, and one which would not be surpassed for more than 50 years.

Though the number of Lake District climbing fatalities had fallen since the four tragic deaths on Scafell Pinnacle—a product of hindsight and improved rope techniques which improved safety—they were still a sad occurrence. One such fatality, on Sunday 26 September 1909 this time involving Millican Dalton's cousin, added to the morbid statistics.

Millican's cousin, Thomas James Rennison, a native of Kirkby Stephen, Westmoreland, accompanied by his sister, Miss Hannah Crosby Rennison, had reached Dalton's Wasdale Head camp the previous day on Saturday 25 September with the good intension of spending a few days walking and climbing in the district.

Tom had been climbing for three years, and during that time had endeared himself to all who had the privilege of climbing with him; especially during the year of 1909, when he climbed more than usual, and his climbing friends had more opportunity of appreciating his kind-heartedness, his extreme generosity, his quiet courage and comradeship. Rennison was a keen sportsman, a clever musician, and a good photographer. In climbing, his undoubted skill, slow deliberateness, and trustworthiness inspired his followers with confidence. Once in Walker's Gully he was dissatisfied with his ascent of the top pitch, and asked to be lowered down so it could try it again.

The Rennisons made plans to accompany Millican and other members of his camp to climb the notorious Pinnacle on Scafell the following day, but later that evening Crosby noticed that her brother was not well; she wanted him to sleep at the Wastwater Hotel instead of camping as he had a cold. He decided otherwise.

Early on Sunday before sunrise, Fred Botterill of Leeds, a climber of wide experience, who had spent the summer in his caravan, "Bertol," on the north shore of Wastwater along and two others—Fred Aldous, a well known climber, and Oliver Thorneycroft, of London—paid a visit to Dalton's camp at 6:00 a.m. intent on inviting Tom to climb Eagle's Nest Ridge on Great Gable, an ascent which he had long wished to make. Dalton and his party were still asleep, so Botterill woke them. Rennison did not take much persuasion and joined them with alacrity, he had led many first-class climbs, and was keenly desirous of leading Eagle's Nest Ridge direct and the North West Climb on Pillar.

Eagle's Nest consisted of three climbs, all of which were difficult, but especially Eagle's Nest Direct. This particular climb was first accomplished in 1892, and subsequently by Botterill, who, since his maiden ascent, had successfully negotiated the route several times. The rocks were regarded by climbers as good, but the holds as very slight. In fact, it was described by one climber, who was well acquainted with the climb, as more of a gymnastic climb than anything else; and experts were divided in opinion as to whether it was really a justifiable route, or whether the risks were too great. As a whole the climb was considered the most onerous in England.

Rennison knew Eagle's Nest by repute, having previously examined it from above when he, along with two friends, had ascended to the Napes on the 5 July 1909, but when rain rendered climbing impossible, he plainly showed his disappointment.

Therefore Rennison was glad of the opportunity on offer, and at 6:30 a.m., after making their apologies to Dalton, the climbing party set out with Rennison remaining behind to change his boots. He left half-an-hour later and then Dalton and his companions went back to sleep.

Rennison was acting curiously, differing from his usual firm way, and during that half-hour period appeared troubled in his mind. For some time previous he had suffered from chest pains, and as a precaution had thought it advisable to see a doctor at

Keswick whilst away from home. Although the doctor forbade him to climb, Rennison felt better and dismissed it from his mind.

Rennison caught up with the party at Needle Gully by 8:50 a.m. The first climb was Napes Needle, but he did not participate, and remained behind instead on a small ledge known as the "Dress Circle" where he changed his boots whilst the other three made the ascent.

After climbing the Needle they ascended the Abbey Ridge in two parties, Thorneycroft leading Aldous, and Botterill leading Rennison. Thorneycroft and Botterill had lead up the Abbey Ridge to husband the energies of the other men for the arduous work to come. It had been arranged to climb Eagle's Nest Ridge coupled in this way, but Aldous and Rennison were to lead. Descending from Abbey Ridge the easy way, the first party was overtaken. Aldous had descended the direct way on a rope, and on returning said that he did not feel sufficiently in form that day to lead the next climb.

This stage of the climb brought the four men back to the Dress Circle, from where springs Eagle's Nest Ridge. Here a light meal was taken and plans were altered somewhat. While Rennison was still to lead, it was decided that Aldous and Thorneycroft should join on to Botterill and bring up the rucksack, the two parties thus combining. Breakfast consumed, Botterill began to go up the first 70 feet of the Eagle's Nest, which is said to be an easy scramble to cragsmen, but of course, something very different for others who walk over mountains.

He was followed a minute or so later by Rennison. At 9:40 a.m. by Rennison's watch, Botterill advanced to the belay pin, which was sixty-five feet above the Dress Circle. Rennison joined him there a minute or so later, and after a moments rest, Rennison took the lead and advanced to the second and worst stage of the climb. "Come back if you feel any hesitation," warned Botterill. Thorneycroft and Aldous had not yet left the Dress Circle, and stood watching those above.

Rennison edged his way tentatively to the left and had advanced upwards a dozen feet, seemingly working carefully for foot and hand holds. His arms were both outstretched, his knees and toes occupying two parallel cracks, his boots within eight feet of Botterill's head. Botterill shouted further instruction knowing the climb well, having seen others undertake it, he wished Rennison to fully realise its difficulty, "Speak to me frequently," said Botterill, "so that I may know you are all right!" Rennison did not respond, he had not spoken since commencing, perhaps three minutes. He had not moved a limb for twenty-seconds when, suddenly, he slipped, all points of contact coming away simultaneously. He made no effort to save himself—uttered no cry—never turned his head—said to be exactly like a man with palpitation or suffering an attack of syncope.

At that moment the knot at his waist was within thirteen feet of the oblong belay of rough rock in an oblique line, the belay being level with Botterill's waist. There was from fourteen to eighteen inches of slack paid out for the leader's next forward step; there was also fourteen to sixteen inches of rope round the belay. Botterill instinctively placed both hands on the rope, feeling sure of pulling Rennison up, and crouched to meet the jerk, but he was not in a good position and unable to lean backwards. There was no time to take in any slack. The jerk came immediately and the rope broke with a loud snap six inches above Botterill's right hand, the total fall before the strain came on the rope being about twenty-five feet.

Time, as it does in such situations, passed in slow motion, and the party observed helplessly as Rennison precipitated to the ledge with a crushing thud, and rolled over the precipice to Needle Gully some 200 feet below. He struck the rocks violently three times in the fall before hitting the bed of the gully, and there, spreadeagled, lay motionless. Panic quickly ensued, but Botterill, after being involved in a similar situation previously, called for calm. The silence resumed, only broken by the grinding footfall and shifting earth of Thorneycroft bolting down the gully getting to him two minutes later.

Thorneycroft, reaching out for Rennison's wrist in a desperate attempt to check his radial pulse, moved his slightly damaged wristwatch to one side in the process, the time on the watch fixed by the impacts, the hands being timestamped at 9:50 a.m. The poor soul showing no pulse, was dead with his neck and thigh broken, and a 14 feet 10 inch length of severed rope knotted around his waist. The knot, being known amongst climbers as an "Alpine knot," or by sailors as a "Fisherman's Bend," had been compressed considerably, becoming very tight, and was only released with considerable difficulty.

Aldous, jittering with shock, was at the scene moments later, and stayed with the body whilst Thorneycroft sought aid from the Wastwater Hotel. Botterill retreating to the belay pin lowered himself to the Dress Circle.

Mr. John Ritson Whiting, proprietor of the hotel, on receiving word of the accident, hastily organised a party of Dalesmen and climbers. They took a stretcher to the spot and conveyed the fatally injured body of Rennison out of the gully, along the rough and precipitous Climbers Traverse, and down the long, steady course of Moses Trod to the sled-gate, then off the mountain to the hotel to await the inquest. The deceased was twenty-nine years of age, and single.

A touching feature of the accident was the fact that Rennison's sister, a school teacher at Millom Secondary School, was also climbing in the locality at the time with a party on Scafell, where she had arranged to meet her brother and his party after they accomplished their climb on Eagle's Nest. She was unaware of the accident until 5:00 p.m., when she and the party arrived at the hotel, and was heart-broken at the terrible news. The next morning, at 4:00 a.m., Miss Rennison drove 26 miles, and reached Kirkby Stephen at noon to break the first news to her parents.

The inquest concerning the death of Rennison was held the day after the accident on Monday 27 September 1909. Family mourners and witnesses assembled solemnly outside the makeshift Coroners Court at the Wastwater Hotel, the legendary, whitewashed, travellers refuge sat proud at the foot of the loftiest cluster of mountains in England—Scafell Pike, Scafell, Great Gable, and the Pillar. The Wastwater Hotel, firmly at the epicentre of English rock climbing, had been an unfortunate regular host to Coroners Courts in the years since the sport began in earnest. The nearby tiny sixteenth century church, and its drystone-walled burial ground—the final resting place to three of the victims from the accident on Scafell Pinnacle—sat subservient to the dark masses above, providing a grim, stark reminder of the extreme dangers of rock climbing, and the limitations of man in those pioneering days.

Mr. Whiting opened the battered black entrance door to the hotel, a clear yet subtle signal of the start of proceedings, whence the assembly were ushered through the entrance hall, cluttered with hemp ropes, freshly greased boots and other climbing paraphernalia, towards the billiard room staging morgue and Court. Mr. Edward Atter, Coroner for West Cumberland, was the last to walk into the room.

"Millican Dalton, of The Camp, Billericay, Essex is called as the first witness" announced the clerk.

Coroner: "Evidence in this court is given on oath. You are asked to swear on the holy book to affirm that you will tell the truth."

MD: "I will not be sworn. I speak the truth, and there is no reason why I should be sworn."

Coroner: "Before we proceed further, can you identify the deceased?"

MD: "Yes, that is the body of my cousin, Thomas James Rennison, who lived at 32 South Road, Kirkby Stephen, and was a chemist's assistant."

Coroner: "When did you last see the deceased alive?"

MD: "I last saw him alive about six o'clock on Sunday morning in the camp which I had made in a wood at Wasdale. Mr. Rennison came on Saturday night, after being about a week in the Lake District. Mr. Bottcrill came round to the camp before we were awake, and awakened Mr. Rennison to go with his party to climb the Eagle's Nest. The party left the camp, along with Mr. Rennison, and my companions and I went back to sleep."

Coroner: "Was the deceased an experienced climber?"

MD: "He had three years experience, but I think he ought to have more. He has done a lot of climbs this year, including the Abbey Ridge, he had done some very good climbs indeed, and always climbed very well."

Coroner: "Was he very well acquainted with the system, and so on?"

MD: "Oh, yes. He knew very well what the climb was. He intended to go about a month ago on the same climb, but the weather so bad they gave it up. Mr. Rennison's boots had been troubling him and he was rather footsore, so he borrowed my boots on Sunday morning to walk up to the climb and then changed to his own climbing-boots, the ones which had been hurting him. He had not climbed the Eagle's Nest before, but he knew how difficult it was. No one was to blame for the accident. He knew the risk, and he had plenty of time to think about this. We had often discussed as to whether it was too risky or not. I had done, perhaps, half-a-dozen climbs with Mr. Rennison, and he climbed very well, being very sure. He had really intended to go second in the climb, I believe, from what he had said, but I knew Mr. Rennison had no objections to going first. This was a very severe climb and climbers had often discussed the question, and the general opinion was that it was unjustifiable for the general public."

Foreman of the jury: "It is unjustifiable for expert climbers to tackle this climb?"

MD: "There is a difference of opinion. Personally, I think, to expert climbers it is justifiable if a man likes to take a risk. To a man like Mr. Botterill, who was with Mr. Rennison at the time of the accident, it was quite justifiable. I believed it has been climbed eight times, and that there have been no previous accidents."

"Mr. Fred Botterill, of Leeds," was called as the next witness.

FB: "I have known Mr. Rennison since last Whitsuntide. He had wished to be in the party to climb the Eagle's Nest, and so I went to him yesterday morning at the camp and invited him to join our party. He arranged to join at once. He had a rucksack, and wore a pair of new boots, and he had another pair in his rucksack. On the way to the climb Mr. Rennison stopped to change his boots, and joined us again on the traverse which leads to the climb.

The rope they used belonged to Mr. John De Vars Hazard, who was staying at Wasdale. Mr. Thorneycroft, Mr. Aldous, and myself ascended the Needle, but Mr. Rennison did not. We all then started to climb the Eagle's Nest Ridge. We then had a second breakfast before starting the next climb. About ten minutes after we started Mr. Rennison, who was about 12 feet from me, slipped. I saw him slip and held the rope hard, so as to arrest the fall. I fully expected it would do so, but the rope broke at the belay. I had made myself quite secure, and was in a position to have held him if the rope had not broken. The rope was 80 feet long."

Coroner: "Can you account for the fall?"

FB: "It was a pure accident."

Coroner: "Was he in a very dangerous part at that moment?"

FB: "Yes, he was in the worst part."

Coroner: "Would it have made any difference if you had gone first?"

FB: "Yes, I like to think it would have made a difference."

Coroner: "He might have slipped, even if he had been going behind you, at the same place."

FB: "Then I should have held him. The rope would not have had such a jerk, because in falling he had to pass the belay twice the distance, which would not have otherwise been the case. I had climbed with him before this and he had negotiated the climbs very successfully and I formed the impression that he was a very good climber. When I look at the climbs Mr. Rennison has done this year I think he was justified in attempting the climb on Sunday."

Foreman of the jury: "Do you think the climb was justifiable for an expert?"

FB: "I am inclined to alter my opinion now. The occurrence was very distressing, and I am inclined to draw the line chosen, and not to attempt severe things. I have climbed the Eagle's Nest five times previously, and led on four occasions. I think it is quite justifiable for climbers of experience such as myself. Mr. Rennison had a perfect nerve. I cannot account for the rope breaking. The rope we were using was an ordinary climbing rope, but I don't think any ordinary climbing rope would have held him under the circumstances. Mr. Rennison had climbed with the rope in question a good bit this season. It had been eighteen months in use, and was a little worn. Had the rope been a new one, it would have broken under the circumstances."

Foreman of the jury: "It was deceased's own wish that he should lead."

"Mr. Oliver Thorneycroft, Manchester," was the next witness called.

OT: "When he slipped he seemed unable to regain his hold. He fell on to the ground which was partly rock and partly grass. I was at the bottom of the climb and the first to get near him, I was there with two minutes, but he never spoke, being unconscious, life was extinct within a few of minutes. I could clearly see the man's neck was broken. I had not seen Mr. Rennison before that morning."

Coroner: "Mr. Botterill's evidence is very clear, and I can take his statement as to how the accident happened. Of course there was no one to blame but the deceased himself. A good many of those who are not climbers might think that it was a very foolhardy pastime, but I suppose it has a great fascination for some people, and of course if they like it there is nothing to prevent them going in for it. It is not for them to say whether it was a climb deceased should have attempted or not. Deceased's life was his own, and he thought fit to attempt the climb which has been heard described as a very severe one. The jury have reached a verdict of "Accidental Death" and remark that no blame attributable to anyone."

Miss Rennison returned to Wasdale that night, and took the corpse of her brother to her home at Kirkby Stephen the next morning.

Wednesday afternoon, 29 September 1909, saw an impressive service take place at the Wesleyan Church, Kirkby Stephen where the deceased's family worshipped, and of which he was formerly organist. There was a large gathering of members of the family, including Millican Dalton who had arrived direct from the scene of the fatality in Alpine attire to form one of the bearing party, along with three of Rennison's old school mates. The committal sentences and a short prayer were offered at the graveside by the Rev. P. Collier, the officiating minister, and just before Rennison's remains were interred in the cemetery Miss Rennison placed a pretty device in white heather, roses, and lilies upon his coffin with the brief message—'From Crosby.'

Many floral emblems were sent, including a choice wreath of lilies and chrysanthemums arranged by Botterill who had decided to remain in Wasdale Head. This climbing fatality, yet another in which Botterill had been involved, had a profound effect on his psyche, and after the accident until his death he withdrew from the rock climbing scene and quietly faded into obscurity. Life was far from simple.

CHAPTER NINE

COMPLEX SIMPLICITY

S tepping off the rollercoaster of life is easier said than done, but there was a large group of people who followed the cult of the Simple Life—a protest against the inordinate vanity and display of the period—in an attempt to ease their time on Earth. Little has been said about this movement, but the opportunity now arises for it to be described by an anonymous author who wrote an article concerning the fifth annual Open-Air and Simple Life Exhibition which ran from 31 March to 3 April 1914, 11:00 a.m. to 10:00 p.m. each day with an admission fee of 1s.—another platform used by Millican and Henry to promote their camping holidays and outdoor adventures.

We hear a good deal nowadays from week to week, from year to year, praise of the Simple Life. It is dinned into our ears repeatedly. Indeed so much has been written and spoken about it that the very phrase has become nauseous and the subject itself to loft severely alone by all save cranks—but exceedingly little is done in the matter of living it. Nearly everybody gives a different interpretation what is meant by the hackneyed phrase, while not few otherwise well-informed people frankly confess ignorance. The Simple Life has become a sort of misleading catchword highly attractive to just those persons who least understand its true meaning even though the phrase has passed into the language.

Some people seem to think it consists of nothing more than walking over ploughed fields, gathering daisies, wearing negligee blouses, living on weird diets, and getting sunburnt in the search for the original Garden of Eden! Others have an idea that the Simple Life means doing without a table-cloth, without a lace cover on your black oak table, without any silver, any shining glass, any flowers, without all those charming adjuncts which make many modern homes so delightful.

The real Simple Life does not seem to be so simple a thing as it sounds. An Englishman living the Simple Life now would find it more difficult to attain to such a trance than if he were content to live like other people. In the first place, says the *British Medical Journal*, it is very difficult to carry out in the midst of a highly complex artificial civilisation. We all know that what is simple for one person may be complex for another, and impossible for a third. The Simple Life is much to be commended when it is not too fantastic in its simplicity, but extremists are beginning to find that, however much the adoption of primitive mode living may conduce to healthiness of mind and body, the present state of civilisation creates many obstacles to its adoption.

The Simple Life has become the fashion across the world after Paster Charles Wagner's first book, *The Simple Life*, published in 1901, enjoyed an enormous circulation on both sides of the Atlantic and with over a million copies sold the craze really gathered pace in 1905 till the end of the decade. Certain royalty, duchesses, society women and even presidents have announced their intention of reverting to Nature and the Simple Life

The Open-Air Exhibition seems at first sight something like incursion into the obvious. Everybody who wants open-air can very easily get it—of kind. But the craft life in it needs illustration. So when I saw that the Simple Life Exhibition was advertised, I thought I would go and try whether I could get any hints as to the bettering of my lot.

Those who wish to live simply, but have been baffled hitherto by the difficulty of doing so, also now have an opportunity at the Horticultural Hall of learning how it is done. Resplendent sunshine whispered "Horticultural Hall" in the ears of scores of folk this morning, who, if left to themselves in the grey of yesterday, would never have thought of the Open-Air and Simple Life Exhibition. But sunshine and simplicity often walk hand in hand, especially when simplicity is translated into terms of rucksacks, open-air stoves, and camps up river.

The Horticultural Hall, crafted from red brick with stone dressings and banding, decorated with Arts and Crafts features and Renaissance details, and its dramatic glass-vaulted ceilings provide a stunning backdrop to the event. This is Edwardian architecture of unmatched spender, and the juxtaposition with the theme of the exhibition seems to the layman as somewhat at odds with the thought of a Simple Life.

Exhibition spaces, such as the Horticultural Hall, are more than just containers for exhibition settings and objects on display. Layout, design and atmosphere are some of the most significant factors in the overall experience of any visit, especially the impacts of spatial elements and their effects. The exhibition stage is also a symbolic space, a place with special aspects which create a frame around the objects.

They form contexts for communicating ideas and for social behaviour which are set apart from everyday life. The exhibition's main function is to supply a cultural information link between the various members of a society. This was perfectly displayed here.

The Simple Life Exhibition is quite an unusual affair. In many ways it is a return to very primitive customs. Guests sit on the floor in circles, tablecloths are paper, and waiters are entirely excluded from the programme, all the dishes are placed on the floor in front of the guests. The platform of the Hall represents a meadow carpeted with grass and flowers. Tents are fixed here, and wax figures recline on the latest hygienic beds. From this unconventional platform addresses are to be given by well-known doctors, and resourceful enthusiasts, and disciples of Thoreau, who carried out a two year experiment in simple living. Experienced exponents of touring in many countries are giving explanations of how to tour in a donkey cart, and others are demonstrating the apparent attractions of camping in the desert.

A few upholders of the creed roam the Hall, brazen to the gaze of wondering Londoners. I found especially attractive the picturesque personage, Millican Dalton, dressed in knobbed boots and corduroy knickers who sat down by me at the opening ceremony. He had cheered up his green sweater for the festive occasion with a tie of red blind cord. He listened very earnestly to Mrs. Leigh Hunt Wallace's thoughtful little address, he himself a "Wallacite," but seemed considerably puzzled by the ballet-dancing which preceded it. I myself feel puzzled. What has ballet-dancing in spangles got to do with sunshine, noon, and the Simple Life?

The Vincent Square venue drew a good attendance, largely made up of people who would have materially to alter their costume if they expected to do anything especially simple living. On the other hand, among the experts in charge of exhibits were some gentlemen garbed in a style which would be calculated to make something of a sensation in Bond Street. It is an unfortunate thing that clothes which merely look appropriate and picturesque when the wearer is roughing it become almost brigand-like among the surrounds of town life.

The exhibition started in earnest on the second day; I arrived early in an attempt to avoid the crowds, but everyone had the same idea, and on my arrival throngs of exhibition-goers already congregated in eager anticipation, all waiting to gain a glimpse into a nonconforming world revisited, a world comprising of alternative characters who had signed their allegiance to a revolution pitted against the perceived luxuries of modern living.

Jostling amidst the crowds, I entered the exhibition through the foyer and was immediately greeted by the incessant chattering reverberating around the Hall, the air within warmed by the spring sunshine radiating through the arching glazed roof, carrying on it the strong scent of musk emanating from the open pores of the dishevelled attendees and exhibitors, who, judging by the number of double-takes from some of the well-heeled visitors, would be more comparable to vagabonds than regular members of civilised society. It was not a scent to caresses the nasal passages.

I instantly found myself in the midst of nut foods and the other curious things on which cranks seemingly feed. Ladies pressed on me pamphlets concerning strange edible preparations. To the left, stalls where every species of sour milk are for sale. Further down I am faced at once by an enthusiastic announcement proclaiming "Wallacites and Vegetarians" are specially catered for. I am offered "vegetarian boots" and others constructed on the sandal principle, and in one little booklet given to me were advertisements for 'Stamina Food,' laxative cereal, soaked evaporated fruits, unfired bread, combination nut butter, protein nuts, and mock white fish cutlets.

Dazzled with impossible luncheon hampers, patent fail-proof stoves, camp galoshes, panama hats, collapsible armchairs, wire covered glass syphons, aluminium utensils of every description, from new fangled devices for condiments, to a rack in the top of your temporary roof tree for sticking umbrellas, and most other things which are significant of the modern impatience with the due routine of urgent affairs, which filled the Hall, I pressed on.

One of the chief impressions which the casual visitor would receive from a study of the exhibits is that the Simple Life consists over-largely of eating. About one-third of the stalls are devoted to foods and not a few others to cooking them, or to literature which deals largely with dietetics. They are not, of course, the foods which one commonly meets with at dinner tables, but vastly more nutritious, condensed, and scientific. Next to the foods in number—and to the ordinary heretic distinctly more interesting—are the camp utensils and equipment. It comes as a revelation to see how much can be done in the way of making furniture collapsible and imponderable. There is hardly anything that does not fold up and is not waterproof, until, for example, a camp chair of aluminium and canvas becomes hardly more cumbersome to carry than a cigarette case.

Besides the foods, health clothing, caravans, and camp outfits, there are many other things more or less directly connected with life in the open-air. Such are the cameras for taking records of your holiday when weather is fine, and Harbutt's Gold Medal plasticine and play-wax presumably to play with when it rains; gramophones, which are perhaps more desirable for the individual camper than for the neighbourhood in which he camps; garden requisites and flower seeds, and miscellaneous objects down to hand-made lace, a silhouette artist, and Mexican woven silver-wire ornaments—the connection between all of which and hygienics seems to be remote.

Cancer, its prevention and cure, town-planning, and garden city building, log huts, fruitarian diets, ideal homes, boats, weekend-cottage exhibits, and the exhibition of light-weight camping outfit by the Amateur Camping Club are all things which are rationally connected with the simple—and better—life movement. I was reminded there is a full programme of lectures and discussions daily, and a Vegetarian Conference each day at 3:00 p.m. and in the evening, with a cooking competition on Thursday afternoon.

One of the interesting exhibits at the Exhibition is a little covered donkey cart. The young couple to who it belong have had no other home since they began their honeymoon in it five years ago. They found the lift so delightful that they have been honeymooning in it ever since. "Contact with the everyday world of toil and mammon," they say, "always destroys love. But with our little cart, as it is drawn about the country, the world is not too much with us, and life is a perpetual honeymoon."

Continuing, nervously dodging the fierce eyes of a resolute man in sandals who had views on the rearing of children, I found refuge in the decorated covered cart of the Rolling Stones—evidently the principle attraction of the exhibition judging by the observing crowd—two young brothers from Birmingham named Foster who themselves built a vehicle, "The Moss," being craftsmen, and trundle it among the Cotswolds, finding odd jobs on farms, and sleeping in their cart at night, they said they would sooner push their portable home about than work at a bench.

"If," remarked one of the brothers, running his fingers through his mediaeval hair, "we can make seven shillings a week we are all right. When we make ten, we have luxuries." As to where they would trundle themselves to in the end with their opinions free as air they had no care; but they declared that they are going to Sussex and Devon this summer, anyway.

The aforementioned "honeymoon caravan," although possessing some merit, was eclipsed by their conveyance which is hauled by the caravaners themselves; a tedious process no doubt, but time is of no object to the born simple-lifer. The two gentlemen who exhibit it are said to have travelled "nearly 300 miles without the use of any other means of traction than themselves" carrying their house with them like snails when it is fine, and getting inside, we presume, when it rains—an obviously simple and compendious arrangement.

Snugly floating on the gleaming polished parquet floorboards in a corner of the Hall lay a dainty craft for two pairs of sculls, waterproof night-awning, bedding, crimson cushions, and novels, all complete. Ah! if the possession of such a craft were linked with an Easter such as today! The poor person finds comfort in the thought that though money may buy the Simple Life, money cant buy Simple Weather. One must journey south for that, and here in another corner of the Hall is impedimenta for Simple Lifers tramping south. Rucksacks and one-man tents light as a feather, canvas baths folded to pocket size, spirit cans warranted not to leak, and to hold just the right amount to escape duty! One could wander over Spain and Italy with one's house on one's back.

Next up was to be found the "Human Snail" who stores a complete camping outfit, including cooking utensils, about his person, and yet claims to travel light. Thus, it was no surprise when Mr. Holding demonstrated "how it is possible to take your bed, tent, and cooking utensils in your pockets, so that one can taste all the delights of a tramp's existence without the attending discomforts." Mr. Thomas Hiram Holding, who is now in his seventieth year, and who has spent the greater part of his life under canvas, remarked that all a man needs to protect him from the weather is a silk tent—which he drew from his pocket, and which was equipped with a sort of fishing rod pole and a set of twelve aluminium pegs.

In this tent it is possible for two to sleep quite cosily, although it folds up into a package measuring only 11in. by 4in., while among other innumerable objects in the way of concentrated comfort Mr. Holding has invented pillows that weigh next to nothing and are blown up like cycle tyres, pots and pans that vanish when they are not wanted, toilet apparatus weighing only a few ounces, and so on.

As a matter of fact, Mr. Holding contends that the whole weight of the outfit for a man who decides on the Simple Life camping out need not exceed 7lb., and this would include cooking, porridge, and frying pans, a stove, water bucket for two gallons, a hairbrush, comb, looking-glass, a set of bags for carrying oatmeal, bread, tea, coffee, and several other minor items. The stove is a tiny oil affair, weighing just over a pound, but capable of dealing efficiently with a rabbit or a beef-steak, while the water bucket can be tucked into a space no bigger than your fist.

"It is wonderful," said Mr. Holding, "what a little ingenuity can do."

"Pooh!" remarked this veteran whose sturdiness would arouse the envy of a man forty years younger: "weather is a matter of complete indifference to a man used to the Simple Life. In the shelter of my tiny tent I can laugh at the rain and have endured as much as 22 degrees of frost, and can now regard snow with composure."

Hidden among crags and cliffs of nut foods was a red gipsy tent and its owner. It's Mr. Millican Dalton again, still sporting hob-nailed mountaineering boots, stood at his stand confidently promoting his wares. Embellished with a fleshpot and tripod, ropes and ice picks all about him and an advertisement of his holidays of adventures this year, Mr. Dalton took no time in explaining he conducts parties of pioneers through the wilds at a most reasonable figure.

A novel programme, which includes such thrills as mountaineering, rapid-shooting, night rambles, bivouacs, and varied hairbreadth escapes (arranged by circumstance), read the handbill of Mr. Dalton, "Dealer in Adventures," as he described himself. "Rapid-shooting" is no empty phrase, as I soon learnt.

Pausing to adjust his stance, leaning forward in a confiding, sincere way, he then offered me more of his promotional material:

"Would you be interested in a Gipsy Holiday? Ireland perhaps? Kenmare Estuary and Killarney? A longshore boating and camping expedition, in a wild, beautiful sanctuary of the sea? I have spaces available for Saturday 27 June, the party arrives Kenmare Station 1:00 p.m., being conducted thence, twelve miles walk to camp on Rossmore Island. The fortnight's program includes boating on the Estuary, alternated with walking, and some hill and rock climbing and bathing; also two days by Killarney, with a boating excursion along the three lakes. Fourteen days tour, inclusive of camp accommodation, transport, boating and fare from London would be £6 10s. An allowance is made for nearer places. There may also be room in other parties starting from Kenmare July 11 and 25, if booking early. I can also offer adventures in the English Lakes, 10 to 29 August, with mountaineering from 26 September; and mountaineering in Scotland and Switzerland in 1915. Austrian Tyrol Tours mid-August to 30 September—Zillertal, Dolomites, Switzerland—£16 each." He also said: "Some of my most dangerous 'mountain climbs' have taken place in— Epping Forest. Two trees are pressed into service for this dangerous pastime."

His holiday arrangements have the breath of the veldt!

It's abundantly clear that the Simple Life folk have achieved the fine art of minimising the work of cookery and of cleaning up, and there are plenty of lessons on cooking without ovens, and other necessities of life on the road.

The exhibition finalised on Friday 3 April at 8:00 p.m with a lecture by Mr. Henry Dalton entitled "Wild Camping in English Lakeland" with lantern slides, but before I left for home, there was on show in another place a caravan with a canvas canoe on top, with appointments luxurious enough to convert anyone to the Simple Life. This was the shallow end of simple living, and some would doubt whether it actually falls into that category at all. Nevertheless, the height of tramp-luxury can be reached, for those Simple Lifers with pockets deep enough, in a Pullman caravan. Once home I think of Joseph Knowles, the Boston artist, who last year survived in the woods of Maine for three months without clothes, a modern Adam, who did not seem to have been engaged at the exhibition, but after all, I suppose, the line of realism must be drawn somewhere.

Millican Dalton

1914 PROMOTIONAL MATERIAL

CHAPTER TEN

THE CAVE HOTEL

The thin line of realism, and exactly where it ends, as anyone will agree, is subjective, but those who had walked through the Borrowdale Valley during the first half of the twentieth century and espied a modern-day caveman would have been left in no doubt that this line can be accurately defined.

Camping at High Lodore had long been considered as the perfect spot, but life under canvas was only really a temporary measure due to the unpredictable nature of the Lakeland weather which made camp life a little difficult and so a search for more permanent possibilities began. During the start of the century, Millican, along with some of his adventurous friends, started exploring caves. Natural caves in the region are rare due to the geological composition of the area, and according to A. Wainwright the only naturally occurring caves are those on Dove's Nest Crags, the remainder being formed by the slate quarrying process of which abound in the Lake District.

These man-made caves offered a lightweight alternative to camping in tents as less gear could be carried and were a further progression from his early experiments with equipment. Benefits of easy access to the crags and fells and the best possible shelter from the elements was provided. A vast, dank and sludgy cavern at Rydal on the slopes of Loughrigg, formerly known as Loughrigg Quarry, was one such option. After being "converted" the cave was then used as a southern base for his camping holidays when alternating between Ambleside and Keswick. Though it may have witnessed overnight stays, it was unsuitable for long term occupancy.

Another option, first discovered in 1901; a disused split-level cave hewn out of the hillside by slate quarrymen long ago, was also utilised. Millican had first started camping in the cave, predominantly during wet weather, and in later years with Rev. George Potts, who said: "When we knew it, it was abandoned place, difficult to find, the other side of the River Derwent from the Bowder Stone. There was a dry ledge in it on which we laid heather and where we slept. There was water dripping from the roof outside for washing and a spring of water inside for drinking. Behind the dry ledge the cave stretched into the hillside, cavernous and forbidding. It was all right while the deluges lasted, but no sooner was the rain over than we would return to the tents."

In time this cave was chosen in preference to the tents and adopted as his main residence where he eventually lived for several months each summer. A more scenic location could not have been chosen. It was amongst outstanding beauty situated deep within the mesmerising Jaws of Borrowdale. A romantic land blanketed with oak and birch woodland, divided by the crystal clear emerald glide of the River Derwent, reputed by some to be the most scenic square mile in the whole of Lakeland.

The cave, situated directly beneath the cliffs of Castle Crag on its easterly flank, acted as a secluded retreat from which to operate. No compromise was made on his choice of 'home,' the cave being one of the largest in Lakeland, with the lower cavern extending ninety feet into the crag, covering an approximate area of 4500 feet square. Here he created his living area tucked up tightly against the cave wall. Inside was dark and damp, but ample dry areas existed. Trees acting as a buffer and the topography around the mouth of the cave provided excellent protection from the wind and driving rain.

Subsequently he made himself at home and claimed the cave as his own, jokingly referring to it as the "Cave Hotel" or "Aladdin's Cave." The interior, in his own words "replete with every primeval convenience," was equipped with a range of junk recovered from Grange tip creatively furnishing his humble abode with Heath Robinson-esque ad hoc contraptions. An abundance of gadgets and wires suspended cookware on and around his fire; planks formed shelves providing storage for books, newspapers and packing cases; tree branches became hat and coat stands, and empty bottles candle holders. Quarried debris covering the floor was used to construct dry stone walls forming his 'living room' with seating and an integral fireplace. His bed was a cold hard slab of stone, softened by a springy bed of bracken or heather.

A fire, which was burnt almost constantly, kept his intimate quarters warm, provided light and was hot enough to cook anything. Ample supplies of timber could be found outside the cave in High Hows Wood. Firewood was cut with a bowsaw and there was always a plentiful supply, stacked and ready to burn.

The water source, constantly flowing through a fissure in the ceiling, provided a year-round potable supply and was the only thing that broke the silence of the subdued ambience. Barrels, again from Grange tip, caught the dripping water which was used for drinking, cooking and on extremely rare occasions washing. Terraces outside the cave, formed by mining operations, also it seems had a use and witnessed the cultivation of potatoes.

Above the 'living room' was the cave's upper chamber, interlinked with the lower and just under half the size, and referred to by Dalton as "The Attic"; this was the guests bedroom. There is no doubt that the Cave Hotel was considered an unpleasant place by most, but it was, in reality, relative luxury compared to life in a tent. Even friends and family agreed after spending a night in The Attic. Board and lodgings were free, which was perhaps a reasonable fee as this hotel had no concierge, room service, public bar; or ensuite bathroom—or any bathroom for that matter—but day trips and evening entertainment were always provided.

Those who cared to find him "at home" were asked to share complimentary black coffee, bread and cheese, and stimulating conversation with him over the fire in his gipsy-like retreat and invited to see over his domain. Speaking in his cultured voice he told the most remarkable stories around his magical campfires that formed the basis of any good evening. Apart from the usual banter regarding climbing and current affairs, Dalton also discussed his theories and as he grew older tried to lure friends into light-hearted arguments, although he tended to be hard to argue with and became progressively stubborn. Those who knew him were well aware of his opinionated personality and rarely took him on. 'In this cave he would entertain his visitors expounding to them the philosophy which was purely Millican Dalton,' added Mayson.

Spine-chilling ghost stories, for which he was noted, provided yet more entertainment. Waiting till after dark he would sit his audience around the fire, lavish them hot drinks and with his most excellent and diverse imagination proceed in scaring their wits out. On many occasions visitors would be so encapsulated in the evening's events that darkness would fall without them realising. Making the point, Mabel M. Barker wrote: 'The charm of his camp fire and coffee and his (increasingly argumentative!) conversation delayed departure till the dusk caught us.'

Friends always knew when the Professor of Adventure was in residence by the blue-grey plume of smoke that emanated from the cave entrance and drifted up the face of Castle Crag. This made a good waymarker as most visitors to the cave remember the difficulty in finding it; over rock; through trees and up scree. Ralph Mayson wrote:

> The approaches to the cave are many, and to go with him there, from Rosthwaite, was always a delightful journey, particularly in the month of June, when the wild roses are gracing the hedges in the lane to the bridge over the River Derwent, and, turning to the right and following the river bank, he would pause to admire the yellow iris in the swamps, and the buck bean rising from the small dark bog holes. He gave special attention to a grove of hazel trees, where the river runs shallow for a hundred yards or more, which to him were especially fine. Some little

distance away a bold rock would seem to terminate further progress, but an exit is found on the left, and the patch indicated along the lower portion would be pointed out as being a very line example of glacier rock. Here, facing directly to Castle Crag, Millican would draw attention to the way Nature was doing her best to clothe the unsightly slate heaps, over which the way lies to a series of three caves. Flowering wild thyme, parsley fern, herb-Robert, and black stemmed maidenhair spleenwort, being amongst a great variety of flowers and ferns.

Access could also be gained from the south via Rosthwaite by following the River Derwent to beneath Castle Crag and then making the steep ascent up to the cave. Alternatively, a shortcut—wet and cold—could be made by fording the river from the Borrowdale Road.

Castle Crag sparkles with many interesting features, but it was the south-side that Dalton particularly loved. The Scotch Firs, High Doat, the ancient deciduous woodland of Johnny Wood and Charity Coppice with its secret waterfall hidden away from the crowds were favourite spots and only a short distance from camp. Sometimes guests would be invited to ascend the northern side of Castle Crag to the summit cairn; an interesting scramble over rough steep ground, rock, and grass and through clinging trees and dense stands of bracken. Once on the summit a full and rewarding panorama greeted all successful initiates. Accurately describing the views Mayson added:

Here Millican would point out, to the north, Derwentwater and Skiddaw with the village of Grange and the River Derwent in the foreground; to the east, Grange Fell or King's How as it is now called, with Helvellyn in the far distance; to the south the head of Borrowdale Valley, with Rosthwaite village, above which Ullscarf stands out on the skyline. The stream descending Greenup Ghyll can faintly be seen with Eagle Crag on the right, which marks the junction of the two streams, Greenup and Langstrath. Rosthwaite Fell and Combe Ghyll come next in turn, overshadowed by Glaramara, then Great End, Scafell, Base Brown and Great Gable, with Grains Ghyll and Sty Head Pass leading out from the hamlet of Seathwaite; to the west, Gate Crag with its wonderful scrambling gullies and short rock climbs and the lovely stream which comes down between Gate Crag and Knitting Howe; in between and down below, runs the track between Grange and Seatoller. All these places were familiar to Millican.

Many people simply visited the cave whilst they had chance before he left for the continent or made his return south. An entry in the FRCC Borrowdale climbing book on 9 August 1914, days after England's declaration of war against Germany, was written by W. Allsop, an occasional climbing partner. He stated that whilst at a FRCC Club Meet in Buttermere he ventured over Honister Pass to Dalton's camp at Castle Crag and then meandered down to Lodore before returning to rejoin the rest of the group in Buttermere. A visitors book housed within the cave even encouraged guests to leave their mark.

To this day evidence of Millican's existence still appears in The Attic in the form of a carved inscription at its entrance explicitly warning visitors: 'Don't!! waste worrds, jump to conclusions!' This particular carving, one of several in and around the cave, is the basis of much discussion. It is rumoured in some circles that the carvings are not those of Millican Dalton but those of best friend, R. Ernest Way.

Ernest, along with his young son Ken, spent the greater part of the school summer holidays with Dalton in his cave. Ken remembers that the two of them were always arguing fiercely over a multitude of philosophical topics and these arguments carried on by letter over the summers while Dalton remained at his cave.

One day Ernest received a letter which really aroused his passions sending him into a rage. Exasperated, he demanded Ken to get into their car and they both drove all the way to Borrowdale so he could remonstrate with Dalton, but he was not at home. Ken's father, in exasperation at Millican's dogmatism, went back to his car, returned with a hammer and punch and antagonistically carved the now famous message above the cave —the context of the quotation of upmost relevance to the argument they were having. Millican, supposedly, tried to stifle arguments and often told his friend "Don't waste words!" or "Don't jump to conclusions!" The carving, it is said, was originally "Don't jump to conclusions!", the second line added at a later date. Curiously, on closer inspection, the inscription is signed M. D. The incorrect spelling of words, a joke between the two friends, was to give the impression of a Scottish rolling "R." Another inscription, 'F. M. A GOOD COMRADE RMD 1935,' attributed here to Millican Dalton, adorns the entrance to the lower cave; it clearly matches his handwriting style and is underlined with a customary wedge, as also seen on his promotional material.

When the author of this book conversed with Ken it soon became apparent he was highly secretive and fiercely defensive (bordering on hostility), of his old friend and mentor who helped shape his opinions and outlook on life. Ken said:

> He was always known as Millican, none of this Mr. Dalton or Dalton, he was always Millican. I met Millican for the first time on the shores of Ullswater in 1935 when he coming from the train station at Penrith with his bike. He was a great reader, very modest and would never blow his own trumpet. We frequently stayed

with him at the cave during the late 1930s and 1940s when I was a young boy, and explored all around Borrowdale and Derwentwater, making fires and cooking our meals. He never, ever cut living trees for firewood, he always collected dead wood. We had great laughs in the cave, men's jokes, commonly about farting—Millican called us "The 5 pop-offs"—and it was even carved into the cave wall along with our initials, though my father had to shout "Joke! Joke! Joke!" after saying something to let him know he was not serious. We climbed around Great Gable and Langdale together, his appearance always attracting attention. He was the most photographed character in the Lake District, but he did not own a camera. I sketched pictures of him and wrote to him regularly in his later years. That's all I'm prepared to say.

During the early 1930s Molly Lefebure, the respected author and former Fellow of The Royal Society of Literature—whose titles included *Scratch & Co.: The Great Cat Expedition*, illustrated by A. Wainwright—and known by Scotland Yard detectives as "Molly o' the Morgue" after her time spent working with the Forensic Pathologist Professor Keith Simpson, wrote in her book *The English Lake District*:

The District's last hermit, a man named Millican Dalton, lived in a cave on Castle Crag, just above the Derwent. As a child I several times saw him walking in the woods at the foot of Gate Crag, or crossing Grange Bridge. I used to think that it would be wonderful to be a hermit here. Indeed, your first glimpse of Borrowdale may seduce you into wondering if you might not try becoming a hermit here yourself; practical reasons will doubtless persuade you against it, but it is an attractive notion.

Charles Rolland, one of the many visitors to the Cave Hotel contributed:

I got to know him in 1936 or '37 or both. We used to have family holidays at Rosthwaite, staying in Rose Cottage which was attached to the village Post Office and Store and was run by Ernie and Grace Plaskett. Millican was living in the cave on Castle Crag and he used to come down to Rosthwaite to mend his boots in Ernie's workshop. There I met him and we used to have long conversations about climbing. I was very keen but had little experience.

He told me about Dove's Nest Caves in Combe Ghyll on Glaramara. He fired my enthusiasm and I set off to explore them and the rocks around them. He did not offer to come with me. I would go by myself complete with candles for the darker recesses.

In the evenings I would find my way through the woods to the cave, equipped with a paper packet of Woodbine cigarettes, two pence in those days. They would keep Millican happy and he would talk to me for an hour or two and ply me with coffee. The cave was very well suited to his needs. Over the fire he had an iron bar from which hung an assortment of cans on hooks made from fencing wire. He did not bother about washing up—there was a special can for each thing he wanted to heat, tea, coffee, soup, porridge and so on. The spoil heap below the cave supplied plenty of slates, which served as plates. They went out in the rain as necessary. I did not see him afloat on his raft, 'Rogue Herries.' My recollection is that he had a bike, which he hid in the bracken beside the track to Grange. He used to go to Keswick on the bike and when he was migrating south the old bike almost vanished under the collection of goods which he hung from it.

There was a large photo of him, complete with felt hat and pheasant's feather in the glass doorway of Birkett's boot shop in St John's Street.

Ernie Plaskett used to show off to visitors. He once asked two ladies if they had seen "the oldest living thing in the valley" meaning the Borrowdale Yews at Seathwaite. He was much amused when they replied "Oh yes, you mean the Cave Man." Millican did not think that was funny.

Amongst Millican's other daily rituals was the morning walk to the Post Office in Grange-in-Borrowdale where he would often be seen sat on the old twin-arched packhorse bridge with his face towards the lake and his faithful red plaid about him. Not only did this jaunt allow him to collect his post and a copy of his favourite newspaper, the *Daily Herald*, it was also an opportunity to catch up on conversation. Political preferences, views and leanings are clearly reflected in his choice of daily newspaper. The leftwing *Daily Herald* commonly portrayed capitalists as devils, never condemned strikers and, unlike other newspapers, took an anti-war stance at the outbreak of the World War I. Importantly the fact that Dalton actually bought a newspaper demonstrates a tie with society and a wish to remain informed of current affairs—not the actions of a true hermit.

Irrespective to the permanency of the Cave Hotel as soon as the Lakeland deluges ended he would not hesitate at throwing up a tent or bivouac whenever the need arose. A large rock, situated between Sourmilk Gill and Lower Seathwaite Slabs, provided the best bivouac shelter in the vicinity and was often used for an overnight stop after Fell and Rock Meets or when on the alternative route to the crags around Great Gable. Stan Edmundson from Seathwaite Farm recalled Dalton sleeping under the rock: "Millican Dalton would come to Seathwaite and sit in our garden, have a pot of tea, scones and cake. He would sleep under a large rock at Seathwaite Slabs. He always wore shorts, army type jacket; never wore socks, just bandages around his feet. Millican got about on a bike for which he made a carrier from hazel branches bound by string. Millican was a wonderful character when Borrowdale was a quiet, beautiful valley."

Dalton's right to camp in the cave long-term on land obviously owned by somebody else is of interest. Did he ever seek permission from the landowner? Nobody remembers, and no records detailing a concession between the two parties appears to exist. Up until 1919 Castle Crag was privately owned, but was donated to the National Trust in 1920 by Sir William Hamer and his family in memory of his son John and the men of Borrowdale who fell in the World War I—they possibly turned a blind eye to his activities. Subsequently, a further bequest to the National Trust was made in 1939, when Lady Hamer gave 18.6 hectares on the lower slopes of Castle Crag, along with its resident 'caveman' and 'Cave Hotel,' as a memorial to Sir William Hamer. In the early days of the National Trust the enforcement of camping bylaws was not a priority. Wild camping was relatively common, but at this point not seen in a bad light. It seems that as Dalton was the only camper in the caves and as he caused no destruction or nuisance, he was left alone, unhindered. Whatever the agreement between Dalton, the Hamers and the National Trust, if any, on returning from the South his 'Aladdin's Cave' would be found intact, undisturbed and uninhabited with all his 'possessions' ready and available for immediate use.

As would be expected, Dalton owned very little. One of his few possessions, probably his most prized, was his sewing machine, which meant the manufacture and maintenance of clothing and equipment was not restricted solely to his southern residences. Although technology was progressing at a rapid rate in the outside world, the Cave Hotel was not left completely behind and the addition of the sewing machine ensured some degree of modernism.

M. D. Entwistle

THE CAVE INTERIOR

G. C. Potts

"HONEYMOON - EDWARD GROVES & MARJORY POTTS" - 19 AUGUST 1923

G. C. Potts

"VIEW INSIDE THE CAVE LOOKING OUT"

G. C. Potts

"LOOKING INTO MILLICAN DALTON'S CAVE"

G. C. Potts

"MARJORY SITTING AMONGST MILLICAN'S POSSESSIONS"

G. C. Potts

"SLATE SLAB BED - MARJORY WRAPPED IN MILLICAN'S BLANKET"

G. C. Potts

"MARJORY ASLEEP ON THE SLATE SLAB BED"

Millican Dalton

CAVE HOTEL SIGN - A GIFT TO A VISITOR

R. H. Mayson

THE JAWS OF BORROWDALE FROM THE CAVE HOTEL

M. M. Barker

TEEPEE FRAME AND SEWING MACHINE

M. D. Entwistle

SHELTER STONE AT LOWER SEATHWAITE SLABS

CHAPTER ELEVEN

YOU'RE MY ROCK

Ever since Haskett-Smith's first ascent of Napes Needle, the pioneering of new routes, including the perceived importance of claiming a place in climbing history, has been viewed by the majority of climbers as the pinnacle of achievement, and, as records prove, Millican Dalton also played a minor role in this subcultural aspiration.

In 1897 Millican, Andrew Thomson and 'E. R.' earned their badge of honour by recording an official first ascent on Dove's Nest Crags in the glacial hanging valley of Combe Ghyll. An initial exploration of the Borrowdale Fells the previous year by Thomson and others from Kendal had led the discovery of the crags, but it was only on returning with Dalton that the pioneering attempt was apparently made. Bentley Beetham, allegedly the spearhead of Borrowdale climbing, described the crag in the 1953 FRCC *Borrowdale Guide*:

> The place is quite unlike anything else in the whole of the Lake District: it is not, as it is sometimes said to be, the result of ancient mine or quarry workings; it is a rare natural phenomenon. A great rock face of a buttress has slipped bodily forwards and downwards; but instead of crashing into scree at the base of the cliff, its fall has been arrested, and it now leans back against the cliff from which it came, leaving cavities and fissures between the detached blocks and the parent rock. It is the 'subterranean' character of the route through these fissures that has made Dove's Nest so widely known. The exploration of the dark passages is interesting; the work is a pleasant mixture of potholing and rock climbing. On account of the sinuous and intricate nature of the routes in both vertical and horizontal planes they are as difficult to describe as they are to follow, and Dove's Nest must be one of the few places in Cumberland where a guide, i.e., a leader who really knows the terrain, is of much value to a party.

If any guide was of value on these crags it was Dalton who, without exaggeration, knew Dove's Nest inside-out, literally. After charting the various routes, both internally and externally, he visited repeatedly to climb with groups of friends, but also, more often than not, on his own. A geological masterpiece for climbers and explorers, it was presented as a prime attraction to his clients who were then granted the rare opportunity to infiltrate the inner sanctum of a Lakeland buttress, a unique escapade they would never forget.

To prove his unrivalled knowledge of the crag he wrote several route descriptions for the *Journal of Fell and Rock Climbing Club* 1914 including the route pioneered with Thomson and 'E. R.' named South or Buzzard Chimney:

DOVE NEST
BY MILLICAN DALTON

The wonderfully splintered collection of problems on this little crag deserves the attention of more climbers than it obtains. On its discovery some 18 years since by the late Andrew Thomson and other Kendalians, the place was felicitously described by them as the "rock gym."

Specimens of nearly every variety of rock climbing are to be found here within a space of 150 feet square—a pinnacle, faces, hand and "stomach" traverses, chimneys galore, with, in addition, an excellent substitute for a pothole.

The crag is situated opposite Raven Crag in the great hollow of Glaramara, and can be reached in three-quarter hours ascent from the Borrowdale Road. Opposite Mountain View the lane for Thorneythwaite Farm leads to a gate, and a path, there, branches to the left and winds upwards to the marshy floor of the Combe. Crossing the streamlet a sheep track leads to the crags.

The most interesting routes on Dove Nest, good enough for expert parties, are as follows:

SOUTH, OR BUZZARD CHIMNEY—Commence with back on left wall, using minute footholds on opposite wall. Twenty-five feet of pure back and knee chimneying brings the chockstone into reach. A bight of rope should then be threaded through, so that it provides a secure handhold, whilst completely reversing the body. The crack on the left of chockstone can then be utilised to complete the pitch.

Above the chockstone the route leads up steep incline to left to the traverse. The second man should belay at the left of the traverse, whilst the leader finishes up a vertical crack rising halfway along. The first ascent was made by M. D., A. T., and E. R. in 1897.

On my second ascent of the chimney I got into rather an awkward predicament. When threading a rope-end under the chockstone, I allowed insufficient length and found myself checked unexpectedly when endeavouring to surmount the chockstone. Not at all relishing any descent, I clung on whilst the situation was discussed with those below. Andrew Thomson finally came to the rescue by climbing an easier route to the top of the chockstone, whence he slung down a noose to me; slipping into this the pitch.

CENTRAL CHIMNEY—A good approach to this is over the ridge of the Pinnacle, thence descending into the chimney foot. The difficulty of the chimney varies according to whether it is climbed well inside, or nearer to the open. At the top of the pitch is the Attic Cave, with a bleaberry patch at its entrance. A long stretch and stride above the chimney takes the leader to the foot of a difficult crack in rather a sensational situation. A careful study of the problem is desirable before stepping off the bleaberry patch to attempt the crack. At the top of the crack a move onto the buttress finishes the difficulty. Hitches for the rope are available at foot of the crack and whilst ascending it.

THE INSIDE CAVE—On walking right into the South Chimney, an arrow drawn on the rock indicates the concealed entrance. As the cave is quite dark, artificial light is necessary, such as an acetylene lamp with hood removed, or an Alpine lantern will serve. String for suspending the light comes in useful at places, and a supply of matches should also be carried.

Continuing forward inside the entrance brings the explorer to a black chasm, about 30 feet deep. The easiest way to reach the bottom is along a ledge on the right-hand wall to its further edge, whence descent is not difficult. The return to the entrance can be made by traversing the chimney at a lower level than the ledge, or by climbing up a vertical hole.

From near the entrance a weird climb of 80 feet, towards a glimmer of light, leads into the Attic Cave and the open air again. A higher and more difficult exit can be reached by continuing the ascent before emerging into daylight. During the ascent the sensation may be heightened by throwing blazing newspapers down the dark abyss! As sound is magnified in the confined space, sensation produced by contact between sharp projecting points of rock and the human head should be carefully avoided!

133

The descent can be made either by the Central Chimney, or by the North Gully. At the foot of the latter, round a corner to the left looking down, is the interesting Inclined Crack leading upwards: and from the top of this, the Pinnacle can be reached by a short descent down a crack, and a swing on the arms across North Chimney.

In addition to the routes aforesaid, sundry problems can be solved:—
Short inclined crack on right wall of North Gully.
Traverse diagonally across central slab from foot of South Chimney.
Chimney on north of Pinnacle.
Chimney on east (inside) of Pinnacle.

The Stiffest problem is the Nose, at the top of North Gully. It has only been done by one party, about 8 years ago, Percy Salter and the late Tom Rennison. Being more difficult that the Pillar Nose Direct, with very minute and insecure holds, almost as hazardous for follower as for leader, a second ascent is not recommended.

For the novice an interesting run is—over the Pinnacle, into Central Chimney, down North Gully, and through a tunnel to North Chimney: thence down behind the Pinnacle.

'One often hears' continued Beetham, 'that Dove's Nest is the place to go in wet weather, and though it is true that by doing so you get out of the rain, it does not follow that you get out of the 'wet,' for water may be found dripping from the roof and streaming down the walls and onto unskilfully shielded candles. It would be better to say that however bad the weather is you can still put in an enjoyable day there.'

Millican certainly took full advantage of this all-weather venue with the caves providing an unadulterated option for when rain thwarted conventional climbing. So much time was spent weaving in and out of the dark cavities that a dilapidated barn a short distance from the crag was adapted as a temporary base; the comfort of a pot-bellied stove allowed wet clothes and boots to be dried before venturing out again.

In the end gravity took its toll on Dove's Nest. Settlement of the buttress over recent decades left the inmost caves impassable and for a period of time the crag unsafe, forever closing the chapter on this underground gem.

Running concurrent with the pioneering developments in the Lake District was an explosion of interest in climbing throughout Snowdonia, Wales. The regions challenging and rewarding routes were deemed equal to anywhere in the world and therefore a hotspot for early pioneers. Millican and Henry were no exception having already camped in the area since the early 1890s, and as pioneering climbers attempted to establish their own climbs.

Over time Millican's efforts, no doubt helped by his social connections, were duly noted and considered to be worthy of membership to the Climbers Club, founded 1898. The Club had evolved from England's and Wales' earliest endeavours to formally organise and muster active participants who were helping to develop the 'new' sport of rock climbing. Millican was subsequently proposed by J. W. Puttrell and seconded by Ashley Perry Abraham, both original members, and elected as a member on 14 February 1902. Shortly after his election he attended the fifth Annual Meeting and Dinner held at Café Royal, Regent Street, London, on Friday 9 May 1902 at which about 40 members attended. Something must have been amiss as successive Annual Meetings and Dinners were avoided.

Persistent extensive exploration and camping expeditions in the Welsh wilderness led the brothers to record a first ascent in 1903 on Craig-y-Cau, set amidst the beautiful landscape of the Cadair Idris range near the town of Dolgellau. Their route, on a remote northeast-facing cliff, rises dramatically above the dark sinister waters of Llyn Cau and terminates beneath the summit of Mynydd Pencoed—"a truly delectable" place, but mere words offer no justice to one of the most spectacular scenes in the Welsh mountains. It was known as Pencoed Pillar, a gigantic 740 feet HVD (Hard Very Difficult) three star climb, considered by climbers as a classic amongst classics. Botanical scrambles past Alpine flowers; greasy grooves; good holds, stances and belays constituted to this great mountaineering route of considerable character and breathtaking exposure. As the climb had never been "gardened," heavy vegetation made the route practically unclimbable during wet weather with conditions only becoming favourable after several dry days, in effect distinguishing the climb as a summer route.

An account of this climb appeared in Rock Climbing in North Wales 1906, written by George and Ashley Abraham, and read:

> This magnificent bastion of rock forms the left-hand retaining wall of the Great Gully. Its north ridge presents a terrific precipice which borders on the vertical in its upper part. When Mr. Jones told us in 1897 that it had never been climbed up this side, he made a statement, which holds good even at the present time and will probably go down to posterity with equal accuracy. Jones had said: "See that fine buttress on the left of the gully? That's Pencoed Pillar. It has not been climbed, and I doubt if it ever will be, up this side."
>
> Several strong parties have looked at it from below and passed on; others have essayed its ascent, leaving no record of their failure. In June 1903, however, Messrs

M. and H. G. Dalton discovered a somewhat circuitous route up the Pillar which "compares in point of difficulty and interest with the Great Gully."

I am indebted to Mr. M. Dalton for a few notes on their climb and for indicating it on the outline drawing of Craig-y-Cau. They started from the grass terrace. By the way of steep heather-covered rocks, they mounted rapidly until the ridge of the Pillar became almost vertical. An overhanging rock "which might have been surmounted had they possessed an ice axe" turned them back, so they retraced their steps until able to traverse upward to the left wall from the Great Gully.

Passing the foot of a chimney which seemed to lead back to the ridge, but which looked exceedingly difficult, they came to a milder looking one heading in the opposite direction. The lower part of this they ascended with difficulty and then traversed out to its left wall, which they scaled "by the aid of friction holds." Steep, bleaberry covered slopes were then followed until a practicable traverse to the right disclosed itself. This enabled them to regain the crest of the ridge, about 200 feet above where they had left it, whence they easily gained the top of the Pillar. They describe the traverse as "extremely impressive." At one point they had to cross the head of an incipient gully, gaining its far wall by means of a hand traverse, one hold on which consisted of "doubling the fist in a crack."

It sounds pretty lively, but if its difficulty be not greater than any encountered in the Great Gully the climb is to be recommended. They explored the ridge for some distance downward, leaving about 150 feet still untouched by climbers.

Years later George Abraham wrote about Pencoed Pillar again in his book *British Mountain Climbs*, 1923: 'Those genial pioneers of real, British mountaineering camp-life, Messrs Millican and Henry Dalton, discovered a route up the Pillar but mostly on its easterly side. The presence of much vegetation and the possibilities of numerous variations will militate against the climb becoming popular.'

With the exception of two further first ascents on Gimmer Crag, Great Langdale in the summer of 1907 with a party from the Fell and Rock Climbing Club, alluded to in the Club's archives, there are no further records anywhere and total the number of accredited first ascents stands at four—a very low number bearing in mind the amount of time Millican spent exploring the various districts. An explanation for this could be he simply did not pioneer any other climbs, or alternatively, unlike most he was not overly concerned in seeking recognition for his achievements or obtaining the associated bragging rights and therefore failed to make official records—something to bear in mind for later. Details of his activities with the Climbers Club also remain sparse, but membership was relatively short lived and before reaching his four year anniversary he resigned on 31 December 1905—there was, however, a more suitable club.

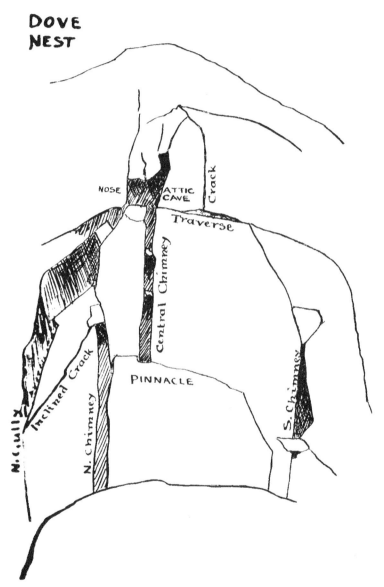

Millican Dalton

MILLICAN'S SKETCH OF DOVE'S NEST

R. H. Mayson

MILLICAN & ERIC BOWSER ON DOVE'S NEST

R. H. Mayson

BELAYING ON DOVE'S NEST

R. H. Mayson

"DOVE NEST" - ERIC BOWSER, MILLICAN & REV. G. C. POTTS

G. C. Potts

"MILLICAN WITH ERIC BOWSER NEAR DOVE NEST"

R. H. Mayson

"ROUND THE CORNER FROM DOVE NEST" (MILLICAN RIGHT)

V. Stimson

MILLICAN & VERA STIMSON CLIMB BOWDERSTONE PINNACLE

141

CHAPTER TWELVE

FELL & ROCK CLIMBING CLUB

S everal references have already been made to the Fell and Rock Climbing Club (FRCC), and so, by now, the reader may have deduced that Millican Dalton was in fact a member of this acclaimed institution, which has a long and illustrious history stretching back to the twentieth anniversary of recreational rock climbing.

Origins of the Club stem from Edward Scantlebury; he had suggested to friend, Alan Craig, who with others travelled to Coniston every Sunday fell walking, that they should form their own climbing club. Initially enthused by Owen Glynn Jones's culturally important book, Rock Climbing in the English Lake District, the pair took up the sport of climbing and as a result of their exploits believed it was a sufficiently good cause for the formation of a club. Two members would never have made a crowd, so they roped in Chas Grayson, G. H. Charter and S. H. Gordon who frequently joined them on their way to Coniston. These five, the real originators of the Club, formed a committee of themselves complete with secretary and treasurer—but it was thanks to Scantlebury that the Club owed its existence. Gathering at the Sun Hotel, Coniston on the 11 November 1906 for the Club's inaugural meeting, with the exception of Gordon who joined a little later, they discussed the aims of the Club. A suitable name, chosen after much debate on a previous occasion, led to the creation of the Fell and Rock Climbing Club of the English Lake District.

Primary aims of the Club included the promotion and encouragement of fell walking and rock climbing within the Lake District and to act as a bonding link between its members. In order to achieve these aims the Club organised a programme of climbing meets at various key locations: The Sun Hotel, Coniston; Wastwater Hotel, Wasdale Head; New Hotel, Dungeon Chyll, Great Langdale; Jopson's Farm, Thorneythwaite, Borrowdale and the Buttermere Hotel, Buttermere constituting the Club's official quarters. Climbing books kept at each of these quarters acted as a log for climbers to record their efforts. Annual Club Dinners provided a social aspect away from the fells and the publishing of an annual journal highlighted new route developments and articles submitted by members.

Attempts to attract new members from a wider audience was the next goal. By raising awareness through the distribution of circulars detailing the Club's existence, membership stood at almost two hundred within a few months. First President, Ashley Abraham, added great impetus to the Club in the early years with credibility of the FRCC assured when the legendary father of the sport, W. P. Haskett-Smith, the renowned G. A. Solly and respected Cecil Slingsby added their names to the list of members.

Notwithstanding Dalton's friendship with several Kendalians and other climbers from South Lakeland he was never a regular to the Coniston area and was only really friendly with one committee member—H. B. Lyon—his status meant little at this point and Dalton did not become a member himself until his return north from Billericay around Easter 1907. Although it is improbable he would have been a founder member it is highly likely that, had he been resident in Cumberland at the time of the Club formation, he would have been in the first wave of membership applicants and perhaps one of the original thirteen ordinary members. Subscription for the first year of the Club was purely nominal with the second and subsequent seasons subscription being somewhat increased—consequently fourteen members resigned.

As already established, Dalton was no stranger to club membership and a competent climber way before the concept of the FRCC; in no way did he join as a novice. Nonetheless he was keen to be involved and wasted no time in participating in the Club's activities.

FRCC archives, currently held at Kendal Records Office, suggest that Millican's first outing was the Club Meet at Seathwaite in Borrowdale between the 3 - 7 August 1907. Attendance was poor with numbers much lower than anticipated despite the fact that Chas Grayson had previously notified all members by postcard. Members present, only eight in total, included H. B. Lyon, Andrew Thomson, Chas Grayson and Edward Scantlebury. Heavy rain ushered in the first day, so the party, staying at Jopson's Farm, amused themselves in the morning by making first ascents up the barn wall into the hayloft; a route highly reminiscent of the "Tiger's" Barn Door Traverse at the Wastwater Hotel. An hour or two was beguiled in the loft with hay climbing, obstacle races and wrestling, then after dinner with the weather slightly finer, they took candles and a lantern from the farm and made a start for the caves on Dove's Nest Crag. During the course of the week, the group climbed popular routes of the day and heading to Great Gable managed to scale Napes Needle, Eagle's Nest Arête and Kern Knotts Chimney; and on Pillar Rock: New West, Slab and Notch and finally Pendlebury

Traverse. Tuesday 6 August saw Dalton and Lyon split from the main group to make a return to Pillar Rock. Miserable, wet and misty weather did not hamper progress and the double act managed to reach the summit via New West descending by East Jordan. Pillar Rock was also the destination the following week, this time with the Bottrerills, the Seatrees and a couple of other friends and yet again headed up New West.

Great Langdale was the destination several weeks later when Millican made the journey from Borrowdale for the first Langdale Meet. Gimmer Crag and a new route pioneered by the Fell and Rock party, including Dalton, proved to be the highlight of the Meet. That same week, on 22 September 1907 the group claimed another first ascent, on this occasion Junipall Gully, a moderate graded climb. With no pause for breath Dalton was off again making a return to the North Lakes where he visited Pillar Rock with P. R. Shannon and J. R. Rennison for a Sunday outing on 29 September, ascending North Climb to the summit and descending via East Jordan.

Next up was an excursion to Coniston on 8 June 1908 but strong gales and mist-covered fells spoilt any good intentions of climbing and so hiking took precedence. Departing early morning from the village centre, A. Gregson, W. Gregson, Chas Grayson and Dalton headed for Brown Pike, Coniston Old Man, Great How Crags, Carrs and Wetherlam. 'The mist lifted and turned very nice later on,' wrote one of the climbers in the Coniston climbing book.

His next Club Meet was at Coniston on 4 and 5 July 1908 at which a turnout of quality climbers attended, included the 'Keswick Brothers' Ashley and George Abraham, G. M. Thorpe, G. C. Turner, H. B. Lyon, C. H. Oliverson, A. R. Thomson, Edward Scantlebury, A. Craig, Chas Grayson and Percy Suller. Climbs on the agenda featured Great Gully, Intermediate Gully, North Gully, Woodhouse's Route and B. Buttress, all on Dow Crag.

Jaunts to Pillar Rock were made many more times over the subsequent years after his first visit, originally with friends and in later years when leading large parties of non-members of up to a dozen people (Sunday 16 April 1911 for example). Evidence of his fondness for Pillar Rock exists in the numerous entries made in the little green climbing book that was housed in a weatherproof container on the summit; this was used for recording routes undertaken, new routes pioneered, climbers names, weather conditions and dates of ascents; and in which some of the greatest names in British rock climbing left their calling cards.

The 1912 FRCC Borrowdale Meet commenced on Sunday 18 August but Dalton did not join the group until the following day when eight members climbed Kern Knotts Chimney. Turning out to be somewhat of a quiet Meet, Dalton did not participate in any other climbs and the entire group abstained from climbing on

144

Thursday 22 August when they all tramped over the fells by way of Easedale to Grasmere Sports; the biggest annual sporting event in the Lake District calendar.

Rock climbing may have still been a relatively new sport, but certain routes, being more popular than others, had felt the burden of large volumes of traffic and become increasingly littered. Concerned about the state of these climbs several FRCC members planned a conscientious cleanup expedition to Walker's Gully on Pillar Rock in 1912.

Their primary purpose was to collect abandoned climbing rope, which had been left behind for a multitude of reasons. Not only was this a blot on the landscape, it also hindered the progress and enjoyment of other climbers. Millican Dalton, W. B. Brunskill, H. G. Dale and H. B. Gibson set out on the climb only to be overwhelmed by the amount of gear to remove and gave up the attempt in despair around the third pitch with their rucksacks full. A much disintegrated packet of sandwiches at the foot of the top pitch; a capacious rucksack; two rock climbing guidebooks and a lady's waterproof were, amongst other items, removed from the gully. One member of the party was so absorbed in the waterproof that he tried it on and although finding it comfortable to wear was apparently a little tight around the waist and shoulders!

Supplementary to the two articles written for the Club's Journal, *A Camping Holiday* and *Dove's Nest*, was a short write-up for Bowder Pinnacle (now known as Bowder Stone Pinnacle), pioneered by climbing partner Ralph H. Mayson, featuring within *Climbs Old and New, Fell and Rock Climbing Club Journal* 1914:

BOWDER PINNACLE, BORROWDALE

On the crag from which the Bowder Stone traces its descent there is a pinnacle, which yields a good climb. The pinnacle, with a chimney on its left, can be picked out from the road below. A traverse leads from the gully on the right, and thence upward the foot of a wide chimney, which is climbed by the back and foot method to the top of the pinnacle.

The pinnacle can be left (or approached) by a very long awkward stride across the chimney to another ridge, from the end of which a short climb up by a yew tree brings the climber to easy slopes. I think Fred Mallinson and Ralph Mayson were the pioneers. M. D.

As the reputation of the FRCC grew so did the number of members, which rose so dramatically that the Club almost became too popular. This also applied to the crags to some extent; the once quiet Club Meets began to develop into mass excursions into the mountains and it was not uncommon to have to wait in turn for many minutes, even hours, on the popular routes during a busy Meet. Totally at odds with Dalton's style, and whilst at ease in the company of up to twenty people, the thought of larger crowds was unappealing and, according to Club archives, he never appeared at a Club Meet in the Lake District again after 1915. Crowded Annual Club Dinners, the highlight of the calendar for many members, were also held in a similar disregard and shown by a persistent non-attendance. Even the Club Dinner of 1928, held at the Windermere Hydro Hotel, Bowness-on-Windermere, could not lure Dalton, despite celebrity guest speaker Hugh Walpole, the Keswick based author, taking centre stage—needless to say Dalton had his own modus operandi.

Later, in the autumn of 1920, a number of enthusiastic FRCC members who lived in the south of England gathered together and discussed the validity of a London Section. Members living in the North questioned the need for a satellite organisation, but after highlighting the difficulties and expense of long distance travel and the post-war slump which necessitated an ever-increased curtailment of weekend excursions to the Lakes, consideration was granted.

After several unofficial gatherings it was decided, with the blessing of the Club, that a London Section was warranted and should be created. Consequently the Section was formed at the end of 1920 with its main intentions to provide monthly outings into the countryside, an outlet for keeping fit and the opportunity for members to talk about all things mountainous. Committee Member W. P. Haskett-Smith was probably the most notable member of the London Section.

Millican followed suit by rekindling his affection with the FRCC during the 1921-1922 season when he too became a member. Not long after joining he was included in a Section foray to Welwyn on 2 November 1921. Of the group, several members decided to head north towards Ayot St. Lawrence, and with Captain Hetherington-Brown acting as spokesman they visited the home of George Bernard Shaw, but he was not in residence. The Irish playwright was much admired by Millican Dalton, a long term supporter since the early days of the Fabian Society, and someone who he considered to be one of the few sensible people in the world. This may come as a surprise considering that Shaw tended to provoke rage and dislike in his younger years through his scandalously subversive opinions and, in his later years, the strong indications that he sympathised with Stalin, Hitler and Mussolini—but no one, including Dalton, disputed his genius. Actually they shared much in common: Shaw admitted he was not suited to work and could not abide the restrictions of being employed; he was a strict vegetarian; enjoyed walking in the Ayot countryside and respected all living things as equals; had a deep concern for humanity, leftwing views and intellectual originality; and opposed war.

146

26 February 1922 saw another London Section outing, this time to Chingford. The party, keen to enter Epping Forest, did so at the earliest opportunity and on their way to High Beech Dalton suggested that tree climbing could be an option, but the damp weather thwarted his plan. Once finished exploring the depths of the forest, the group stopped and ate a soggy lunch before setting off for Ambresbury Banks where debate between the knowledgeable members focused on whether the forest's hillfort was in fact razed in AD 60 by Iceni, Queen Boudicca, and her tribe of Ancient Britons, rather than the site where she made a galant last stand against the Paulinus led Roman army. To conclude the excursion Dalton offered to provide tea; most accepted but several found themselves so engrossed in the topical discussions of Everest and oxygen that they found themselves lost, but nevertheless managed to meet the rest of the party at Chingford Station.

Future years witnessed a surge in membership of the London Section and in consequence, sometime in the 1930s or 1940s, his subscription was left to expire.

Reverting to the topic of tourism, a progressive influx of thrill seeking excursionists visiting the Lake District after the turn of the twentieth century saw the establishment of other guiding businesses looking to take advantage of the burgeoning numbers of people wishing to enter the fells. Modern tourists were, in general, far less daunted than the early Victorians and much keener to experience the 'savageness' of the mountains. No longer the domain of shepherds, gentleman explorers or pioneers, mountains had become an attraction for mass tourism.

The flamboyant and controversial character J. E. B. Wright seized the opportunity and established The Lakeland Mountain Guides (LMG) in 1925. Jerry Wright, 'The Keswick Guide,' based his business at Seatoller House, Borrowdale, at the foot of Honister Pass. Guiding was primarily for groups or individuals who wished to hike, but he also catered for those wanting to experience rock climbing, which in later years became the mainstay of his business.

In 1927 the Journal of the FRCC contained an article in the Editor's Notes relating to a pamphlet titled *The Fell Guide to the English Lakes*, which it branded as 'American advertising and the cheap press, that is perhaps only to be expected in our modern age.' High pricing and the strong advertising medium was highly frowned upon which according to the Journal: 'Makes rock-climbing a sport for plutocrats, instead of what it essentially is, the most democratic of all recreations.' The pamphlet, Wright's creation— his idea of a forward thinking approach to advertising in order to attract increased custom—was akin to a menu listing plainly and simply the available routes and tariffs. Fees seemed rather high with guiding services priced at five guineas per day for each guide for specific courses as selected by Wright on Pillar Rock. Wright's retort to the

FRCC article was one of contempt and in an act of defiance glided up Napes Needle in sixty-five seconds—a more than impressive feat. Needless to say, Wright made several enemies.

Stanley Watson, a native of South Shields, was one such enemy. Watson, formerly employed as a guide by Wright, was in direct competition having established the British Mountain Guides (BMG) in 1933 and originally based his business at Grosvenor House, Blencathra Street, Keswick and later at Newton Place opposite the Borrowdale Hotel. Adopting a similar advertising format to the LMG, Watson placed posters around the local area, charging up to £1 per day, per person for a typical ascent of Napes Needle and up to five other equally difficult climbs, all dependant upon conditions of the rock and ability of the climber.

A resulting dispute with Watson left the LMG considering legal action against alleged libellous statements in a BMG poster that ambiguously referred to Wright and his business. Advised accordingly, Wright chose not to pursue the action, but this left resentments.

Occasionally, during the mid-thirties, Dalton was employed by Watson to help out when overburdened with work. For this he received 15s. per day to guide parties up routes on Great Gable or Pillar Rock, as advertised on posters of the BMG. Although employed in his late sixties he was obviously regarded by Watson as a competent and prudent leader, more than capable of the job role; he was longest serving mountain guide in the Lake District after all. No other person could have been more suitable; a steadfast old hand, who needed no Bartholomew map or magnetic needle to point the way, he knew this district like the back of his hand.

Except for occasionally relieving the BMG, Dalton's own programme remained full with the period between the two world wars the best trade; he had built an extensive client base, many of who returned year after year. Clearly the Professor of Adventure competed with both the BMG and the LMG but as custom was high he remained unconcerned about sufficient trade; he certainly cared little about the spat between Wright and Watson.

As far as can be gathered, Dalton escaped criticism for his approach to advertising. Considering that his advertising medium was just as 'Americanised' as Wright's and actually preceded it by at least twelve years, it is of interest why he was never condemned or challenged by the FRCC with the same distain. What seemed to have passed unnoticed within the hierarchy of the FRCC is the fact that Dalton's article, *A Camping Holiday*, was nothing more than blatant advertising; a clear adaptation of his work programme that managed to manipulate the Journal into a free advertising medium.

148

FRCC Collection

GRANGE BRIDGE, BORROWDALE (DALTON SECOND FROM RIGHT)

FRCC Collection

"ON THE WAY TO GIMMER." - A FELL AND ROCK PARTY IN LANGDALE.
(DALTON, FRONT ROW SECOND FROM RIGHT, ROPED TO HIS COUSIN
T.OM RENNISON, MIDDLE ROW SECOND FROM LEFT)

149

A CAMPING HOLIDAY.

By MILLICAN DALTON.

One of my favourite camps is a steep fell
commanding a perfect view of a perf
framed by mountains on each
Skiddaw in the distan
sunsets from th
dined i

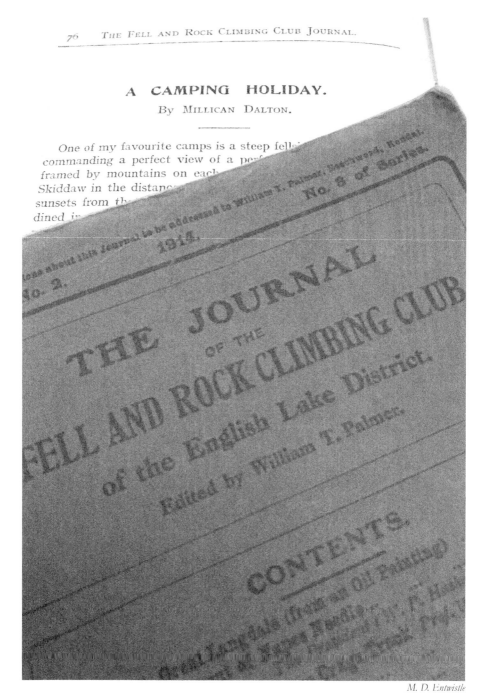

M. D. Entwistle

THE JOURNAL OF THE FELL AND ROCK CLIMBING CLUB

CHAPTER THIRTEEN

THE EPPING FOREST CAMP

Meanwhile back in deepest Essex, Millican had come to the conclusion that having spent several years living at The Camp in Billericay a change of scenery and a return to his childhood roots was in order to be closer to his ageing mother. Over the years, Epping Forest, due to its accessibility and resources for adventure, had become one of his favourite areas to camp; after all it was the Dalton brother's first training ground where their voracious taste for the great outdoors was born. Every inch of the forest had been explored, from ancient earthworks and ponds to coppices and former roads; he knew all the darkest recesses.

And so, in the region of 1910 or 1911, making the 15 mile journey westward, he followed in the footsteps of many other like minded people before him and set up camp in the forest. Proving an ideal situation, the forest was not only a huge maze of almost ten thousand acres in which it was easy to escape, it was still convenient for shops, transport links, friends and family. Left without a permanent base, he occasionally spent time at his mother's home and used her postal address for several seasons as a mailbox for his guiding business.

April 1913 then brought with it the death of Frances Dalton; chronic bronchitis ending her life at the age of eighty years whilst at home at Elm Villas. Brothers Joseph, Millican and Henry, all included in the resulting Will and Testament, received approximately £700 each, which also incorporated a share of the legacy from their late grandfather, Tinniswood Millican. Succeeding his mother's death, Millican moved into 8 Lincoln Terrace in the village of Loughton, sited on the outer limits of Epping Forest adjacent to Woodbury Knoll, though, unsurprisingly, this did not bring an end to his adventures within the forest.

Prior to the Epping Forest Act 1878 the forest was a similar situation to Thornwood and Billericay in the fact that many gipsies, hawkers, vagabonds, hermits, men of the road and Simple Lifers camped within its boundary. The Act was commissioned by the

City of London Corporation to govern Epping Forest as Conservators. Upholding a duty to ensure that forestland remained unenclosed and preserved for the enjoyment of the general public was the Act's primary mission. Preservation of the natural aspect of the forest through the protection of wildlife, trees, plants and the ancient earthworks, was achieved by the prevention of wood cutting, the removal of earth and resistance to new construction on forest land. Forest Keepers, sometimes referred to as Woodmen, were the boots on the ground assigned to actively enforce compliance with the Act and ensure that such damage to the forest was prevented. Therefore as the majority of travellers caused much destruction and disturbance, they became looked upon with great disregard. Their wish to live in the forest was refused and they found themselves removed along with their dark barrel tents and carved, elaborately painted caravans on a regular basis.

Yet, curiously, a close friendship with the Forest Keepers in which they would turn a blind eye allowed Dalton to camp in the forest unhindered and regardless of the Epping Forest Act he was rumoured to be the only person allowed to light fires by special arrangement.

Originally consisting of only a tent, the encampment, located towards the eastern edge of the forest, soon took on different guises. Always proficient in achieving comfort, even in the most challenging circumstances, the tent was superseded by the luxury of a small, two-roomed wooden hut, barely larger than a garden shed. It was constructed from overlapped timber, featured a hinged door, an internal hearth from which the grate had been removed, and was equipped with everything he needed—cooking utensils, food and coffee; his library of books, journals, letters and photographs openly available to both visitors and passers-by alike. The walls of his hut were festooned with Alpine ropes and ice-axes; his bed the uncovered floor. A companion in his Simple Life, a woman he referred to as "Pixy," lived alongside his hut in a tent. She was Pixy Poole, a fellow devotee of the great outdoors. Those who knew the forest suggest that at one point his Epping camp composed of a strange treetop dwelling of his own devising—presumed to be some form of tree house high in the canopy.

Dalton was well known in and around Epping Forest; a well-respected character amongst local residents, Forest Keepers, colliers and other woodland workers, with whom he became particularly famed for his love of tree climbing when he often alarmed the unwary by abseiling down trunks. He was however remembered above all as a kindhearted and hospitable man who would share whatever he could. Treats for guests at his retreat included merry singsongs and jovial parties around his fire with food and constant servings of hot drinks. "Tree boling" also provided entertainment with all new ascents named and the favourites climbed repeatedly.

Generous with his own extensive knowledge, he was ever happy to teach folk about Nature or the techniques associated with the construction of debris shelters, bivouacs, rope ladders and swings; the use of lassoes, bows and arrows; and the skills involved in "tree boling" and tracking to anybody who wanted to listen. Such enthusiasm for free tuition was unheard of and the opportunity to experience innovative and daring escapades soon gained him a following.

Changing seasons brought with them new and diverse challenges particularly during the winter months when the forest was transformed into a crisp, white wonderland creating even more resources for fun and adventure. Undeterred by the warning signs posted around the many ponds signifying: 'Danger! Thin Ice,' he would be the first to don his crudely fashioned homemade wooden skates and glide effortlessly across Baldwin's Pond, and when the thaw set in and the 'rinks' turned to nothing more than slush he would be the last to take them off. Dalton was said to be a most impressive and natural skater whose balance was insurmountable, but which was fine-tuned with the aid of a cigar, which was humorously claimed to assist! Even more impressive were his long, handmade skis with which he zipped down the gentle slopes of the forest. Visits to the Alps had introduced Dalton to this hairbreadth sport and, as a particularly rare sight in Essex, mesmerised the local youngsters, especially the boys—never mind the igloos!

Life in the forest was not all fun and games and when September 1914 ushered in World War I it immediately curtailed day to day enjoyment for the majority of the population, in particular outdoor pursuit enthusiasts. Some were already involved in one of the armed forces, some volunteered and others had priorities away from sport. At the age of 47 Dalton was too old to fight but, as an ardent pacifist, would have refused anyway.

Directly before the outbreak of war and the imposed restrictions on international travel Millican and Henry had managed one last expedition enjoying a camping and climbing trip to the mountainous wilds of Corsica, without bicycles, where they "purchased a 'moke' a very little ass, to transport the baggage."

On returning Millican chose not to flee the events of the war until the end of the hostilities, which carried terror to London and the surrounding counties, and instead watched events unfold from Loughton, though he was far from safety. Irrelevant to the lack of threat posed to mainland Britain from a land invasion, great concern arose from the extended strategic bombing campaigns by the German Empire's fleet of airships. Their slow speed may not have frightened the public in the same way as the enemy's aircraft did, but their presence still unsettled a population who had never before experienced the arrival of war on the home front. Resolute, Millican decided to live his life as normal and defiantly persisted in travelling between Essex and Cumberland to meet up with friends and continued to conduct domestic camping tours.

Irrespective of his non-participation in the conflict, the war still had a direct effect on him. A bizarre incident occurred in the autumn of 1914 in which Police arrested Dalton under the suspicion of being a German spy—though there was never a more unlikely secret agent. Whilst going about his own business at the Epping camp, a hiker, who had spotted him and become suspicious of his homespun appearance and nocturnal forays in the forest, informed the police. On their arrival they found Millican perched in a tree, which must have looked dubious as the constables dismissed his innocent claims of being a camper and sequentially detained him. The next day he appeared in the dock before Woodford Magistrates Court where it took the persuasions of several friends and reliable witnesses, who took the stand in his defence, to have the charges dropped.

From May 1915 onwards Zeppelin bomber raids concentrated on London became an increasingly regular occurrence in what has become known as the 'First Blitz'. As the flight path from the North Sea crossed the home counties there were isolated incidents that saw Epping Forrest fall under the shadow of the passing airships. Loughton folk saw two of these balloon 'baby killers' pursued by incendiary fire and meet their doom with almighty explosions. On the night of 3 September 1916 the war arrived with a bang in the small village of Cuffley, only a few miles from the Waltham Abbey Royal Gunpowder Mills, when a Schutte-Lanz airship, tactical number SL-11 (a wood and wire airship lighter than a Zeppelin) was successfully attacked by a small biplane using a new type of incendiary ammunition. SL-11 plunged like a giant flaming torch out of the night sky becoming the first airship shot down on British soil drawing huge crowds from London.

T.P.'s WEEKLY
VOLUME 25, PAGE 629, 1915
ADVENTURES, superior to War.
Camping Holidays, Mountaineering, Rapid-Shooting,
Night Rambles and Bivouacs in British Wilds,
25s.—30s. weekly.
Particulars of PETER PAN, 8, Lincoln Terrace, Loughton, Essex.

With Lincoln Terrace facing demolition, Dalton, forced to move, resettled in one of several cottages clustered around the Foresters Arms on Baldwin's Hill, Loughton. After the dawn of the twentieth century Loughton, as with many areas north of London, developed into a sanctuary away from the mushrooming conurbation. Loughton was certainly a quiet retreat with the population, even as late as 1921 standing at a mere 360 people. Prominent artists, freethinkers, members of the scientific community, wealthy merchants and assorted intellectuals were particularly attracted to The Hills area characterised by its steep hills, narrow lanes, ancient trees and high holly hedges, primarily due to its close proximity to both Epping Forest and London.

A common non-conformity adopted by these residents in terms of religion and outlook was particularly apparent. Residents, including Jacob Epstein amongst others, although not remembered individually, contributed to a wider revolution in popularising arts and crafts and a display of sympathy for the workingman.

It was in The Hills area that Dalton's home, Walnut or Camp Cottage—a white weatherboarded, red tile-roofed gardened tenement with many charming architectural features—was located in a small row known as Stony Path. Immediately opposite Stony Path lies the forest boundary affording a tranquil atmosphere and allowing for unequalled and unrestricted access. This close proximity to Nature, it seems, was a prerequisite and even with the luxury of Camp Cottage, he continued to camp and bivouac in the forest, satisfying his preference for the outdoor life.

DAILY HERALD
11 JULY 1919
HOLIDAY CAMP

ADVENTURES—Camping Holidays, Mountaineering, Rapid Shooting,
Night Expeditions, Hair-breath Escapes
Particulars, Millican Dalton, Stony Path, Loughton, Essex.

DAILY HERALD
11 JUNE 1921
HOLIDAY CAMPS

ADVENTURES for All! Camping, Boating, Mountaineering, &c. Inexpensive.
Programme of Dalton, Stony Path, Loughton, Essex.

Visitors to his camp could simply marvel at the transformation wrought by a short plunge into the woodland. There was just the distant echo of civilisation for a short time, but that died away on entering upon a new world, a refreshing change from the dusty roads and hard pavements, where the delicate green of the pollard hornbeam contrasts with the sombre holly, whist the graceful silver birch forms a canopy of green, through which the sky of richest blue is hardly visible. The briars and thorns, and fragrant, climbing honeysuckle mingle their tints of emerald, and give cover to the birds and roe deer, whose presence is everywhere. These were the delights of Mother Nature that Millican was ever keen to introduce to others—friends and stranger alike—as became clear in an article published in *The Weekly Dispatch*, 19 April 1925 *(Mirrorpix)*:

TOO SIMPLE LIFE

ADVENTURES OF ONE WHO TRIED IT

FOREST CRUSOE

"Will you come with me?" asked Mr. Dalton, Professor of Adventure, mountaineer, vegetarian, philosopher, and disciple of the Simple Life. "Will you come with me to camp in the forest and sleep beneath the stars, to shoot the rapids and navigate the whirlpools, to climb the crags and tramp the highways, to search for a new adventure every day?"

"Perhaps, when the weather is a little more settled"—I began.

"The weather?" boomed Mr. Dalton. "Who cares for the weather? You must learn to sleep in the snow, to light a fire in the pouring rain, and to sing for the joy of life when the wild north-easter's blowing. It's grand."

"It must be." I said. "What other simple pleasures will there be?"

"There will be tree-climbing," mused Mr. Dalton. "We shall, of course, climb most of the different trees in the forest."

"Of course," I agreed. "I shall enjoy that."

"Sometimes we shall use ropes," added Mr. Dalton.

"What for?" I asked. "To hang each other with?"

Without replying to this question Mr. Dalton slung his rucksack over his shoulders and ordered me to accompany him into Epping Forest.

The Professor of Adventure lives on the edge of this beautiful spot in a very simple cottage furnished in the simplest possible manner.

He is 58 years old, wears a beard and is variously nicknamed "Robinson Crusoe," "Sinbad the Sailor," and "Peter Pan."

"We will have tea in the forest," announced Mr. Dalton.

"I shall need it," I answered gratefully.

"It will be your first adventure," said Mr. Dalton.

But he was wrong. Before we had walked another yard I had sunk deep in a ditch filled with beech leaves and felt the water oozing round my ankles.

I stooped to brush some leaves away, and when I rose the Professor of Adventure had vanished.

Then, far above me, a voice shouted, "Here I am!" and I observed the grey-haired professor swinging himself happily from branch to branch of a tall oak.

When he reached the earth once more he ran up to another tree with a cleft in its trunk which he raked vigorously with a stick.

"What's in there?" I asked, peering into the cleft.

"Bees," he said joyfully.

Taking my face away with the greatest possible speed I ran across the clearing and hid in a thicket. From there I observed the professor turn away disappointedly from the bees' nest and search anxiously beneath a fallen tree truck.

"What's under there?" I shouted from the safety of the thicket.

"Snakes," he shouted back.

I went further into the thicket.

Later on we met again and the professor made a fire and brewed some tea.

"What shall we do next week?" I asked, when the meal was over.

"You can choose," he said, "between sleeping in the forest, shooting a weir in an open boat, or climbing the most dangerous rocks in the country."

"Thanks," I replied. "I'll think it over."

N. H. G.

That same summer another news reporter tracked down Millican at his forest retreat; his article featured in *The People*, 16 August 1925 *(Mirrorpix)*:

BACK TO NATURE'S GREAT GIFTS
MEN WHO RENOUNCE THE WORLD AND FIND TRUE HAPPINESS

Is life under modern high-pressure conditions worth living? There are some men, weary of motor cars and aeroplanes, telephones and wireless, who declare we pay too high a price for the luxuries and so-called advantages of civilisation. The vast majority of us will say that life is worth living in any ordinary conditions and will continue to pay tribute to the god of things as they are. What happens to the rebels who have defied convention and made new laws for their own governance?

There is a man who has decided that modern life is not worthwhile. On the edge of a green sea of oaks in Epping Forest, the representative.

The People came upon a tiny wooden hut.

A man, bearded and tanned, stood in the doorway. He wore an old pair of breeches and a green shirt, open at the neck. He is known far and wide as the Sage of Epping Forest and to his intimates as Millican Dalton, Professor of Adventure.

He is the eternal boy. Ask him why he lives in the forest and he laughs and says: "Because I grew to hate the City years and years ago when I was an insurance clerk."

Millican Dalton spends his days climbing trees, tramping, chopping wood and studying the life of the birds and animals of the forest. He is sixty, but looks forty. And he eats nothing but raw fruit and nuts and wholemeal bread.

"Civilisation," he says, "has nothing to offer me that I want, so instead of becoming a disgruntled member of conventional society, I prefer to do the honest thing—live as my instincts tell me I should live."

Had Millican really discovered the rot of modern life? Had he, like Thoreau, solved the problem of how to be happy without any of those stimulants upon which we depend under the modern conditions of life? This question may yet be unanswered. But one thing this surreal, lonesome adventurer appears to have discovered is the way of perfect health, how to break up the dulness and monotony of conventional-bound life and habit, and reveal in all the glory of freedom.

Fire eventually destroyed the Epping hut in which his collection of photographs, letters and early volumes of the *Fell and Rock Journal* were lost. Laid-back as ever Dalton made light of the situation and simply commented that at least he would not have to bother replying to the letters!

Archives

MILLICAN AND PIXY

158

Archives

MILLICAN STITCHES A RUCKSACK OUTSIDE THE EPPING HUT - c. 1925

159

CHAPTER FOURTEEN

MY FIRST LEADER

Time honoured clichés are not always warranted, but the utterance "birds of a feather flock together" summarise some relationships precisely; a term especially relevant in the friendship of Millican Dalton and Mabel M. Barker. The birth of their relationship was rooted in 1913 when Mabel wrote to Millican regarding the possibly of hiring tents and equipment.

Barker, a school teacher, acting as leader for a party of students from Saffron Walden Ladies' Training College, Essex, was proposing a camping expedition to Seathwaite, Borrowdale. George Morris, friends with Millican, had told Mabel about him long before they ever met during a discussion on literature. "I know the original of the chief character in Rest Harrow" said Morris, "At least, he is like enough to have suggested him." W. G. Hanson had made the same comparison in his article *A Gipsy Holiday* with his reference to Maurice Hewlett's Jack Senhouse, who, for clarity, is the chief character in *Rest Harrow*. Morris, also working in education, was a Science and Geography Master at the Friends' School, Saffron Walden. Overseeing the introduction of 'Nature Study' and botany into the curriculum, he organised school tramps to the countryside each year, but reputedly, when Dalton tried to lure him onto the rocks he persisted in declining.

Ever keen to help out in his area of expertise, especially where women were concerned, Dalton was only too pleased to provide the impedimenta. Late one afternoon, with the camp underway, he walked from High Lodore and visited Seathwaite to check on the welfare of the twenty-five female party members, referred to by Barker as the "Walden Gipsies," and the performance of his equipment. 'Then and thereafter" wrote Mabel, "he reminded me of pictures of Robinson Crusoe.'

That evening, with darkness falling and the flames of the campfire rising, he took position and, habitually, set up a billycan arrangement and brewed-up forthwith. 'He was at home throughout his life by any campfire; certainly so at mine' added Mabel.

Over the course of the holiday one of the "Walden Gypsies" had a pair of walking boots that required mending. Forever offering assistance, Dalton took them away to Plaskett's store in Rosthwaite, but unfortunately the shop had closed for the day so he left them, trustfully, on the doorstep. To the astonishment of the students, who doubted his better judgement, they returned in due time; safe, sound, repaired and ready for use.

Something definitely clicked and the two of them maintained a friendship joining forces later that year after he had quite casually offered to take any one of them climbing, 'I could hardly believe my ears' exclaimed Mabel. Arriving at Needle Gully in some force on 31 July 1913 Barker and her group prepared for a day on the rocks with their newly discovered friend. Climbing had officially started for Barker; the fells and rocks being the original and abiding link between them both. Napes Needle, an impressive introductory ascent, was her first roped climb on which she took second behind Dalton's lead. 'Several more of the party, including a young Japanese student, who took excellent photographs, were taken up in turn. But while he was on the rope I wanted to get a photograph of the top, and have still a faded old print of a startled Dalton turning towards the camera, level with the top block from somewhere on the Needle Ridge. Later in the day he took eleven of us up the Ridge on one rope—rather an achievement—and a test even for his immense patience' added Mabel.

Only a week after their first roped climb some of the same party met up with Dalton again and, feeling more confident, tackled the problems on Kern Knotts, proving to be their last climb of the season.

Dalton and Barker had hit it off straight away because she was somewhat like him— rather unconventional, very well educated and in possession of love for Nature and the outdoors. Dr. Mabel Mary Barker, Litt.D., B.Sc. gained her geography diploma at Oxford and her B.Sc. in geology at London University. Born at Silloth in 1886 she ultimately made home in Friar Row, Caldbeck where she maintained an organised mess of books, papers and photo albums which enveloped her living space. At one point she rescued an injured Jackdaw that became a domesticated pet named Johnnie. Generously hospitable, she would share anything with anyone and whilst at home would keep a pan of broth on the stove for the benefit of lucky and hungry hikers who would tramp past her door. Mabel was fascinated by Millican and his primitive mode of life and it is possible her educational theories were influenced by him. She had an interest in prehistory and the evolution of humanity; in Millican she had a living template that she espoused in her work.

A further twelve months elapsed before they happened to meet up quite by chance in September 1914 when Mabel and friend, Norah Geddes, were walking the Borrowdale Fells. His eagerness for non-stop adventure led them both by 'glimmering and guttering candles' through the caves on Dove's Nest. On that ascent, and so lit, Mabel was 'greatly impressed' to notice the seat of his shorts to which had been sewn a large patch of Willesden canvas to ensure that his waterproof groundsheet went with him! Norah Geddes, incidentally, was the daughter of the distinguished Scottish Renaissance man, Sir Patrick Geddes—ecologist, town planner, biologist, philanthropist and sociologist—who employed Mabel, his god-daughter, for several years prior to the outbreak of World War I to assist him at Edinburgh University. Eagle's Nest Ridge and Arrowhead Ridge finalised the summers climbing before the interruption of World War I, putting a temporary stop on the Dalton-Barker climbing partnership.

With World War I spilling blood over Europe, Dalton, upholding his anti-war stance, thought there must be a peaceful solution to the conflict. Pacifism was a subject which stirred strong emotions from within, to such an extent that his disagreement with the government's actions during the conflict was clearly evident in a correspondence to Mabel. The letter dated 14 June 1915 sent from his home at Lincoln Terrace stated: 'I wonder when, if ever, the British government will have sense to propose peace.' Pacifism, literally 'making peace,' is a core Quaker value and, although not technically a Quaker, he was raised by their beliefs.

Mabel's camping and climbing exploits were paused in their entirety and a trip to France appears to be her last for the duration of the war. Subsequently, she temporarily left teaching behind to nurse and traveled to Holland where she assisted the Society of Friends with the escalating refugee crisis.

Returning from Holland, she resumed lecturing and took up a post at King Langley Priory, Hertfordshire, in an attempt to deliver education that would change society and guide mankind away from future wars. Whilst working there she began making weekend visits to Epping Forest to join Dalton and other friends where they visited his woodland hut, climbed trees, and, as with every other mountaineer that time, discussed the chances of success for the proposed Everest recognisance expedition. Mabel did not encounter many accidents, but she did carry a tiny scar from a cut whilst climbing the trees in the forest.

Post-war excitement had witnessed the return of normal life, eventually reviving the Dalton-Barker climbing partnership. In 1919 they once again picked up the rope and scaled Walla Crag and Mouse Ghyll, situated on the outskirts of Keswick. Mabel recalled: 'At the exit from the latter I remember being very tired and coming on the rope. Only twice again, in a fairly long innings, do I remember doing that, and in both cases it was anticipated!' Around the same time they had mooted the possibility of a joint adventure, which culminated in a planned Alpine mountaineering expedition to Austria.

162

'I had no other climbing partner, nor did it occur to me to seek one, though, as always, I walked and scrambled alone whenever possible. Millican was my only contact with the rope in those early years' explained Mabel.

Around the same time Millican visited Friar Row. Concluding a lengthy evenings discussion it was arranged that he was to stay overnight to save the homeward journey in darkness. Mabel, knowing his unorthodox choice of sleeping arrangements and not wanting to offend, was unsure whether to offer him the best bedroom, the garage or a tent in the garden!

Never far from all things unconventional, it will be of no surprise to learn that Millican was best man at the strangest of ceremonies when Mabel's brother, Arnold and fiancée Madge Owen married in the last week of summer that same year. Mabel had originally introduced Arnold and Madge and so both were friendly with Millican. Desiring a service with the minimum of fuss but still in a church, the couple carefully chose to conduct their wedding at St Andrew's Parish Church, Rosthwaite. Throughout the run up to the big day the four met on a daily basis climbing and hiking around the Borrowdale Valley.

Two of Dalton's friends from his office days had also travelled to join in the celebrations and were, in effect, the best man congregation. On the eve of the ceremony Madge and Mabel camped out at High Lodore between Grange Fell and the Borrowdale Hotel.

Meeting on the morning of 16 September the quartet headed for Rosthwaite looking more comparable to a climbing party than a wedding procession. Abandoning the tradition of morning dress and white wedding gown, the bride and groom opted for the comfort and practicality of tweeds; Millican, as expected, in complete climbing costume with boots, rucksack, rope, but most uncharacteristically—a pair of socks. Apparently he endured with the discomfort of the socks until the end of the service, but, on emerging from the quaint church, sat down and removed them immediately! A quick photograph was followed by a wedding reception breakfast held at the Cave Hotel. The "wedding breakfast," prepared and cooked with an open mind—by Dalton the staunch vegetarian—befitted the simplicity of the occasion and consisted of nothing more than a chicken boiled in a billycan. Sporting activities concluded the Happy Couple's day with all enjoying an afternoons climbing in and around the nearby quarries.

'I had a few more days with him on the fells' wrote Mabel, 'strange it is, on looking up dates, to realise how very few and precious they were, and how far spaced...For a few days each summer, hesitating to intrude among the gods least my slower pace should keep the party back and I be a hindrance to them'

Days together were indeed far spaced and a further two years passed before their next meeting during a camp at Taylor Gill Force—the fine foaming cascade at the head of Seathwaite—when Dalton led a small party including Mabel in 1921. The famous blue bicycle again acted as a porter's trolley and transported the majority of their gear past Seathwaite Farm to the foot of the Force where they pitched their tents; the camp, adjacent to the Sty Head packhorse route, being convenient for the high fells and crags such as Scafell Pike and Great Gable. Whilst exploring the area a member of the group serendipitously encountered a stash of tinned food hidden deep among grass and boulders. Rusty and without labels, it appeared that the tins had been long forgotten about. Claiming the stash as their own the campers proceeded to excitingly open the tins to check their mysterious contents. Unfortunately for Millican, most contained meat products, so the majority of the spoils went to the others.

Mabel's climbing ability and confidence had gained in leaps and bounds since her first roped climb. It was later in the summer of 1921 that, in addition to climbing Dove's Nest, Eagle's Nest Chimney and Needle Ridge, she undertook her first lead— Kern Knotts Chimney. On another occasion that summer Ralph Mayson accompanied Millican and Mabel to Great Gable to climb Napes Needle, Kern Knotts Buttress and Eagle's Nest Direct. As Barker had become a good friend, competent climber and female ambassador for the sport, Dalton and Mayson talked openly about proposing her for membership of the FRCC (Rule number five—'All candidates for membership must be proposed and seconded by members of the Club, and will be elected subject to the approval of the Committee').

'That same season' continued Mabel 'joined by Coward of Keswick, we did the climb now called Black Crag Buttress, but then Troutdale Buttress; and on another day had some fun on the Ennerdale face of Gable. For the first (and most certainly the last) time, I was inveigled into that detestable affair called Smugglers' Chimney. Dalton, very knowing about it, kindly gave the lead to Coward. Then he went round to the top, and sat there making sarcastic remarks about how long we took and "Snugglers" Chimney, while we fought and gasped in what should really be called "Strugglers" Chimney.'

By 1922 Mabel had blossomed into an accomplished climber with outstanding ability at a time when only a few women ventured onto the crags; nothing stood in her way and membership to the FRCC was duly granted. What she lacked in physical strength was made up for with her exquisite style; her capability exceeding that of many of her male counterparts. Without a shred of doubt Dalton was fully confident in Mabel's ability and happy to let her take full responsibility, she explained: 'When we climbed together it was rather a shock to find that I was expected as a matter of course to take the lead.'

Passions for the outdoors ran high, but Barker's close bond with Millican never progressed past friendship; her favourite companion was in fact C. D. Frankland. They may not have exactly been in love but they rejoiced in each others company and spent significant time together camping and climbing around the British Isles. Frankland was the man responsible for taking her climbing ability to the next level and from this period forward Mabel racked up an impressive series of pioneering firsts.

In August 1924 Frankland led Mabel up Central Buttress (CB) on Scafell Crag, which according to the FRCC *Scafell Guide* published that same year 'ranks among the world's hardest.' Hyperbole? Most certainly, but it was the undisputed hardest route in the Lake District. Until their ascent, CB had only been climbed three times before, but more importantly it was the first ever ascent by a woman, with Mabel leading the crux pitch past the Great Flake. Then, twenty-four months later, in August 1926 again with Frankland, she became the first woman to traverse the Cuillin Ridge on the Isle of Skye. Mabel continued to climb extensively with Frankland right up to and including his untimely death in 1927 mid-climb on Chantry Buttress on the Napes when a hold broke loose. Trauma did not dissuade her from the sport and latterly, in 1936 aged fifty, she became the first woman to descend Central Buttress. Barker well and truly etched her name in history, leaving a legacy of twenty-seven first ascents.

However, teaching had not been forgotten and remained at the forefront of her life. Between 1925 and 1927 she had supported Geddes at the University of Montpellier where she achieved a doctorate for her thesis on education written in French entitled *L'Utilisation du Milieu Géographique pour l'Education* (*The Use of the Geographical Environment for Education*). For a period Mabel acted as housekeeper to Geddes until his marriage to Lillian Brown.

Reverting to England in 1927 she set her focus on outdoor education and opened a private school at Friar Row. Caldbeck and its rural setting was the ideal platform from which to encourage her pupils to explore the woods and rivers nearby and learn about the environment in which they lived. Adventurous Lake District trips to Scafell and Great Gable supplemented her teachings, instilling in her pupils the need to respect and protect the countryside leaving no trace behind.

When World War II broke out Mabel's students, the majority of which came from across Europe, made a return home before the borders closed; inevitably the doors to the school were also forced to close. Temporarily leaving education behind she turned to nursing once more, this time round to help out at Garlands Hospital in Carlisle, before returning to education where she taught in Peterborough.

Whilst nursing Mabel developed arthritis, which prevented any further climbing; it also signified a premature end to the Dalton-Barker climbing partnership, but they remained good friends. "In all the later years, up to the outbreak of the last war" said Mabel, "we met from time to time." Thereafter they maintained their friendship by post.

M. M. Barker

MILLICAN WITH RUCKSACK AND TENT, SEATHWAITE - 1913

M. M. Barker

"THE WALDEN GYPSIES - 2nd WEEK, THE TRIBE"

M. M. Barker

A LAZY MORNING BENEATH THE 'EAGLE DISPLAYED'

M. M. Barker

DALTON & BARKER ASCENDING THE NEEDLE - 31 JULY 1913

M. M. Barker

ON TOP OF THE NEEDLE AS SEEN FROM NEEDLE RIDGE - 1913

168

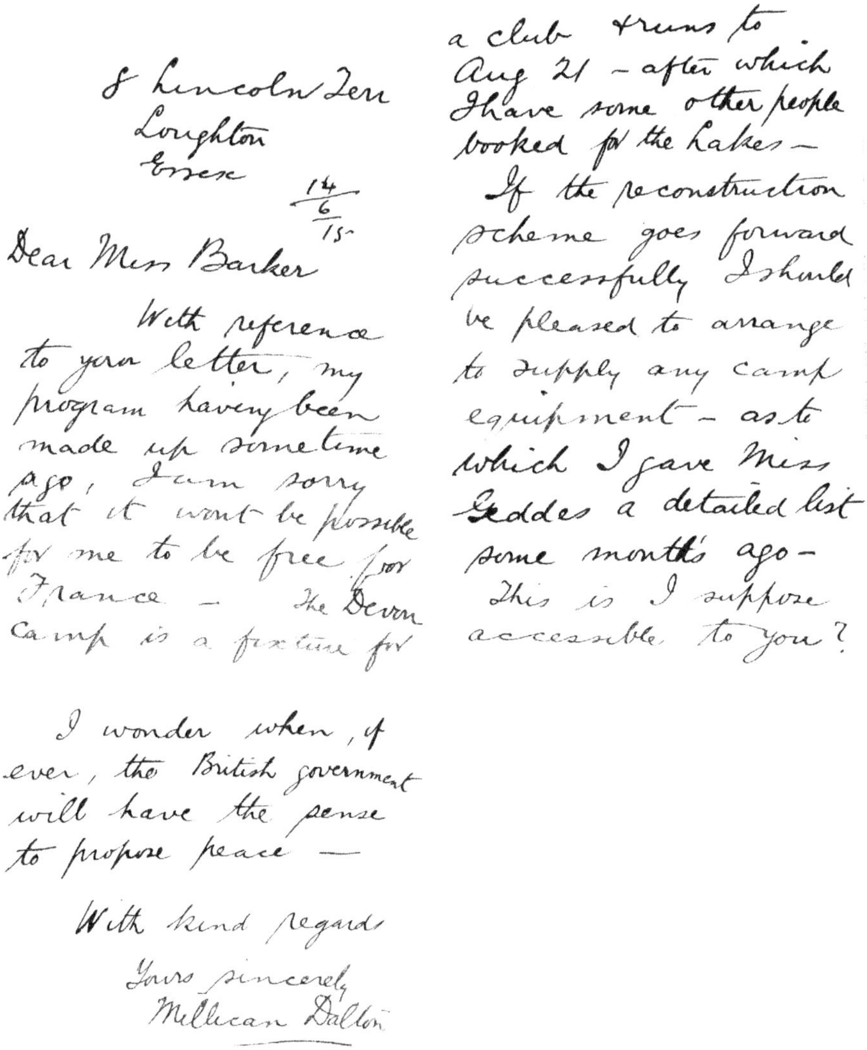

8 Lincoln Den
Loughton
Essex
$\frac{14}{6}$
15.

Dear Miss Barker

With reference
to your letter, my
program having been
made up sometime
ago, I am sorry
that it wont be possible
for me to be free for
France — The Devon
Camp is a fixture for

a club & runs to
Aug 21 – after which
I have some other people
booked for the Lakes —
If the reconstruction
scheme goes forward
successfully I should
be pleased to arrange
to supply any camp
equipment – as to
which I gave Miss
Geddes a detailed list
some months ago –
This is I suppose
accessible to you?

I wonder when, if
ever, the British government
will have the sense
to propose peace —

With kind regards

Yours sincerely,
Millican Dalton

Millican Dalton

DALTON'S LETTER TO BARKER
CLEARLY IN FAVOUR OF A PEACEFUL SOLUTION TO WWI

M. M. Barker

"BEST MAN CONGREGATION!"
DALTON WITH FRIENDS FROM HIS OFFICE DAYS
SHEPHERD'S CRAG - 15 SEPTEMBER 1919

M. M. Barker

"OUR CAMP IN BORROWDALE" - MADGE, MABEL & MILLICAN - 1919

M. M. Barker

THE HAPPY COUPLE, CENTRE, WITH MABEL & MILLICAN

M. M. Barker

"WEDDING BREAKFAST CAVE" - 16 SEPTEMBER 1919

M. M. Barker

"SPORTS AFTER WEDDING BREAKFAST" - 16 SEPTEMBER 1919

M. M. Barker

MILLICAN CLIMBS KERN KNOTTS CHIMNEY

M. M. Barker

"TEA BY THE RIVER"
MILLICAN, JEAN BROWN & MABEL BARKER - SEPTEMBER 1935

CHAPTER FIFTEEN

PRIZED SUMMITS

The Matterhorn, standing at 14691 feet in the Pennine Alps on the Swiss-Italian border, climbed by Dalton on the first occasion sometime prior to 1914 was the jewel in the crown amid a stellar array of summited Alpine peaks. Mystery surrounds his initial trips to the Alps; the later expeditions also being deficient in detail, but the diaries of friends Mabel M. Barker and Rev. George Potts leave a valuable insight into his Alpine mountaineering adventures.

As briefly mentioned, whilst at the Epping camp in 1919 Dalton and Barker had discussed the possibility of a continental holiday. Barker suggested that she would organise a group if Dalton chose the objective and acted as guide. Post World War I Europe was a devastated place, but one which had witnessed vast reconstruction. Tourists began to return and financially the strength of Sterling against foreign currencies made for cheaper travel and therefore provided a means for many to visit overseas destinations. As agreed, the plan came to fruition in August 1922 with the Austrian Tyrol, or more precisely, the Zillertal Valley—considered the cradle of Alpine mountaineering—the chosen destination with the intention of staying for a month. Mabel made the most of her part of the deal, and enlisted a group of thirty people on the expedition, a party ranging from small boys to middle-aged women. Evidently, it must have been a hastily arranged trip as Millican had already placed adverts in the *Daily Herald* for that season's Alpine holiday tours.

Assembling at London's Victoria station, the party caught the train destined for Dover, making the three-day journey in reserved carriages. Millican, unconcerned with the paperwork, left the clerical side to Mabel who was responsible for the distribution of passports and tickets. They left Dover and after a charming Channel crossing the sea "still as a millpond"—arrived at Ostend and continued their rail journey at 4:00 p.m. managing to cross the Belgium countryside in daylight which now looked "wonderfully prosperous and industrious," according to Mabel. Due to problems at the Belgian-

German frontier the party had to delay their onward journey and spent the evening in their carriage for no apparent reason. As part of routine post-war checks all baggage was examined and receipts issued for money carried. Eventually they changed trains at Cologne at the stroke of midnight for Würzburg only to be greeted by a German family occupying their seats in the reserved carriage. "It's open—we come in" said the husband. "That's the policy that didn't work, isn't it?" snapped Barker scornfully. Their through train eventually arrived in Munich, and after spending time recuperating from their long journey, they set off the next day and began the scenic and dramatic approach to the Alps and Mayrhofen.

On reaching Mayrhofen on Thursday 3 August the group's luggage was transferred to small carts and pack mules, which then made the eight-mile journey on foot to the camp at Schliffstein, finally arriving in the evening. All were astonished to find that, after such hectic travelling, not one of the thirty people or ninety pieces of luggage was missing! Their route followed Rosshag, Breitlahner, Grawand, Alpenrose and Berliner hüttes where rates averaged 1/- for a bed and two meals, but as a cheaper option the group prepared to base themselves in tents and hired a plot of land for a small ground rent. Due to the lack of flat camping ground, all of which was used for agriculture, their pitch was far from ideal; it was sloping and rather exposed. Dalton, the professional camper, was unhappy with the site and wanted to move to an adjacent pitch, but the owner, who lived in the Berliner Hütte, wanted too much money so they decided to stay put. Upon an initial scouting expedition they arranged to take a large party up to the Grawand Hütte on the 6 August for a couple of nights, that for most would be their first experience on a glacier. Once there, Dalton taught the group the skills involved in negotiating glaciers, snowfields and the use of ropes and ice axes.

Further expeditions followed on 10 August when a party of ten set off for the Greizer Hütte; a much wilder situation high above the Floitenkees Glacier, surrounded by a ring of jagged black peaks. The party climbed to approximately 9000 feet on the slopes of the Löffler, but for one reason or another did not reach the summit. Interestingly Mabel's fourteen-year-old half-brother, Pat, also with the group, made friends with a young boy called Franz Knefel from the English Kinderheim in Vienna, who spent a year with George Leigh Mallory at Godalming.

Next morning Dalton led the whole party on a day outing to the Riffler Hütte and two days later, after visiting a folk-festival in Mayrhofen, on 13 August Miss Mayer organised a camp festival, during which two young girls performed a short play, finalised with jolly singing and dancing around the campfire. Early the next day Dalton, Miss Hamilton (an old friend of Patrick Geddes) and Gertrude Walmsley (an ex-Saffron Walden student) departed for the Furtschaglhaus, with Mabel and a Miss Hirst from

175

Portsmouth meeting up with them the following morning. Skies were clear, the sun shone bright and all had good intentions to cross by the Schönbichler Horn to the Berliner or Alpenrose Hütte in the adjacent valley. Unfortunately, the party drifted slightly off track and ended up on a ridge on which they traversed too far to their left. By now they were lost. Mistakenly, they had climbed a mountain that was not the Schönbichler Horn but the Talggenköpfe. Continuing along the ridge, the weather changed for the worse with heavy winds and hail hindering progress, making the consultation of map and compass difficult, and in haste the group proceeded downwards along a rough ridge on the wrong side. For reasons of safety the three novices of the party were roped together; Dalton led the way and Barker was at the rear for most of the time attached to the tail end of the rope. Time was running out and it was obvious that they may not make it back in daylight. Conscious of this, one of the women asked whether they should unrope for speed; Barker quick to respond, suggested they should not.

Fortunately Barker's sound advice proved valuable when a few minutes later a large rock came away in the hands of Gertrude Walmsley and carried her down a steep slope. She was hoisted up all right, but had injured her leg, subsequently slowing the party further and as a result darkness fell whilst they were still on the glacier.

Finding a sheltered position nestled amongst the rocks, and although soaked and chilled to the bone, they had no choice but to settle down for the night and proceed in the morning. It then decided to snow, definitely stranding them high above the Alpenrose Hütte at around 7000 feet. Somewhat ill prepared by modern standards, with only half inch of candle in a lantern, food and cigarettes, the group sought refuge under a mackintosh. Huddled together for warmth, they spent the long night in good spirits singing and story telling. Barker commented on Millican: 'His passion for making tea and coffee in all sorts of queer places was more than useful, but when his brew would have been more than welcome than manna from heaven the apparatus was missing.'

Luckily for the sporting bunch there was no wind that could have made the situation life threatening, however, a customary violent thunderstorm arrived with most curious and exciting effects. As a rule they all stayed under the mackintosh, but on leaving the bivouac to rearrange themselves they realised their hair was electrified. Gertrude stood up against the sky and had a halo—every strand of hair had a spark of light on it. Adding excitement to the situation were lightening-strikes, one of which struck their ice axes later that night. Regardless of the discomfort, all remained cheery, good tempered and in high spirits. 'It sounds rather an awful experience, but in point of fact it really wasn't' wrote Barker. Some managed to grab a little sleep, but all rose as soon as dawn emerged to a wonderful white world and thankfully nobody 'woke up dead.'

When the light came, heralded by a glorious sunrise, dreaming of their beds and lots of hot coffee, they headed off still in comparative darkness from the shadow of the mountains. On the way down flocks of tame sheep mobbed the party; Dalton, in no mood for wrangling, thought it necessary to defend himself by shepherding them away with his ice axe, which the others thought was a strange spectacle.

Eventually, the party made it to the Alpenrose Hütte arriving at 7:00 a.m. where the staff made them most welcome and ushered the five explorers straight to bed and brought them tea, to which they added spirit without asking. Dalton's reaction is unclear, but the kindness of the Hütte's occupants was noted. Most of the day was spent asleep in bed, thawing out and regaining energy after their night's exploits. Once recovered they returned back to camp and the rest of the main party later that evening. Travelling down to the camp in darkness was an experience in itself as nobody had a lantern. In order to ensure a safe descent Dalton ingeniously tied a white handkerchief around one ankle and held, conveniently, a lit cigarette as a makeshift beacon. Fortuitously nobody was the worse for wear as a result of the unplanned adventure and even Gertrude only had a bruise. "Hairbreadth escapes arranged by circumstance" aside, this was a calamitous navigational error on Dalton's behalf, and huge a black mark against his professorship.

Come 18 August, unperturbed, Dalton, Barker, Gertrude Walmsley, Dr. Thomas (lady) and Miss Venables embarked on an expedition to the Grawand Hütte and, with none of them feeling particularly energetic, stayed the night. The next day Dalton returned to the spot where he and the other four had been stranded several days prior to find and retrieve a climbing rope that they had left behind on the glacier as it was frozen stiff and impossible to coil. On returning to the Alpenrose Hütte, their accommodation for the night, two of Millican's friends—Wallie and Lottie Camelus—had arrived and wandered up to find them. The group, including the new arrivals, agreed hike over the Schwarzenstein the next day following a party of English boys and their guide up from the Berliner Hütte. Rising early and departing at 5:00 a.m. they sailed up the slopes because none of the climbing was difficult, but according to Barker, Lottie struggled with the steep snow slopes because she was 'small and fat!' Ascending for six hours over pure-white snowfields with a clean atmosphere and cloudless blue sky, they reached the Italian frontier at 11500 feet after six hours. Soldiers had also been up that day marking the frontier with red paint circles on the rocks, so recent in fact that the paint was still wet! A long time was spent there where Dalton found some waste wood and made a fire.

He baked a cake and brewed coffee, whilst all admired the distant views into Italy, Switzerland and away over the Tyrol. A descent down the other side to the Greizer

Hütte in the Fententhal was much steeper with the route heading over a glacier—'poor Lottie had a stiff time!' quipped Barker in her outwardly unrestrained language. Arriving back at camp around 8:00 p.m., the group felt tired and hungry, but terribly pleased with themselves. Wallie and Lottie left the party here and set off for Mayrhofen. Around this time Lewis Mumford (native New Yorker internationally recognised as one of the most distinguished urbanists of the twentieth century) and his wife Sophia arrived at the camp. Mumford was an ardent admirer of Patrick Geddes and a friend of Gladys Mayer.

With the holiday drawing to a close, Friday 25 August was the last opportunity for a serious expedition. Dalton, Franz, Gladys, Reps (a German student from Leipzig), Mr. and Mrs. Mumford, Miss Hamilton and Barker went up to the Grawand Hütte where they said farewell. The planned trek over the Schönbichler Horn the following day was thwarted due to severe thick mist; rather than miss out, another night was spent at the Alpenrose. Continued misty weather the next morning restricted the group's activities, so the afternoon was spent playing on the Horn Kees, the glacier adjacent to the Berliner Hütte. Mr. and Mrs. Mumford, ill equipped for climbing, did not last long, and in the glorious weather of the following day they returned to Schliffstein and onto Mayrhofen. The rest of the group managed to tramp over the Schönbichler Horn, with the path passing directly over the summit. Mindful of his previous blunder, this time Dalton ensured they stayed on the right track without getting lost, and spending another night stranded on the glacier. On the top he found wood, lit a fire, made tea and coffee and then dispersed it between the group and the other tourists lucky enough to be on the summit at the same time. All members of the party signed their names in a book that had been left on the top and then descended to the Furtschagelhaus.

Mabel and Miss Hamilton escorted Franz back to Vienna, where they spent three days, but Dalton decided to precede them to Cortina where Mabel would meet him later. The group relaxed and took in the sights around camp concluding their stay in the Tyrol. Winding up camp at Schliffstein on 30 August, the party then set off on the weary 15-hour 2/- journey from Mayrhofen to Vienna. Seated in second class was uncomfortable and to top it all they spent the night in the corridor, which was fortunately fitted with seats and wide-open windows. Mabel returned and to finalise the holiday a small number of the group crossed the Brenner into Italy for a view of the Dolomites. Barker and Millican, being the only two remaining climbers, according to Mabel 'had a small taste of the lovely quality of rock.' At the end of the venture Dalton was very tired—not all that surprising at 55 years old. All remaining members of the party returned to England at Tre Croce, except for Dalton who went his own way to meet a friend.

M. M. Barker

MILLICAN & FRIEND, COLOGNE CATHEDRAL - AUGUST 1922

M. M. Barker

"BROTHERS MILLICAN & MUEL AT THE BREITLAHNER"

M. M. Barker

"THE RULING PASSION" - DALTON MAKES COFFEE

M. M. Barker

CHECKING THE BILLYCAN

M. M. Barker

"BREWING UP AT 11500 FEET"

181

M. M. Barker

BOYS & WOMEN (DALTON SECOND FROM RIGHT)

M. M. Barker

MILLICAN TEACHES ROPE TECHNIQUES

M. M. Barker

TAKING A BREATHER (DALTON SECOND FROM RIGHT)

M. M. Barker

CROSSING THE SNOWFIELDS

DAILY HERALD

7 AUGUST 1922

HOLIDAY CAMPS

AUSTRIAN TYROL TOURS

Mid Aug.—Sept. 30.

Zillertal, Dolomites, Switzerland.

For particulars apply Millican Dalton, Loughton, Essex.

DAILY HERALD

11 AUGUST 1922

CAMPS IN SWITZERLAND

Millican Dalton, well known in the Labour movement,

has vacancies in his Austrian Tyrol and Swiss camp parties.

Those wishing to join him must write at once to

Camp Cottage, Baldwin's Hill, Epping Forest,

in order to secure passports and visas in time.

DAILY HERALD

7 JULY 1923

"A NEW HOLIDAY" TOURS—TYROL. Camping (or inns).

Alpine walks; glaciers; mountaineering. £16 fort.

Millican Dalton, Loughton, Essex.

Three years later Millican's friendship with Rev. George Potts led to an eighteen-day expedition to the Alps between 6 and 24 July 1925. Their relationship had begun in 1917/18 after George had been wounded and invalided out of the Border Regiment whilst fighting as an infantry solider on the battlefields of France. Having met in the mountains of the Lake District, where Potts acted as a guide for the CHA at Newlands Vale Guest House, they became climbing partners despite the thirty-one year age gap, though it served him well and he learnt much from Millican. In-between Potts' study at Keble College and Cuddesdon Theological College, both in Oxford, and being ordained in Carlisle in 1923, they climbed and camped exclusively in the Lake District. But as Potts' experience broadened so did his horizons, and he set his sights on the highest peaks in Europe. On this expedition, where Potts once again acted as the professor's pupil, among other peaks they decided to tackle the mighty Matterhorn—a highly desirable ascent for any serious mountaineer. This was a meritorious effort by Dalton who, by now, was fifty-eight years old. Potts wrote in his diary:

184

There have been many consequences of my Cumbrian childhood and upbringing. I must select but one, my passion for the mountains under whose shadow I spent those happy years with my excitement in exploring new country, experienced in the first place by following the hounds. I was bought a second-hand bike and promptly set off for the hills I had so longed to climb. First there was Binsey Fell.

The vision I had seen from Binsey led me inexorably in the course of years to other hills and other countries. But before I went further afield I gained an intimate knowledge of the Lakeland Fells as a secretary and guide, during Oxford long vacations, with the Holiday Fellowship, then based at Newlands, and of Snowdonia from their centre at Conway. There was rock climbing with Millican Dalton, now of legendary fame, on Gable's Ridges, Scawfell Face, Doe Crags out Coniston way, the Pillar, and Birkness Combe overlooking Buttermere, accompanied at times by Ralph Mayson, the well-known Lakeland photographer. There were visits to Snowdonia with the gullies and buttresses of Tryfan, days on Y Lliwedd Face, and forays out to the crags of Carnedd Llewelyn. We rock climbed then only with the help of nailed alpine boots, a rope of manilla hemp, and an ice axe if needed, nothing else. To us, rightly or wrongly, anything else would have been sacrilege. Your modern rock climber with his clattering ironmongery would have horrified us. Of course it had to come. My generation of rock climbers had tackled and conquered all the routes that could be done in nailed boots. Younger men felt rightly that they must go further than we had gone, turning our impossible into their possible. We had our day with the gullies and the ridges. They now have theirs with the hold-less slabs and the forbidding overhangs. But, as with much else, simplicity has given way to complexity.

My opportunity to encounter the Swiss Alps came during an extended holiday with Millican Dalton. Amongst with other Alpine Peaks, we tackled the giants of the Alps, the legendary, prized summits. We climbed Monte Rosa, second only in stature to Mont Blanc, the highest peak in Western Europe, and the Matterhorn by way of the northeastern Hörnli Ridge, only to discover that at the Solvay Hut, precariously perched just below the shoulder of the Matterhorn, it was not possible to brew tea. Water boils at a much lower temperature at this altitude. I should have recalled this from Physics lessons at Oxford, but Physics in a college laboratory is one thing; Applied Physics at 13000 feet is quite another. A comfortable night was spent in the Hut, and next morning while the moon and stars still shone bright, we rose from our bunkbeds well prepared for our summit assault. With darkness retreating from the morning sunshine slowly edging over the sawtoothed horizon, we departed for the pinpoint summit, eventually, after much careful rope-work, reaching our goal shortly after noon. Panoramas from the top are a delight to behold, and which one will never forget.

Those of you who know Millican Dalton, our very own "Professor of Adventure," and his ragged, colourful and outlandish garb, will not be surprised to hear that we were arrested and gaoled in the small, scenic town of Interlaken. "Vous êtes mal habillé messieurs!" hailed the officious Swiss policeman. They must be sensitive souls, as we were apparently 'improperly dressed' wearing shorts with our knees showing! "Il parfum!" he added, as we gazed with forlorn interest into a most superior photographic emporium, thereafter watching our own peculiar detainment in the window's warped reflection. I am told such French doesn't exist, it should have been "Qué pue!" and I must have misheard what he said. Maybe he was just trying to speak English. Maybe he did "parfum," and so did we. The three of us had just completed two weeks arduous camping and climbing in those high mountains above Zermatt without even a sniff of soap.

We subsequently spent several hours in the police station trying to persuade a number of Swiss policemen and detectives that we were merely "mad Englishmen" and nothing worse. Our main trouble was our clothing. It was not only that it was too ragged for this most elegant city, but that it was insufficient. "Three weeks guileless camping and climbing explain the former, while the heat and the "Skipper's" delight in bare legs explain the latter. But bare legs are not permitted in Interlaken, and the passport photograph of the Skipper's companion dressed as a most respectable Clerk in Holy Orders only added to our difficulties. Dalton's 'suit' came in for various critical remarks until at last he retaliated on the chief interrogator via the clergyman interpreter, "Ask him if he made his suit, because I made mine!" We were ultimately let out by Dalton agreeing to cover up his bare legs with a pair of the clergyman's puttees. Our incarceration meant we missed our planned ascents of the Jungfrau, the Mönch, and the Eiger.

Common-sense eventually prevailed and we were released without charge, but only on condition that we left town. The police escorted us to the station and we boarded the next train bound for Kandersteg. We spent time exploring the area looking for a camp for the night, and discovered a most hospitable cave above that loveliest of mountain tarns, The Oeschinensee.

Each morning, not long after daybreak, a goatherd, seeing the wispy, curling plume of white-grey smoke from our fire, came along with his tinkling, bleating, herd of long-horned, black and white goats to give us milk drawn straight from the udder, and cheese cut straight from the presses. Food doesn't come much fresher. We happily exchanged pleasantries without difficulty, he spoke American learnt from a long stay in the United States, and he was delighted to talk his 'English' with us again.

There, before breakfast, while coffee was brewing and porridge cooking on the open pinewood fire, Millican would take what he called an "Air Bath," which consisted of his standing in the open air for fifteen minutes, clothed only in his ragged, dark green shirt, and letting the wind and air flow over him—apparently a fashionable "Nature tonic," intended to harden the body and create vital resistance against cold and chills. No, we had no butane gas stoves then. What the modern sophisticated generation of campers miss! Convenience is not the last word in camping. It misses "the wild" which is everything. Some time, someday, you modern campers, go and frizzle a kipper over a wood fire with a forked stick. Then you will know! Or change your pneumatic air bed for springy sweet smelling heather. It will take more time to assemble than will the blowing up of an air bed. You will learn the secret with patience. But you will sleep soundly and awake refreshed to the unforgettable scent of the hills.

Millican had a brain wave one morning as he considered the police and their dislike of us. "If they come again we'll show them our ropes and say we are acrobats. They let acrobats go anywhere in Europe." It would have been fun to try, but we never got the chance.

In view of Dalton's evidential ability and longterm interest in Alpine mountaineering, it may come as a surprise to learn that he never became a member of the venerable Alpine Club, formed in 1857 and based in London—though in all fairness the Club was rather elitist and generally more conservative—rendering any further explanation unnecessary.

G. C. Potts

"NEAR THE TRIFT HOTEL. MILLICAN WITH 9 SHEEP IN THE SNOW"

G. C. Potts

"THE ROAD TO MONTE ROSA"

G. C. Potts

"SKIPPER HAS GROWN A TAIL AND THE REVEREND SAYS HIS PRAYERS"

G. C. Potts

"MILLICAN ON TOP OF THE COULOIR GLACIER, UNTER GABELHORN"

G. C. Potts

"M. D. UP A SNOW RIDGE ON THE UNTER GABELHORN"

G. C. Potts

"SUNSET ON THE GORNER GLACIER"

191

G. C Potts

"MILLICAN ON THE LYSKAMM ACROSS FROM THE GRENZ GLACIER"

G. C. Potts

"ON THE LYSKAMM"

G. C. Potts

"MILLICAN TAKES AN AIR BATH OUTSIDE THE HERMIT'S CAVE"

194

G. C. Potts

"13000FT - THE HIGHEST POINT, SO FAR"

G. C. Potts

"MATTERHORN FROM GORNER GLACIER" - MILLICAN, POTTS & GUIDE

G. C. Potts

"SECOND BREAKFAST AT THE TRIFT GORGE"

G. C. Potts

"ABOVE THE CLOUDS ON THE TRIFTHORN LOOKING TO MONTE ROSA"

G. C. Potts

"MILLICAN & THE MATTERHORN FROM RIFFELALP"

G. C. Potts

"MILLICAN MAKES CAMP NEAR TO WINKELMATTEN"

G. C. Potts

"MILLICAN'S TENT COMES DOWN AT THE WINKELMATTEN CAMP"

201

G. C. Potts

"MILLICAN PERCHED ON THE HÖRNLI RIDGE, MATTERHORN 9490FT"

G. C. Potts

"DALTON & POTTS HEADING TOWARDS THE MATTERHORN SUMMIT"

G. C. Potts

"ON THE SUMMIT - THE MATTERHORN, HIGHEST OF ALL"

CHAPTER SIXTEEN

NEGLECTED CLIMBER

In spite of Millican's mountaineering accomplishments—soloing Napes Needle on his maiden attempt; climbing the hardest routes in the Lake District; early expeditions to the Cuillin Hills or ascending the highest peaks in the Alps and Dolomites—certain sections of the climbing community were of the general opinion that he was rather overcautious and lacked the nerve and ability of the "Tigers."

Whilst climbing for slightly different reasons than most, Millican's nerve and ability was every inch that of the "Tigers," exemplified by undertaking the same routes in and around Wasdale and pioneering his own climbs. Chronologically he was not far behind the recreational pioneers of the 1880s and had claimed an official first ascent when the sport was still only eleven years old. The very concept of searching for new routes to pioneer differentiates some climbers from others and elevates pioneers into a league of their own. Unknown climbing on virgin rock and the lack of knowledge of the next move or the whereabouts of the crux dissuades many who prefer to read guidebooks and follow in the steps of others. Pioneering requires courage and a high degree of skill in reading the climb, selecting the route in the first instance and firm belief that it can, more likely than not, be climbed to the top; this all requires steely focus and an unfaltering trust in one's abilities. Dalton's first ascents of Buzzard Chimney and Pencoed Pillar are prime examples of such nerve and ability. His route descriptions for Dove's Nest predominantly outline climbs suitable for experts and, as one of the routes is his, it becomes apparent that he considered himself an expert. In his 1913 holiday programme he once again refers to himself as an 'expert mountaineer.'

Although no innovator of new techniques or equipment he was never averse to their adoption as they were gradually introduced. Even though there was still an eccentric resistance to clear technological advances that often occur in human history, latterly he even wore plimsoles acknowledging their superior grip on dry rock. In the first instance the equipment used was no different from that chosen by other climbers. He employed the same nailed boots, pure Manila hemp Alpine rope and long wooden-shafted ice axe which was carried year round to "garden" routes of vegetation and loose rock. The ice axe was an integral piece in any kitbag essential on virgin rock or unpopular routes, and could be utilised as an "artificial aid" on which to stand and reach the higher holds otherwise out of arms-length. Tricouni nails and hemp ropes were at the forefront of climbing technology. Whilst the nailed boots offered satisfactory grip especially on wet rock, the rope—a ticket to wild and high places, the metaphor for everything that is truly meaningful in this vertical sport—had a terrible strength-to-weight ratio, poor durability, low elasticity and snapped easily, more often than not resulting in a painful death.

The slogan of the era: "the leader must not fall" were not just hollow words. There was no margin for error, remember, these were the days before dynamic nylon ropes, helmets, carabiners, cams, ascenders, slings, chalk-bags and hands-free two-way radios. Even the humble harnesses had not been invented and the only way to tie onto the rope was by knotting it tightly around the waist. If a climber slipped and the fall did not kill them, the rope probably would through serious injuries sustained to the abdomen, diaphragm or unprotected head. Without a helmet debris raining down from above compounded the risks. To add more doom to the scenario: there were no official Mountain Rescue Teams ready to respond to an emergency, and should an injured party require assistance it could take hours for help to arrive at the scene—and that was only half of the rescue. This was an incredibly dangerous pastime.

As Disraeli said long ago in one of his early novels 'Adventures are to the adventurous' and so Millican, along with every other hardcore thrill-seeker, having assessed the outcome of reward versus danger willingly accepted the risks to life and limb. A reporter investigating for the *Sunday Chronicle* in 1933 was told by Dalton "I have had many hairbreadth escapes from death. Once while on a rock climbing expedition I slipped, and but for the prompt action and presence of mind of another member of the party I would have been dashed to death." Whilst no comparisons of ability can be made between Millican and the likes of Owen Glynn Jones, he had, demonstrably, the same aptitude as the "Tigers."

In the modern era critics suggest he routinely disregarded client safety and failed to use belays. These allegations of bad practice are based on the misinterpretation of a promotional photograph that unequivocally depicts an unsafe belaying technique supposedly with a second climber in tow.

Upon first sight of this photograph, if unaware of Dalton's vast experience, it is understandable why a prejudice could easily be formed. Nevertheless this photograph, taken by Ralph Mayson, was nothing more than a publicity shot with Dalton merely posing for the camera, and in reality no other climbers were involved. Had he been bringing up the second he would have most definitely created a belay by threading the rope around a chockstone or with a bight of rope around a spike of rock. This was common practice and the principle lesson learnt from the 1903 accident on Scafell Pinnacle. It is an incredibly basic concept—without the security of a belay, a falling climber would drag their companions with them.

Important to the defence of his reputation is the highlighting of the Keswick Boot image. Immediately recognised as the same location as the aforementioned postcard there is, intriguingly, no rucksack and this time he appears in a seated position. Would he really have belayed from such an awkward and ineffective position? Other poses on this pedestal, possibly only a matter of feet from the ground, complimented the portfolio of Professor of Adventure merchandise indicating that the photos were simply dramatic art.

Contrary to these misconceptions he was actually a very safe climber who, although a thrill-seeker, never took unnecessary risks when guiding and was, admittedly, rather cautious, but this is not necessarily a negative. Understandably as a guide he would never put clients under his duty of care in any danger and would not take a novice on climbs that were beyond their physical or mental capabilities. Boundaries existed and under no circumstances would a novice be allowed to take the lead. Supplementary to teaching the basics of balance and movement he also passed on his knowledge of safety, demonstrating the physics of belays and the correct tying of knots. Showing the trustworthy length of a pitch, he would indicate practicable methods to care for the leader and the wellbeing of the whole party.

If anything, his unhurried, methodical and simplified approach ensured that students comprehended his instructions, increasing the safety aspect of his tutelage. Dalton was an extremely patient and natural teacher whose encouraging manner allayed fear. Questions, more than welcome, received answers in a cheery tone—precise and clear explanations relieving nervous beginners of their concerns. Folk, young and old, of differing abilities and aptitudes, sought his enlightenment and all were warmly accepted on his courses.

Millican possessed the lightest of touches and handed down his knowledge to many first-rate climbers; Mabel M. Barker, for example, developed into one of the best British women rock climbers of her generation. She had full faith in his teaching abilities and wrote: 'I was never really happy in the use of any knots but his...Probably, by modern day methods, he was overcautious, but it's a good fault...He was not ever, I think, among the great climbers. He had no ambition to be so. In a way he had no ambition at all.'

All students had confidence in his ability, proven by a full work programme and lack of adverse publicity. Talk of accidents occurring under his guidance was unheard; a testament to his excellent safety record considering he guided hundreds, if not thousands, of people throughout his long and eventful career—something that could not be said for all Lakeland guides.

Climbing club members, undisturbed by hearsay, also trusted their own judgements. As an illustration, just one of many, accomplished climbers Ashley and George Abraham, Edward Scantlebury, Chas Grayson and seven others climbed with him on 4 and 5 July 1908 at the FRCC Coniston Meet suggesting he was a contemporary.

Upon realisation of Dalton's priorities, it becomes apparent that he climbed for self-gratification and not for the approval of others, and because of this his skills as a cragsman may have been overlooked—it is likely he had a more substantial influence on the British climbing scene than was first realised. As a commendable achievement well worth highlighting, Buzzard Chimney was only the sixth recorded first ascent in Borrowdale. Only the Abraham brothers, O. G. Jones, W. C. Slingsby, J. W. Robinson and a couple of other climbers had earlier recorded ascents in the valley. As already suggested, it was common for Dalton not to record first ascents; climbing and having fun with friends was more important than claiming a first, indicating a distinct lack of self-glorification. Interestingly, Buzzard Chimney was not recorded officially until 17 years after the pioneering climb when he wrote-up the route description for the *Fell and Rock Journal* 1914. Other variations on this route purportedly pioneered by Dalton were left unrecorded, as were the climbs in the quarries around Castle Crag after Arnold Barker's 'wedding breakfast.'

More interesting still is the fact that a further twenty-four years passed before the accomplished climber Bentley Beetham made his mark in Borrowdale with Woden's Face Original Route in 1921. Incidentally, only five other routes were recorded in Borrowdale between 1897 and 1921. Apparently the explorative instincts and zest shown by Beetham necessitated a separate Borrowdale guidebook. Until his appearance on the scene the number of recorded climbs in the valley were few and far between and therefore grouped with the more comprehensive *Great Gable Guide*.

The FRCC *Guide to Borrowdale* 1953 written by Beetham, contained 131 of his own routes; he certainly took great satisfaction in recording his ascents, of that there is no doubt. The Editor's note asks why, considering Beetham's 'astonishing efforts,' Borrowdale was overlooked when Keswick, being of such close proximity, offered easy access to the rock for the many competent climbers who lived there. Moreover, the Editor states that Beetham could claim, without exaggeration, to have almost created a new climbing ground. Beetham had achieved this by tearing through the Borrowdale

Valley clearing overgrown crags of vegetation, either by raking or burning, in what would now be classed as 'environmental vandalism.' This exposed new routes, previously deemed unclimbable due to the undeveloped nature of the sport. Dalton is rumoured to have climbed extensively with Beetham on these new routes, though no evidence has yet come to light.

The majority of early climbers had concentrated on areas around Wasdale Head with few venturing to Borrowdale specifically to climb due to its distance from the popular and challenging cliffs abounding Scafell Pike, Great Gable and Pillar Rock. Even those who passed through Borrowdale, purportedly, ignored the few 'credible' climbs amongst the dearth of exigent rock. In theory the Abraham Brothers should have more routes credited to them in Borrowdale, but found themselves busy climbing in Wasdale, concentrating on more difficult rock and their professional photography. This lack of attention to the climbs in Borrowdale left them open to be claimed.

Shepherd's Crag, positioned between the Borrowdale and Lodore Hotels, was supposedly one of Beetham's finest discoveries. Lying only one hundred yards from the road, the crag affords the most easily accessible rock in the whole of the country with stunning views to match. Yet, according to Beetham, because the crag was immediately disguised by a band of trees and lush, green vegetation, droves of climbing parties had walked parallel to it completely oblivious to its existence for 36 years since the sport began in earnest. Shepherd's Crag, it seems, according to the guidebooks, was not discovered until 1922. Beetham along with climbing partner C. D. Frankland, on returning to Keswick from Wasdale, caught a glimpse of a spur of rock that looked appealing. After an initial investigation they climbed it and thought no more of it. This route was named Brown Slabs Arête.

Without detracting from Beetham's evidential dominance in Borrowdale, it is of great surprise to learn that, remembering his explorative instincts, a return to Shepherd's Crag was not made until 24 years after his first visit when he eventually noticed the far better standard of climbing to the south of the crag.

Of great significance, and a total contradiction to Beetham's claims on Shepherd's Crag, was Dalton's visit to the south of the crag in September 1919—27 years before Beetham's discovery. Dalton, photographed with friends from his office days, is clearly seen taking afternoon tea dressed in climbing regalia replete with nailed boots and a half-coiled rope slung over his shoulders; his female companion in breeches; all except the gent appear to be taking a break from climbing. He was not on the south of the crag looking for Scotch mist, neither was the rope for decoration—he was pioneering climbs! In fact his achievements on Shepherd's Crag may never be fully realised, but by any stretch of the imagination clearly preceded Beetham to this 'new climbing ground.'

209

Thinking logically, Dalton, based on the slopes of High Lodore Farm for many summers, could not have missed the bulging south end of the cliff.

Similarly with most other crags in the valley and knowing Dalton's taste for exploration it seems highly improbable that he pioneered no other routes in Borrowdale. Imagine, for example, passing the shadowing cliffs of Walla Crag, Falcon Crag, Shepherd's Crag and Black Crag conveniently lined up one after another like a guard of honour along the Borrowdale Road—would Dalton, who had the spirit of the hills in his blood and who knew the fells as other folk know their own street, have simply cycled past and not been tempted to uncoil his rope? It was well known that he was happy to potter about; surely he must have investigated further or did he just travel over fell and dale blinkered? What Professor of Adventure would simply stand back and observe from afar?

Borrowdale was his base, the hub from which he operated in the Lake District. Dalton was not merely a fleeting weekender or day-tripper, but a seasonal worker whose time, both free and working, revolved around the outdoors, with a particular emphasis on climbing. He was a real mountain man; mountains were his life to which he had devoted everything. When he saw a mountain, or anything that looked like a mountain, it had to be climbed. As a matter of fact, climbing was so appealing to Dalton that he was once travelling along London's Embankment quite contently with a friend, a clergyman from Cumberland, when, upon passing a famous landmark he stopped and looked up with a twinkle in his eye. "All went well," said the clergyman "till we were passing Cleopatra's Needle. Then he paused, looked longingly at it and I had to drag him away in case I found it listed in the next edition of 'Abraham's *Rock Climbs in the British Isles*.'" They continued their onward journey and the opportunity of a remarkable first relinquished.

Unlike many he would venture out onto the rock on his own and sit in wait. Should anyone pass-by he would opportunistically shout down and encourage them to climb with him. In the late 1920s Vince Veevers was in the process of carrying his bike up and over Sty Head to Wasdale, having cycled to Borrowdale from Bolton, when he spotted a climber on a crag. Curious he went over to watch when a voice beckoned from above: "Can you tie a bowline?" "Yes!" replied Vince. He lied; he had no idea. After asking a passing climber to show him, he managed to tie-on and scale the climb, Kern Knotts Chimney, and on pulling himself over the top was shocked to be greeted by Millican tied the other end of the rope.

This all leads to the question: Where does Millican Dalton feature in the history of British mountaineering? The answer: Nowhere, he is a neglected climber. He may be recognised as a participant in the sport, but certainly never any given credit for his contribution to rock climbing or mountaineering; this is a travesty because in reality scores of climbs were discovered, inspected and attempted with successful conquests left unrecorded. Obviously such records are at the discretion of the pioneer and act as the only real proof, but, however controversial, in the opinion of the author based on circumstantial evidence, Millican Dalton could have been the true pioneer of Borrowdale!

Favourite climbs amongst his personal repertoire included Scafell's: The Keswick Brothers' Climb, Slingsby's Chimney and Moss Ghyll. On Great Gable: Arrowhead Ridge, Eagle's Nest Ridge, Abbey Buttress and West Chimney; Dove's Nest and its caves at the head of Combe Ghyll and in Langstrath: Gash Rock, Sergeant Crag Gully, and the bouldering problems of the Woof Stones which he delighted at. Of all the climbs in Lakeland his favourite was without doubt Napes Needle; so popular was this climb that he scaled it well over fifty times.

His fiftieth ascent of Napes Needle was made during the last week of August 1920 and to celebrate the occasion in style he carried water and a pile of sticks to its spectacular and exposed summit. There he made a small fire and brewed coffee for himself and the friends who accompanied him, and topped it all off with a couple of Woodbines. Quelle surprise!

The next day Millican made his fifty-first ascent, this time joined by a south-countryman who announced to the "gallery" of spectators sitting in the "Dress Circle" opposite the rock that he intended to celebrate his maiden ascent. Living up to his promise, the cragsman thereupon produced a razor, then lathered and shaved himself. To understand what this means is perhaps best conveyed by a picture of the Needle, on the top of which three people form a crowd, and which can only be reached by means of a climb that looks, to the uninitiated, particularly dangerous, not to say impossible, and something not easy of accomplishment.

Napes Needle—geologically termed an aiguille—the symbol of British rock climbing, stands free from the gigantic rock buttress of Napes Ridges, and sits tucked away 2000 feet above the Wasdale Valley on the south-west face of Great Gable. Access to the Needle can only be made by the rough and precipitous climbers' track known to the cognoscenti as the Gable Traverse. Standing sixty-five feet high with a loose, rocking top block, it was one of the most difficult climbs in the British Isles and to this day remains the most celebrated in the Lake District; one which all climbers set their sights as a rite of passage.

From its pinnacle, the view, a finely proportioned scene with varying tints and deep quivering shadows, comprises of Scafell with its Peak, Pinnacle, and Pike towering above its crags, below divided by the dark rift of Piers Ghyll; the pleasant, green, patchwork fields of Wasdale Head; the shimmering steel-grey levels of Wastwater far below, with the Wasdale Screes plunging down beneath its gloomy depths; and the Irish Sea twinkling in the far distance—the ultimate backdrop against which to celebrate a successful ascent! Millican certainly celebrated in style, but Napes Needle has witnessed many stunts over the years in a long series of chest-thumping displays of manliness; oneupmanship was routine in those days. Competition was intense; the one hundred and one showboating performances including a record breaking 85 second speed climb up and down by J. E. B. Wright, who also scaled it 750 times; a nonchalant blindfolded, unroped ascent and descent by Stanley Watson; and a show-stopping forked headstand on the top block defiantly executed by John Geoffrey Ball to mark his first attempt.

Most would be pretty impressed with Millican's celebrations on Napes Needle, but concerns were raised during the annual dinner of the Fell and Rock Climbing Club held at Coniston on Saturday 6 November 1920. This time he fell foul of the Club's purists who commented: "The foolish freak perpetrated on the Napes Needle, and published in many newspapers as 'climbing,' was an action which, at best, is derogatory to the true sport of mountaineering." The meeting was in strong agreement with universal condemnation passed. Even the clergyman from Cumberland had an issue: "I don't mind old Dalton having his tea parties on the Needle, but I do wish he would put the fire out, I put my hand on it last time I was up."

Never one to be disheartened, for each subsequent birthday Millican returned to the summit of the Needle for a brew and a smoke in the same fashion.

H. G. Dalton

NEGLECTED CLIMBER

R. H Mayson

THE CREVICE, SLINGSBY'S CHIMNEY, SCAFELL (MILLICAN CENTRE)

R. H. Mayson

CLIMBING ON SCAFELL PINNACLE (MILLICAN CENTRE)

214

R. H. Mayson

"ASTRIDE THE RAZOR RIDGE" - MILLICAN LEADS

H. G. Dalton

CLIMBING THE COOLIN HILLS - "THE WILDEST CORNER OF SKYE"

216

G. C. Potts

"TOWARDS THE SUMMIT OF WESTMORLAND CRAGS" - 7 OCTOBER 1920

CHAPTER SEVENTEEN

HIGH HEAVENS CAMP

As everybody knows, fashions come and go, including the Charleston which had continued to rage across Britain with more bent knees and twisted feet on dance floors than cigarette ends, but with the Roarin' 20s nearing its abrupt end, a Mr. C. J. Brake advertised some of his leafy Buckinghamshire estate for sale in London's evening newspapers. The land was in the secluded valley of Marlow Bottom situated in the Chiltern Hills, one of Buckinghamshire's wildest spots, where plots costing up to £50 could be obtained.

Families from London, not only looking for a better way of life in the countryside but also through destitution, moved to the valley from the 'big smoke.' The once open meadows and farmland had suffered from the continued effects of the agricultural depression with plots of land being sold off in phases from around 1916. In complete contrast to the towns and cities across the Southeast, Marlow Bottom was a spacious, peaceful, clean and safe rural valley with a dusty track for a road, no electricity, gas or mains water, but dense beech woods graced the valley sides and wildflowers grew everywhere. The surrounding areas were blessed with quaint villages, leafy lanes, furze commons and soft, rich pastures running up to the rolling hills which commanded glorious views of this delectable land—the green heart of England.

At first, holiday homes and weekend getaways made-up the majority of dwellings, but some folk lived there full-time with most residents making their homes from tents, wooden huts, or shacks from asbestos and corrugated iron sheets, resulting in the area becoming known locally as "Tin Town" or "Shanty Town." Apparently, all those who lived in Marlow Bottom appeared to be of a strange disposition, leading people to initially assume that the district was full of down-and-outs and gruesome characters. To others it had become known as a neighbourhood of intellectual dropouts.

It proved very appealing to Dalton, and wishing to be closer to his brother Henry, who had already married and moved to the nearby Quaker village of Jordans in 1922 also acquired a plot of land around 1927. Henry first met his wife-to-be, Elsie Harman, on one of Millican's guided camping holidays to Loch Lomond, Scotland around 1913. She was to share Henry's passion of outdoor life for the rest of her days, appearing regularly in his writings and photos. Affectionately known as "Goldie" or "Goldred" on account of her flame red locks, they had two children, Nicholas and Nancy.

Excerpts from literature available from Mr. Brake's estate, which Dalton must have read, stated:

> Particulars of Cheap Freehold Land for Sale on The Marlow Estate—The prettiest part of Buckinghamshire, only 28 miles from London, 19 miles from Uxbridge, 25 miles from Ealing and 27 miles from Acton. The County of Buckinghamshire is considered by those of authority to be unrivalled for its many beauty spots, amongst which the Marlow District stands pre-eminent, whilst its climate is unequalled, being particularly noted for its bracing character and tonic-like effect. Prospective clients should not miss this unique opportunity of securing some really excellent land in this pretty and most healthy neighbourhood, so readily accessible to London and its suburbs and entirely unspoilt.
>
> Sportsmen—have plenty of scope: good boating, fishing and bathing can be enjoyed to the usual sports. Numerous rambles through shady lanes and footpaths and beautiful woods may be enjoyed without being isolated. Conveniently, the Estate is situate adjoining the Town of Marlow in the Rural District (thus escaping Urban Rates) and is within ten minutes walk of the Station and River and occupies a truly delightful position high up on the spur of the Chiltern Hills, thus enjoying views of the Quarry Woods and overlooking the Thames Valley. By reason of its altitude the land is perfectly dry. Thus the land especially appeals to the City Worker and others requiring rest and quietude away from the hustle and bustle of the Metropolis.

Ironically, although produced as a circular, these particulars could have been written specifically for Dalton, the erstwhile City gent who had been searching for quiet places to live for the past 30 years. At this point a definite pattern becomes apparent; as one area became overpopulated he liberated himself and relocated to another more peaceful location. Evidently, he purchased one of the more affordable plots away from the busy Main Wycombe Road, the particulars specified them as:

> Cheap plots—other choice plots having frontages to pretty secluded roads are for sale from £10 each upwards. The majority are 20 feet by 200 feet and at this absurdly low figure represent more than value for money.

Millican's plot was a long strip running from the edge of High Heavens Wood to High Heavens Lane, on which he first lived in a tiny improvised tent close up against the woods in a sort of bohemian camp, delightfully named "High Heavens Camp" for obvious reasons. Water, as with every other plot, was supplied from a well. He lived alone, but neighbour's homes were close by and he was not isolated in any way. Amongst the scanty population was a collection of differing personalities: Mr. and Mrs. Hockin, his nearest neighbours, lived in the luxury of a small brick and flint bungalow; Doctor Durrant owned a large sanatorium at White Hill; and Mr. Lane, owner of a little wooden shop on the edge of Munces Wood, sold food and paraffin, and acted as milkman. Other provisions could be obtained from baker, Billy Hunter, who sold fresh bread from his pony and trap.

Following Dalton to Marlow Bottom was Pixy Poole, supposedly "a queer nattering woman who seemed something of an invalid. She was also unconventional and similar to Dalton in certain ways." Helen Mary Poole, as she was formally known, was Irish and from a titled background. Pixy resided in a caravan and travelled around on a bicycle; she had also opted out of society and chose to live a solitary existence on her own means, though oftentimes she worked at the Post Office in Marlow Bottom to boost her income. On her land grew vegetables, kept a goat and lived no more than 30 yards away from where Millican had his patch, living on the opposite side to the Hockins.

According to one resident, though the pair were friends and led similar lifestyles they tended to have nothing to do with each other, but this was more through Dalton's choice than hers, mainly because Pixy chased him everywhere having fallen in love years earlier. As time passed she became increasingly irritable and often crept about insulting anyone within earshot. Millican was also a target, and it was well known that the two of them had the most dreadful rows. On one particular occasion Pixy was seen running around in her nightdress in the early hours screaming and causing a great disturbance— Dalton, by all accounts, had been in her caravan; though nothing came of the accusation, and there was no proof he had actually been inside. Either he had been in her caravan; all the fuss was a result of her ailing faculties; or as a friend and one of her closest neighbours he may well have just been made a scapegoat? Who knows?

DAILY HERALD
24 MAY 1928
ADVENTURES for Holidays! Camping Tours: Mountaineering, boating; fine scenery; English Lakes, Alps, Thames (whirlpool rapids).
Dalton, High Heavens Camp, Marlow.

"Old Dalton," as many knew him, was frequently seen pushing, sometimes riding, his famous old blue bike—rumoured to be a woman's bike—along the valley or on his infrequent trips through Badgebury Woods and down Oaktree Road to Marlow where he would travel for supplies. More often than not, he was seen to walk much more than he cycled, especially on journeys to High Wycombe where he would visit the library or meet up with friends for coffee. Close contact with family was maintained and he made a concerted effort to visit Henry and "Goldie" in Jordans, which was within walking distance across the fields from Seer Green village. Occasionally, when Millican was a little short of money, Henry would slip him a £5 note as a gift on the understanding that he need not repay it. This was to the amazement of Millican's nephew, Nick, whose weekly pocket money was only one penny! Although more than welcome, he never stayed more than a night as he could not bear to be under the constraints of a roof for long. During visits to Jordans he would scope the village wood, which contained plenty of holly trees—or as he saw it, an abundant source of tent pegs!

Pottering around High Heavens Camp or the valley; developing his plans for further thrills; working on his programme; contemplating new theories on life, creation, and the world in general; and searching for wildlife formed much of his day. Growing older and slightly reserved he became less famed for his free and comprehensive outdoor instruction to local townsfolk. Generally he tended not to mix with other locals all that much and rarely went out of his way to speak to other people, though he would often pass the time of day with anybody he chanced to meet on the road. However, when he returned from guiding on the continent the children of the valley always acted as a keen audience. Foreign travel was still relatively uncommon; this made Millican something of a maverick. Gathering anxiously at his camp, the children would sit silent and wide eyed listening intently to his jaw-dropping tales of adventure in wonderful faraway places. Oohing and aahing intensified as the stories unravelled and photographs shuffled around the audience adding to the excitement—his ripping yarns simultaneously passing through a haze of cigarette smoke and into legend. Of particular amusement to the children were his puttees, which always left his knobbly knees bare.

DAILY HERALD
1 JULY 1935
HOLIDAY CAMPS
ADVENTURES—Thrilling. Camping, Mountaineering, Boating—
rapids, etc. English Lakes (£3 5s). Highlands, Wales, Switzerland.
Chilterns beechwood, real camping, tents with kit 7s. 6d. wk., hut 10s. 6d.
Dalton, Camp Hostel, Marlow, Bucks.

Millican was very much liked by the locals and it was of the general opinion that he was a delightfully interesting man, who was harmless with nothing frightening or untoward about him. They thought he spoke beautifully, was honest, well educated and a real gentleman who never bothered anybody and kept himself to himself. It was obvious that he came from a good family and all respected him, even though some thought he was something of a hermit in a pleasant way. Valley residents rarely knew where he would be, as he would come and go, but during fine weather he would often be seen seated on a bank at the side of the road, his bike propped up, enjoying a smoke and reading a newspaper. Quitting work remained an achievement of which he was proud and repeatedly reminded his neighbours "I used to work in the City but felt stifled."

In future years Dalton was to build himself a hut for use in the colder months and forfeit the tent for something a little more comfortable. His self-built, larch weatherboarded, red tile shack—free from all extravagance—was similar to the Epping hut and again housed a fire. In the centre of the hut was a metal grate on which he burnt large logs, with smoke left to escape through an opening in the roof directly above the grate. On some occasions the logs, over six feet in length, protruded outside the hut. Each log was carefully nurtured, rotated, kicked now and again and produced terrific heat always burning to dust, which left visitors to his home shaking their heads in disbelief with his seemingly unconcerned burning of solid fuel in a highly flammable wooden hut!

Millican tempted fate once too often and was eventually rendered homeless when his hut at High Heaven Camp was burnt to the ground on Thursday 27 April 1939. Away from home, the fire was first spotted by a group of children playing nearby who raised the alarm, their high-pitched screams and fervent shouting alerting the neighbours who then attempted to quell the outbreak with pails of water, but fuelled by a strong northerly breeze the flames quickly gained a hold. The Marlow Fire Brigade were called, but on their arrival the roof had already fallen in, and shortly afterwards the walls collapsed, leaving the building a complete ruin. It had been impossible to save any of the contents of the building. Faced with adversity, not for the first time it may be added, a new home was soon fabricated—branches from the beechwood, trimmed and bowed, formed a bender tent frame, and a number of wool blankets donated by neighbours made a flysheet. This was just another day in the life of Millican Dalton and normal business was resumed for a while.

Living dangerously does have its consequences and his somewhat reckless behaviour eventually led to more than a burnt hut and lost possessions. One winter whist camping out he was involved in a devastating tent fire and sustained severe third-degree burns leaving him hospitalised. Remaining ignorant of the threat to life, he sent a number of good humoured letters from his bed to R. Ernest Way in which he expressed surprise at himself for 'enjoying' his stay. The letters indicate he was a realist when confined to hospital; he did not show any signs of frustration, complain in any way, or suggest that he was particularly incapacitated. Instead he accepted his situation with good grace and total cooperation, though he did find it a little amusing to be pushed in a wheelchair, which he considered totally unnecessary.

Millican's stint in hospital did have its perks; he thoroughly appreciated the meals and revelled in the feminine company of the nurses and their care towards him—for the first time in decades our ageing protagonist was pampered and, perhaps, saw a glimpse of the joys he had rejected as he was in no rush to be discharged. Was this the first sign of a blip in his resolve?

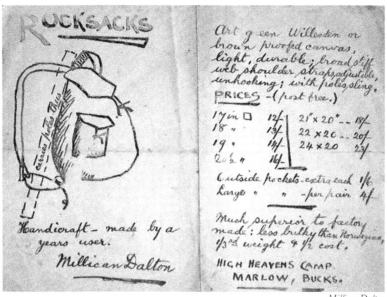

Millican Dalton

HANDICRAFT - MADE BY A YEARS USER

Archives

"MR. DALTON CLIMBING A LARGE TREE NEAR HIS CAMP" - 1933

Archives

"HE WORKS THROUGHOUT EACH WINTER AS A TENT-MAKER" - 1933

Archives

MILLICAN CONSTRUCTS A GIPSY TENT - 1933

CHAPTER EIGHTEEN

A NEW WORLD ORDER

High Heavens Camp happened to host one of the most eccentric, uniquely British, progressive social youth movements Britain has ever seen during Easter 1927 when a small group gathered for an event prearranged by Millican. Without digressing too much from the narrative, it is imperative to expand on the exceptional subject of John Hargrave in order to understand the tantalising nature of the organisation to which Millican was partisan.

John Gordon Hargrave, artist and author, social reformer and inventor, is today a name known to few, but had his dreams become reality the modern world would now be unrecognisable. Born in 1894 he was raised in an unconventional fashion. Having spent part of his upbringing in the Lake District, where he was educated at Hawkshead Grammar School, he garnered a passion for Nature. As a precocious child with a gifted intellect, learning was easy, and additional self-education through literature, art and the natural world instilled in him an avant-garde outlook on life. At the age of twelve he moved with his family to Latimer, Buckinghamshire and in 1908 joined the First Chorleywood Scouts.

Capitalising on a proclivity for art, his career as a published book illustrator embarked with several vignettes for a 1910 edition of *Gulliver in Lilliput*, published by Thomas Nelson & Sons. Twelve months later his exceptional skills as an artist gained him employment as chief cartoonist on the *London Evening News*, becoming, at seventeen, the youngest illustrator on Fleet Street.

Combined interests in Nature, Scouting and art led to the production of his first book, titled *Lonecraft*, published by Constable in 1913 under his woodcraft name "White Fox." His inspiration was Ernest Thompson Seton or "Black Fox," the British-American whose "woodcraft," a caricatured version of Native American life, was adopted by the Scouts as a sideline to their usual teachings. Acknowledged by the Scouting fraternity as a natural talent, he began a journey ascending through the ranks and en route penned further books on Scouting and woodcraft for C. Arthur Pearson Ltd. Subsequently, a job offer from Pearson resulted in his first salaried position as staff artist.

At the outbreak of World War I, Hargrave, a Quaker and committed pacifist who refused to see active service as a solider, enlisted in the Royal Army Medical Corps serving as a stretcher bearer on the battlegrounds of Gallipoli. Exposed to constant shellfire and haunted by ghostly snipers, he worked day and night on the long carry of wounded men. Falling victim himself, he was discharged on medical grounds yet despite recovering from the physical injuries, his horrific experiences left him emotionally and morally wounded. From this point he was convinced that modern civilisation had lost its way and a remedy for many of the present day evils was a necessity.

Post-World War I, he resumed his role with the Boy Scout movement, climbing further through the ranks to its upper echelons and once there become a well-respected expert on woodcraft earning the position of Commissioner of Woodcraft and Camping at Boy Scout Headquarters. At one point he was even mooted as the future Chief Scout, but disillusioned with the militarisation of the movement and their neglect of their own founding Woodcraft principles, he started to make his discord known. "Be prepared," the subtly ambiguous Scout rallying-call to ready themselves for war, and his distain at the lack of democracy within the organisation were among many issues to irritate Hargrave.

A global unease in the wake of World War I remained even though the mincing machine had stopped turning mainly fuelled by fear and uncertainty of the future. In light of this, there were many optimists who dreamt of a new world order of peace and prosperity, a new era for mankind, and within the Scouts grew an inner rim of men who were striving hard to improve the physique, citizenship and safety of future generations. Though, perversely, the majority of the population still supported the governments route and their half-baked peace talks. Nonetheless, Hargrave had audacious ambitions and his own plans in place for new a global movement: a subset anti-war wing of the Boy Scouts.

Hargrave's brainchild was a world peace brotherhood, the Covenant of the Woodcraft Kindred remodelled, a woodcraft tribe as mysterious as its appellation—The Kindred of the Kibbo Kift—an old Cheshire expression defined as 'proof of strength.'

Word of the Kibbo Kift started to appear in Hargrave's writings and in August 1920 the group was formed. In 1921, not long after the group's creation he was expelled from the Scouts by Baden-Powell after wealthy financiers made threats to withdraw their funding if Hargrave was allowed to continue in his role, and so, as a result, the Kibbo Kift became a standalone organisation. Initial internal quarrelling over ideologies and

227

personal differences saw Hargrave emerge from the ruckus as the sole leader, or "Head Man," in 1924.

The Kindred of the Kibbo Kift held a belief that they could forge a new post-war world based on the principles of a distinct and complex philosophy. Healthy outdoor living encompassing camping, hiking and physical training; self-reliance through handicraft; peaceful fraternity achieved by unilateral disarmament; economics by adopting a single currency; self-education reading recommended texts, rituals incorporating myth and magic; and politics with the goal of a one world government were all purposed to enable the regeneration or urban man.

Their Covenant, a lengthy declaration, was signed on acceptance, but a shorter version was developed with children in mind: "I wish to be Kibbo Kift, and to camp out and keep fit, help others, learn how to make things, and work for world peace and brotherhood." It was not only necessary for those over eighteen years of age to agree with the Covenant, they had to be ready themselves to execute certain duties and fulfil them honourably. Training was undertaken as member of a tribe, a 'roof tree' (family group), or a lone kinsman. A Kibbo Kift tribe composed of at least two clans.

To call their vision Utopian would be an understatement; it would have been all well and good in an ideal world, but as history has proven time over it is a deluded concept very unlikely to ever succeed as it is virtually impossible for a minute group of people to change the mindset of billions.

Relentless, Hargrave would try his hardest to convert the population to his way of thinking; he was, after all, an adman and knew the power of aesthetics and the use of propaganda. An experienced commercial freelance illustrator in the advertising industry, he had designed book covers for Mills and Boon in 1922, and then in the late 1920s produced promotional material for Boots the Chemists, and Lever Brothers for whom he designed soap packets.

Imagery of the Kibbo Kift was therefore meticulously thought-out in an attempt not only to catch the eye but to distinguish the group as a superior body; a select few who would lead humanity towards a new beginning far away from the perceived grubby industrialisation and consumerism blighting society; and to act as an exciting appeal to a weary audience living aimless lives during the drab inter-war period where the memories of conflict was to reverberate through the next couple of tormentous decades.

Creative designs were based on a perplexing blend of influences from Anglo-Saxon, Native American, Norse and Egyptian cultures which were appropriated in an attempt to retrieve the earthly qualities that civilisation and its quest for progress had stolen from them. This quaintly garbed fraternity wanted to be, and indeed saw themselves as Intellectual Savages.

228

If one met a man or youth dad in green or brown with a Saxon jerkin and cowl upon his head, a long cloak and shorts, a staff in his hand, and a rucksack on his back, he would be recognised as a kinsman of the Kibbo Kift; women wore a similar outfit. This, their everyday attire, must have caused a commotion in the English landscape of the early 1920s when marching two abreast along lanes with their standard raised leaving observing members of the public utterly bewildered—but this paled into insignificance compared to the rest of the Kibbo Kift's wardrobe.

Handicraft elements to the Covenant meant that individual members or 'roof trees' were duty bound to fabricate their own clothing and ceremonial regalia to specific designs strictly dictated by Hargrave. Kinsmen were also expected to make their own lightweight, one-man hiking tents and equipment.

By the late 1920s Art-Deco's prominence morphed their ceremonial garb, required for the quarterly meetings of the various tribes, into outrageous mystical modernist designs, which when coupled with animal masks and rituals that were overloaded with symbolism resonated shades of the occult. Coincidental? No, Hargrave was a firm believer in magic being inspired by the beliefs of Frazer's *The Golden Bough* (1890), the works of Aleister Crowley, and the rising theosophy movement. Highly coloured decorative tents, this time with symbolic designs of members' own devising, carved staffs and totems, and illuminated manuscripts and banners continuing the vivid theme created a chasm between the browns, greens and khaki hues of their everyday wear.

Ceremonies played an intrinsic role in the training of the Kibbo Kift especially at the seasonal gatherings known as Althing (national meet) during Whitsuntide, Gleemoat in Autumn, Kinfeast in winter, and the great Easter Hike. Once there, when all kinsfolk had gathered at camp, the rituals began with the "ceremony of the greeting of the kin." The beater of the tom-tom, standing proud in surcoat, beat the rally tattoo, whereupon the kinsfolk, clad in their ceremonial garb, assembled at the council circle, ready for the Chief of the camp to greet them with words of welcome. The Chief would then say: "Brothers, let us proceed to the four corners of this our encampment, that the ceremony of the beating of the bounds and the dedication of the camp may be performed." All kinsfolk, in silence, would then proceed slowly in single file, with the keeper of the encampment bringing up the rear before continuing with the days ritualistic events and archery or wrestling contests. Then, in the evening, seated around the council fires the kin would indulge in storytelling and the airing of disputes whilst the tom toms reverberated around camp and the flute melodies caught on the wind intertwined with mumming and chants from the Kiftie's songbook.

Other events involved paying homage to the ancestors of mankind by visiting significant sites—plaster cast skull bearing parades at Piltdown, the site of the supposed 'missing link' remains, and Druid-like assemblages at Stonehenge—where they held ceremonies in accordance with their traditions and commemorated the importance of the occasion. Weekly meetings, puppetry and mumming plays, and weekend camping trips or hiking excursions into the countryside provided an opportunity to leave their normal lives at home and step away from their full-time white collar positions as teachers and office clerks. 'Picturesque and dramatic public speaking' was also encouraged.

Hargrave had assembled an impressive collection of well-known names to the Advisory Council who added serious credibility to the Kibbo Kift, comprising of high-profile writers, artists, politicians, scientists and no less than five Nobel Prize Winners including Maurice Maeterlinck, Norman Angell and Rabindranath Tagore. Dr. Somerville Hastings, H. G. Wells, Stephen Graham, Henry W. Nevinson, Julian T. Huxley, Patrick Geddes, D. H. Lawrence, George Bernard Shaw, Havelock Ellis and many other prominent individuals were approached and subsequently offered their support to varying degrees indicating that the Kibbo Kift intended to build the foundations of their reforms on intellectual ideals. H. G. Wells was never a true member of Kibbo Kift, he tended to lend his endorsement to an enormous amount of progressive societies at the time, and along with the majority of other names on the Advisory Council simply acted as legitimators of the organisation. Few on the Council actually attended hikes or camps, and there is no evidence that they ever met with Hargrave in person, and some may only have sent a generic reply to his letters asking for support. Others, however, were involved in the day to day business of camping, Emmeline Pethick-Lawrence for instance, whilst T. E. Lawrence supposedly allowed Kindred members camp on his land. A working agreement with the No More War movement, and affiliation to the Regional Survey Association bolstered creditability.

Others were not so supportive, and some critics, based on their observations, labelled the Kibbo Kift a cult. Indeed, Hargrave's charismatic and intellectual yet intense, blinkered, humourless, domineering, unbalanced and swollen-headed personality with monumental delusions of grandeur to match, had all the hallmarks of a cult leader, and certainly made rational people think twice. George Orwell was not impressed and came to the conclusion that they were "cranks" and "sex maniacs"; thoughts he probably derived from their mixed-sex activities and body-exhibiting costumes worn during outdoor physical exercise that would have even made Adam and Eve blush.

Elaborate modern dances required participants to don delicate slips and peploi fashioned by the Ancient Greeks, whilst the clothing, or lack of it, for group workouts was even more daring. Kinsmen sported prettified buttock-skimming breechcloths and

230

thongs, which barely hid the nether regions; whilst the women, or 'Kibboettes,' exercised in brassiere-style tops twinned with diminutive, inner-thigh revealing painted skirts—forget the comparatively tame issues of grown men in shorts and women in breeches, these costumes were highly provocative for the period. D. H. Lawrence whilst in general agreement with Hargrave's principles was largely unsympathetic considering his ultimate goals unachievable.

The organisation's choice of name, often a contentious issue at the best of times, raised some concerns; its acronym and their Saxon cowls drawing dubious parallels with a darker organisation from the opposite side of the Atlantic. Though this was far from the truth and an accusation Hargrave later publicly denounced on many occasions, though not too convincing. "In some ways," he said, "it is a sort of Ku Klux Klan, but it is more closely resembles an English edition of what is happening among the youths of Germany, except that the Kibbo Kift is anti-military."

Regardless, the Kibbo Kift offered membership to men and women, boys and girls of any age, class or creed, who agreed with the ideals laid down in the Covenant. Kibbo Kift was non-political, owing no allegiance to any political party and pagan, being unconnected with any religious body. This may have been the theory, but in reality membership election was a strict affair to ensure that only the 'correct people' were enrolled.

Greeting of "Huh!" accompanied by an outstretched arm, open handed salute derived from the Native Americans were adopted by the group which, with hindsight, also carry an unfortunate, albeit innocent echo of a later fiendish group and their Der Deutsche Gruß gesture. Moreover, heavy connotations surround the then fashionable pseudo-science of eugenics—a rather odd aspect to Hargrave's vision considering his Jewish heritage—though selective breeding in this case reportedly revolved around health: fit and healthy individuals would be in an advantageous position to develop a more acceptable world, rather than the creation of a master race.

Regardless of these personal opinions, many notable subjects applied for membership including, lo and behold, Mabel M. Barker, who was a committed member from the earliest days, and one of the guiding spirits behind the Kibbo Kift's Regional Survey work in the early 1920s. She was an intellectual influence and a well-connected individual, her relationship with Patrick Geddes and his work with the Regional Survey Association being a prime example. Barker's standing within the Kibbo Kift is apparent by the substantial amount of articles she wrote for their newsletters, commencing from the very first of their publications in 1922.

Hargrave, being involved in outdoor education and Scouting from around 1914 heroised certain outdoorsy, adventurous older men, some of who he admired from afar, and others who he saw as the potential backbone to the Kibbo Kift; Millican Dalton one likely hero. It is highly probable that Mable introduced Millican to Hargrave, but there is no evidence available to prove either way. The Kibbo Kift were one of many small groups operating at the time with similar ideas, and it is possible that they moved in the same circles.

Although the Kibbo Kift left an extensive paper trail there is little relating to or produced by Millican, the exact dates of his membership are therefore uncertain. His name does not feature in any early documents to suggest that he was there at the outset, and this part of Kibbo Kift is very well documented, even mythologised. Neither did he write for any of the regular periodicals.

However, offering a crucial milestone, in 1922 Hargrave painted Millican's portrait, and the event immortalised on camera in an alluring photograph set in his cluttered art studio. Dressed in full Kibbo Kift costume rather than his usual linen artist's smock, the photo was clearly choreographed with significant symbolism on show, for Hargrave did not paint many portraits. Since Hargrave painted Dalton in 1922 it would suggest that he was a member from the early days, although there is still the possibility that he may have initially admired him from afar.

Following the lead of "White Fox," personal names were dispensed with in favour of an adopted woodcraft, or Kin name, in a push for equality that added to the fantasy of the organisation. Plain old Paul Jones became "Old Mole," and Emmeline Pethick-Lawrence was "Lotosa." Millican Dalton became "Adventurer" and Mable Barker "Ken-Ea"—her person symbol included the Plough constellation.

At some point a group of Kibbo Kift members, including Hargrave, paid "Adventurer" a visit in the Lake District indicating that he was an active member in the fact that he attended camps and hikes, though there is some uncertainty as to whether he went to weekly local meetings, the annual Althing or was part of the small number of lodges that were mostly located in the south of England. Bereft of facts, it would be relatively safe to assume that he was a lone Kinsman, if his membership was even formalised as such. The Kibbo Kift also had a 'Kin Reserve' for elder members who were unable to attend camps and hikes as frequently as younger members, though once again there are no references in their archives.

In comparative terms the Kibbo Kift was short lived, and despite a few thousand members signing the Covenant over the years, membership at any one time only reached the low hundreds though the exact numbers will never be known. Membership records were a closely guarded secret and held in a sealed, carved oak chest evocative of the Arc of the Covenant from Biblical times, known as "The Kist"—still sealed to this day—and now an irretrievable item lying dormant in the vaults of the Museum of

London. Newspaper reports from September 1920 stated that the organisation already stood 100000 strong; an error which Hargrave, the propagandist whose stock-in-trade was exaggeration, conveniently ignored.

Hargrave had an autocratic personality, there was only ever one "Head Man," and was certainly no egalitarian showing little respect towards those would not subscribe to his ideas. He did not like the thought of other people determining the direction of *his* movement; his own masterplan forever sacrosanct, and one which he edited at will to suit his own agenda. These changes had started to take shape in 1924 when Hargrave was introduced to C. H. Douglas' economic theory of Social Credit. From hereon in his belief on how to reform mankind lay in the rectification of the economic system.

This dictatorship coupled with his diverse personality repelled many sympathetic, dedicated and loyal members over the years, and a portion of the remainder looked to breakaway and form their own movement; all rather ironic considering his dislike of the Boy Scout Movement's lack of democracy. A splinter-group was formed, The Woodcraft Folk, founded in 1925.

In terms of influence, Dalton and Kibbo Kift were aligned in many of their interests: Nature, pacifism, self-determination, outdoor living, natural health, physical hardihood, and so it is speculative whether one influenced the other, though Hargrave was certainly impressed by Millican's input as expressed in an account written by the "Head Man" in May 1927 for *Broadsheet*, one of the Kibbo Kift's periodicals; Dalton significantly referred to as 'Our old Kinsman.' 1927 was a creative year in Kibbo Kift's life, and Millican would have seen many of the most colourful and spectacular outputs of the group, including their original Glee singing in full ceremonial costume.

BROADSHEET
MAY 1927

The Wikinp—a monthly pow-wow and illustrated supplement
for the clans, tribes, and rooftrees of the Kindred K. K. by White Fox

Saturday 16 April 1927
The Spring Festival Hike at Eastertide.

The finest Glee Mote the Kin has ever had was performed at High Heavens Wood, near Marlow, on Saturday night. Our old Kinsman, Millican Dalton (Adventurer), had seen to it that huge logs were ready for the fire, and we all sat round on beachen trunks. However, I must not go on—I could fill the Broadsheet six times over in telling you what happened. A brief report appears on another page…

…At 11:00 a.m. on Good Friday morning a party of about two dozen Kinsfolk and friends assembled at Berkhamsted for the start of the Easter Hike. White Fox gave a short address of welcome and ceremonially handed to Little Lone Wolf authority to act as Hike Chief. Camp was made the first evening on Coombe Hill near Wendover. Much familiar ground was covered on Saturday on the way to Marlow, the midday halt being taken on Bradenham Common. The camp fire on Saturday evening was the best ever held by the Kin. The setting was glorious. A huge fire in the woods, a full moon and an hour and a half of Kin songs, mumming etc. (The advance made on the Glee side of the work of the Kindred during the last few months has been tremendous). The going on Sunday was hard. Almost the whole seventeen miles from Marlow to Ascot was along roads, some of them newly tarred. But no-one fell out and when the women were met, a song was still forthcoming.

Towards the end of the 1920s Hargrave reengineered the Kibbo Kift into a soapbox from which to promote social credit bringing the obscure economic theory to the mainstream. By 1932 Hargrave had changed direction completely and turned the Kibbo Kift into Green Shirt Movement for Social Credit. Exploiting the economic and social mayhem of the 1930s they became a paramilitary organisation marching and campaigning on the urban political battlefields of London and were later involved in the notorious street brawls against the Black Shirts of Oswald Mosley's British Union of Fascists and the Red Shirt supporters of the Communist Party of Great Britain.

Understandably this proved too much of a change for the majority of members, especially those who had been attracted to the Nature, health and camping aspects of the original movement. They in turn left to join other groups and Hargrave had to be content with his remaining hardcore members and the pursuit of their anti-fascist, Social Credit based agenda. The Public Order Act 1936 which outlawed the wearing of uniforms by political groups curtailed any further action. After one last name change World War II disrupted any further plans and eventually Hargrave's fractured organisation was disbanded in 1951.

Millican did not advocate this and left well before the Green Shirts were formed returning to his one-man progressive counterculture. Hargrave had fascinated the liberals of that era through the promise of simplicity, pacifism, faux primitive and an obsession with the advantages of outdoor life—though he did not take his own beliefs to the extreme limits—unlike Millican Dalton who was, of course, living a wild and free life decades before the creation of the Kibbo Kift, and long after its demise. "White

Fox" had made a gallant effort at making changes to society, but the huge leaps required happened too early in history to make a difference and were, by and large, too far ahead of their time.

Moving on, Millican simply continued with life as normal and remained more than a common sight exploring the outstanding natural beauty of the Chiltern Hills, and throughout Buckinghamshire was known by repute as "The Robin Hood of the Chilterns." Much enjoyment was had wandering carefree through the abundant beech woods, chocolate-box villages and down the leafy lanes, rucksack over shoulder and cigarette in hand.

DAILY HERALD
14 SEPTEMBER 1934
CRITIC OF SCIENCE

Science is not wisdom. Even professors do not understand the anti-science arguments. Only a small proportion of scientific knowledge is useful for human life—much is too abstract, useless, and even disruptive. Scientific specialists lack the guidance of wisdom, and have no talent or qualifications for guiding reform.

MILLICAN DALTON
Marlow, Bucks.

DAILY HERALD
16 SEPTEMBER 1934
SCIENCE AND US

No one understanding what Science means will agree with Millican Dalton's letter, except in so far as he is attacking much that passes for science. What can be demonstrated as true both of external nature and of man is useful for human life. Existing injustice, however, does not permit its diffusion, and, in fact, so stunts the mental development of the great mass of the people that they have not the capacity to avail themselves of it. This results from man's failure as yet to achieve liberty in the economic sphere and, in view of the present strong retrogressive tendencies, he may lose the little in the political sphere he has gained so painfully.

MANOJ, Liverpool

JOHN HARGRAVE PAINTS MILLICAN DALTON

CHAPTER NINETEEN

ROGUE HERRIES

For centuries the Lake District has been graced with the presence of an endless list of outstanding wordsmiths such as William Wordsworth, Samuel Taylor Coleridge, Robert Southey, Thomas De Quincey, Harriet Martineau, Beatrix Potter, and Arthur Ransome; and in the more modern era, Alfred Wainwright and A. Harry Griffin. Some were native to the region and others chose to relocate from elsewhere—but all used the quietude and outstanding beauty of the landscape to fuel their creativity.

New Zealand-born Hugh Walpole, another revered author who features in the annals of Lake District literature, was one such incomer drawn to the region and it was Keswick's attractions that incited him to purchase Brackenburn at Manesty, beautifully sited above Derwentwater, in 1923. Precious childhood memories of family holidays to the Lake District had developed a longing to return, and Walpole's purchase of his "little paradise on Catbells" subsequently provided a retreat from his hectic literary lifestyle that saw him in great demand, travelling feverishly between London and the USA to attend various functions.

Upon arrival in Keswick he was keen to be involved in all aspects of day-to-day life and soon became a respected figure of the community. Despite staying at his idyllic home in the Lakes for generally no longer than a fortnight, his visits and accompanied social interaction at local events still enabled him to become acquainted with most colourful personalities of the area, including the most colourful of them all, Millican Dalton.

On Christmas Eve 1927 Walpole commenced writing his family saga novels, the *Herries Chronicles*, and the first of the four books, *Rogue Herries*, was published in 1930. This splendid work of fiction, depicted in eighteenth century Cumberland, is a fine, adventurous and wonderful story of a split family set amidst throngs of strange characters, romance, murder, weddings and feuds. Walpole had an excellent geographical knowledge of the county, which became more than apparent in his works. Locations, panoramas and famous landmarks abound giving the reader an authentic sense of reality. Taking the leading role in the story is Francis 'Rogue' Herries, known as the Dark Angel of Borrowdale.

Typically, the source of inspiration for many authors is a result of real-life encounters. Indeed Walpole's familiarity with Millican provided him with a ready-made character. Millican fit the bill nicely, he looked as if he had been plucked straight from the eighteenth century, and his time warped eccentricities therefore resulted in his inclusion as a character in *Rogue Herries*.

Rogue Herries
Part Two 'Forty-five - Into the Cave

[About Herries] He woke to a strange sense of constriction. He moved and found amazingly that his arms and legs were tied with rough rope. He raised his head and stared into the eyes of a man who sat motionless on a rock near him.

[About the man] He was a man with a thin dry face, long shaggy black hair, a coat and breeches of some colour that had faded into a dirty green. He looked like part of the fell. His legs were thin and long and sharp. He was not young, fifty years of age maybe…The man was, from his voice, not of the North. His tone was firm, quiet, reflective…He was of great height and very thin with a long nose.

[About Herries] He saw then the grey opening of a cave in the hill, fenced with dead bracken and furze. At first he could see nothing, but could smell cooking food, an odd sweet scent of flowers and a musty animal tang. The man had his hand on his arm and very gently, as though he were speaking to a child, said: "Sit you there. You can sleep if you will. The straws dry." Francis turned back, shifting the bracken a little and the sun flickered on to him, dancing before his eyes…He sat up and looked about him. The sun streamed in from the fell. He could see all the cave, which was not indeed quite a cave, but rather the opening of some deserted entrance to a long-neglected mine. In the black cavern beyond him there was a fire and on the fire a round black pot.

Comparisons between Walpole's 'fictitious' character and Millican Dalton are compelling and manifest themselves to be more than coincidence. It does not take much analysis to draw parallels.

238

Looking from an analytical perspective: Obviously Dalton did not bind people but he was renowned for routinely carrying an Alpine rope. His black, grey streaked hair was longer than the usual, fashionable "short back and sides" of the day; it was shaggy and never appeared to be combed. Describing his outward appearance identically Mabel M. Barker said his clothing was of "…a dull green, toning with the fells." His legs were thin and long and sharp. In addition, by the time Walpole penned the first words of *Rogue Herries*, Dalton was not young. He was sixty years old, sufficiently close to the estimated fifty years of age. Although having lived in Cumberland for the first thirteen years of his life, when Walpole arrived in Keswick Dalton had spent the previous forty-three years living in the south of England and had lost his northern accent, he spoke in cultured tones giving the impression he was not from the locality. He was tall and thin— in excess of six foot tall and of a lean physique. Interestingly, access to the Cave Hotel is gained by a walkway, which in summer becomes encircled with towering fronds of bracken and nettles. He may not have used hay for bedding, but bracken, taken into the cave, formed the basis of his sleeping arrangements. Finally and probably the most defining comparison is the fact that the Cave Hotel is not a naturally formed cave, but the remnant of a long terminated stone quarrying process.

Furthermore to Walpole's composition, it is well known that the "Skipper" constructed many rafts, the most significant being the one he proudly christened 'Rogue Herries.' On first impressions this rough watercraft would not inspire any confidence or assurance of safety in any modern-day sailing instructor or sea dog, this was clearly no Kon-Tiki, but undoubtedly functioned as it was used to sail down the River Derwent and across Derwentwater.

Constructed principally from a combination of tree branches and old rope, the addition of four empty red and green oil drums recovered from Grange tip then provided the necessary buoyancy. It was steered by the provision of a tiller, propelled by a mast and red junk-style sail, and adorned with a handwritten name plaque on the bow. Was the naming of this raft coincidental? Unlikely! Of course Millican will have enjoyed the book; the excellent reading which encapsulated loved and frequented locations was in the right style; but ultimately the naming was not merely a casual nod to a compelling piece of literature, but a discreet acknowledgement to Walpole of his inclusion in a best-selling classic that was recognised on an international stage.

Photographic artist Ralph H. Mayson ensured that this acknowledgement was captured on film in a series of photographs presenting Dalton sat astride his raft at a point on the River Derwent known as Gowd Dub. Whether or not the photographs were purely stage-managed, there was an element of theatre on show and a definite play made to the camera as, conveniently, the lettering on the name plaque was suitably sized and pointed directly towards the photographer. Thanks to Mayson's imagery these iconic images of Millican Dalton, with their underlying significance, became some of the most influential photographs in Lakeland after being sold by as publicity postcards and posters to unsuspecting tourists through his Lake Road Emporium.

Descriptions, similarities and acknowledgements of this nature are not simply a twist of fate and without doubt Dalton was immortalised in literature as Hugh Walpole's character, George Endicott.

R. H. Mayson

AFLOAT ON ROGUE HERRIES

R. H. Mayson

"SHOOTING THE RAPIDS"

R. H. Mayson

IN THE SHALLOWS AT GOWD DUB

CHAPTER TWENTY

THE ETERNAL BOY

Thomas Criddle Stephenson also had literary connections with the Lake District, and although not known for poetry or novels and nowadays somewhat forgotten, his power with words helped forge the Lake District National Park into the area as it is known today.

Born 1893 in Chorley, Lancashire, Stephenson was a keen walker and climber who used the countryside as a means of escaping the increased industrialisation of the northern mill-towns, but he quickly realised that vast swathes of open land were out-of-bounds to public access. He was not alone, and the issue of access to the open countryside eventually became mainstream news after five walkers were imprisoned following the organised protest and Mass Trespass of Kinder Scout in the Peak District, 24 April 1932.

In 1933 Stephenson took up a position as journalist for the *Daily Herald* giving him the opportunity to write articles about his passion of walking. Around the same time he became involved with the National Council of Ramblers Federations, ultimately becoming Secretary of the Ramblers Association, the organisation he had helped to create. Dismayed with continued access restrictions, he vowed to establish new rights of way, and to ensure existing footpaths across the nation remained open to the public. Through his efforts he became one of the prime movers in the long campaign against landowners to open up forbidden moorlands, particularly in the north of England.

The *Daily Herald* supported his activism and championing of walker's rights with the Ramblers Association, providing him with a national platform from which to promote campaigns, such as the mass trespass of Winnats Pass, or to highlight the injustices suffered by individual walkers. In future years, using his political and journalistic skills he relentlessly lobbied parliament playing an instrumental role in the composition of a report that became the blueprints for Britain's system of National Parks. He is now accredited with playing a key role in the eventual passing of the National Parks and

Access to the Countryside Act 1949 and for inspiring the creation of the Pennine Way which officially opened in 1965.

Stephenson first mooted the idea of the Pennine Way in an article for the *Daily Herald*. This thought provoking piece, heralding the birth of the open access movement, was written in 1935 and titled *Wanted: A Long Green Trail*, the same year in which he wrote an article concerning Millican Dalton:

DAILY HERALD
31 AUGUST 1935

PETER PAN OF THE MOUNTAINS

In a shop window in Keswick, among climbing boots and alpine rope, there is a very fine camera study of a cragsman, a portrait which daily attracts the attention of passers-by, and one which must have made many an artist wish to meet the man depicted.

It is twenty-five years ago this month since I first saw in the flesh this most picturesque mountaineer. In those days, as an impecunious youngster I had begun to roam the Lakeland fells, wandering where fancy led, sleeping "rough" in barns, or in the open, and feeding as cheaply as possible.

One evening at sundown I saw a tall, well-built man with a coil of rope and a red plaid over his shoulder striding up from Sty Head towards Esk Hause. I well remember admiring his nailed boots and watching him walk with the slow, seemingly-effortless, rolling gait of the experienced fell-walker. Though we two were alone in the evening silence of the hills, with the clouds lowering on Gable and Great End, we passed without a word or greeting. I was too shy to speak, and I have since discovered he suffered from the same affliction.

After watching the retreating figure I descended into Wasdale and, in the dark, crossed Burn Moor into Eskdale. The night turned cold and wet and, unable to find shelter, I made a vain attempt to sleep on the lee-side of a wall rolled in a groundsheet.

About 4:00 a.m., soaked and shivering, I was stamping about to regain some warmth when my mountaineer came strolling down the dale, apparently bone-dry and looking cheerful and comfortable. This time I found courage to say "Good-morning" as he passed.

Though in the intervening years our paths must have crossed, not until last week did we meet again.

244

With A. B. B. Sutcliffe, a lithe young fellow who has succeeded Jerry Wright as Chief of the Lakeland Mountain Guides, I was spending the day on Great Gable. At Kern Knotts we met one who might have passed for Robinson Crusoe or a Lakeland Caveman —a tall, sinewy fellow in strange attire. Although considerably older there could be no doubt about this being the same person I had admired a quarter of a century ago.

His beard had turned iron-grey, but that was the only sign of years gone by. Lean and active looking, with clear blue eyes and face tanned with sun and wind, carrying no superfluous flesh, here was a man who refused to grow old. This time I had no hesitation in greeting the stranger and telling of our previous meeting.

Thirty-five years ago Millican Dalton was "something in the City," but he cast off the shackles, took to the Simple Life, to vegetarianism and the open-air, camping, bivouacking, living in caves, mountaineering, communing with the world of Nature and settling, at least to his own satisfaction, many of the problems of life. He believes:

"The blue spiral incense of the blazing Camp Fire reddening the stems of the pines, with the infinite starlit dome above, transports you out of the monotonous, commercial world, far back to the old, ever-fresh, primeval world of Romance, Freedom and Adventure at the untamed heart of Nature."

245

Later that same afternoon we met at the foot of the famous Napes Needle, that splendid tapering rock spire on the flanks of Gable.

There we sat down and looked down on Wasdale and the glimmering Wastwater, and these two, Dalton representing the old brigade, and Sutcliffe the modern school of climbers, talked of men and mountains.

With equal enthusiasm they discussed various climbs, the changes in technique and various mountaineering topics.

Then, to show he still retained his vigour and prowess, the elder man took the lead, and the younger one followed him to the summit of the Needle.

Twenty-five years ago I admired Dalton, and once more I salute him fervently, hoping that I may retain something of his strength and the ability to climb the Napes Needle at the age of 68 lightly and surely as if he had been forty years younger. *(Mirrorpix)*

Two years later Stephenson once more had a chance meeting with Millican, then aged 70, in Wales, April 1937:

"There were cold winds blowing from those snow-streaked Welsh mountains, but this weathered old man of the hills had pitched his flimsy tent in the valley and cared not for wind, rain or snow. Lean and muscular, his eyes still bright with enthusiasm and knees as brown as his khaki coat, he talked of his climbing plans, oblivious of his years and unconsciously testifying to the health-giving regime he had followed so long."

CHAPTER TWENTY-ONE

THE CAVEMAN 1941

Another four years passed but Millican still remained impervious to the elements and neither snow, ice or subzero temperatures could prevent his occupancy of the Cave Hotel over the winter of 1940/41. World War II was well underway and although the evacuation of thousands of children to the Buckinghamshire countryside was considered to be a safe option, its close proximity to London presented too much of a threat. Unlike his determination throughout World War I to carry on with normal life, the increased risks posed by the heavy aerial bombardment of the Luftwaffe and the high possibility of invasion resulted in his own evacuation to Borrowdale in the summer of 1940, and then decided to stay put for the winter months. The Cave Hotel was one of the best air-raid shelter in England and provided an ideal retreat from the Blitz devastation in and around the capital, though whether it offered the same appeal to many others was another matter! "It's about the safest place you could find these days" he told visitors, with a reassuring twinkle.

Keswick residents, familiar only with his summer visits, became aware of his uncharacteristic out-of-season residency down the valley. As a welcomed member of the community there were those who cared about his wellbeing and checked-up on him from time to time.

Mindful of his presence, Christmas even came early for Millican when a group of local school children paid a surprise visit to his cave and sang carols. News of his winter stay quickly piqued the curiosity of others including the media. By this point it was evident that Dalton never shied away from press coverage, instead taking pleasure in relaying his unique story, but one thing is clear, he always maintained a degree of mystique, never divulging any personal information. However, no matter how unpretentious the Professor of Adventure was, he could not escape some greater amount of publicity after featuring in an article in the national tabloid newspaper, the *Daily Mirror*, on 21 January 1941 whose circulation figures had reached 1.7 million. The article, titled *The Caveman 1941*, written by a special correspondent, described how war could not touch him:

> Millican Dalton threw up his job to live among the hills of the Lake District. He didn't look for a country cottage overlooking a lake. He chose, at Borrowdale, a cave as high as a three-storey house set in the wooded crags above the river. Today this seventy-three year old hermit is less affected by the war than any man in Britain. Peep into Millican's home. He wears a Tyrolese hat decorated with a heron's feather, a plaid over a brown coat, green corduroy shorts, puttees and climbing boots. He makes tents, builds rafts and is a Lake District guide.

Rationing posed few problems mainly due to his simple living, ability to reap wild food and manufacture his own clothing. He told the correspondent "My only luxury is coffee, for which I pay 2s. 2d. per lb. I sleep on a bed of bracken and need only my plaid and an eiderdown to keep me warm. I don't burn a light, though I lie in bed from beginning to end of blackout." Unlike other civilians living conventional lives it was clear Dalton cared nothing for the blackout. After failing in an attempt to contain the light within the confines of the cave, he sacrificed the obligatory campfire and refrained from burning candles.

However, his decision to remain in darkness was not through his own choice. One night in 1940, an ARP Warden for Keswick, patrolling the Borrowdale Road towards Keswick, observed a bright, flickering, incandescent light on the flank of Castle Crag. He promptly walked up to the cave by way of Hollows Farm curtly reprimanding Millican on arrival for infringing the blackout regulations shouting "Put that light out! You are permitting light to be displayed from this cave!" Picking up a large, rusting tin of water the fire was extinguished without argument casting the cave into instant blackness, and the forced blackout implemented.

This infuriated Millican and incited him to write several letters to 10 Downing Street. They detailed his disapproval for government policies and demanded Prime Minister, Mr. Winston Churchill, to call an immediate end to World War II as it was interfering with his liberty! Yet despite Millican's efforts, his nemesis ignored the pleas from a cave in the back of beyond and rightly or wrongly continued with the Allied offensive. Millican never did elicit a response.

"Seven hours sleep is enough for anyone. The rest of the time I just lie and think and listen," said Millican who had become one with his surroundings, not just in appearance as by now he looked as rugged as the landslide on which he lived, but also with his affection for all things wild, claiming "You can't feel lonely with Nature as your companion." If that was not enough to keep him entertained there was always the pitter-patter of water dripping from the ceiling of the cave and the crashing of icicles from the crags above the cave entrance.

Accompanying his expenditure on coffee was food and tobacco that came out of his weekly allowance of 22s. His weekly income is well worth analysing. Through a study by the Ministry of Labour, of which figures became public on 14 January 1941, it was ascertained that the average man in the street was spending 10s. 10d. per week on rent and 6s. 5d. on lighting and fuel. In comparison, Dalton must have been reasonably comfortable on his 22s. considering his minimal living expenses.

Two photographs featured in the article—he looked a striking figure. The main photograph, taking up nearly a full page, pictured Dalton outside the lower portion of the cave against a curtain, nay a portcullis, of impressive ten-foot long icicles. Not forgetting that the great man was now aged 73, he still wore shorts while the rest of Borrowdale's residents were sat cuddled up in front of their raging coal fires; he was as hard as the nails on his boots. In the second smaller photograph he was captured stirring his pan of porridge with a burning cigarette clamped between his toes in an attempt to prevent ash from falling into his breakfast—proof if ever it was needed that he was a chain smoker.

The *Whitehaven News* then sent their own reporter to the cave and published an article on 30 January 1941 with the headline '*Borrowdale's caveman cooking a meal.*' The article read:

Meet Mr. Millican Dalton. He is one of the creatures of the wild. He lives in a cave high up in one of the wooded crags that are the glory of Borrowdale. In the photograph he is stirring the porridge he is making, taking care to put the cigarette he is smoking between a big toe and a smaller toe that the tobacco ash may not drop into the breakfast. Mr. Dalton is 73½ years of age, is tall, spare, hard as a fell toad and if you were to meet him you would agree that in his Tyrolese hat, decorated by a heron's plume, his plaid drawn over a brown tweed coat, his green corduroy shorts, sinewy legs, sometimes encased in puttees and climbing boots, he looks a fine figure of a man.

We last met him 20 years ago at the foot of Taylor Gill Force in Seathwaite. Then, as on this day, he was stirring porridge in precisely the same fashion. He was conducting a climbing party on the Napes Ridge and, joining us, did a Kern Knott climb, the Napes Needle and the Arrowhead Arête. One experience that day is unforgettable. Mr. Dalton had with him a man who lost his nerve and would neither go forward nor backward and in the pitch in which he lay stuck we had to climb over his body, leaving his guide to extricate him as best he could. We asked Mr. Dalton if he remembered the incident and after a while, for 20 years is a long time, the memory of it came back to him

It was on the coldest and bitterest day of this year that we renewed our acquaintance with this man of the wilds. The icicles hung like a curtain across the mouth of a cave high as a three-storied house and roomy enough to hold one or two companies of soldiers. Water, which seeps through the roof of the cave, was also icicles and divided it into two. Millican Dalton's part of it is only a few yards square. It is walled in by slate offal. Everything within is "wondrous neat and clean." Cleverly packed is the cave-dweller's camp equipment and the cooking utensils, which have all been picked out of village dumps. There was a place for everything and everything was in its place. In one corner was Millican Dalton's lying-up place. Bracken for a bed and a plaid and an eiderdown for covering. And on this deadly cold night Millican had, as is his wont, taken off his day clothes before he stretched himself out to sleep. Which of us accustomed to the luxury of a bed in a well warmed house would not have been frozen stiff? But Millican makes light of all severe kinds of weather.

And Millican glories in the life he leads. "I was a clerk in a London office. The life stifled me. I longed to be free. I gave up my job and ever since I have camped out. Today I live rent free, rate free, tax free. It's the only kind of life worth living." And a question about the 14 hours of black-out, without even the occasional glimmer of candlelight, he said, "Well, I don't sleep much, and while I am awake I lie and listen and think. There's a lot to think about just now, isn't there? All the sounds of the night, the roar of the mountain stream, the barking of cur dogs and foxes, the cries of birds, how can I be lonely with such company?" Millican told us a good deal about his philosophy of life, but that, of course, is not for public reading. Suffice it to say that the more you hear of his conclusions the greater your respect for the man.

Our curiosity about his domestic ways was, of course, keen. Soon we discovered that Millican is a vegetarian and believes that we can live on wholemeal bread. And, delving into one of his packing cases, he produced a bag of wholemeal flour and began to make it into dough, mixing with the flour the sultanas and currents soaking in water in tin canisters depending on an iron rod ingeniously suspended between the slates. The dough was a slab twice the size you could hold in your fist. Then, drawing together the birch logs smouldering on a rock, he fanned them with the lid of a flat canister. In a moment or two there was a bright fire, with the blue smoke curling up the rock face as though Nature had designed a perfect way of getting rid of it. It was still a mystery how the dough was to be baked. From another hole in the slates Millican pulled out a long-handled wire tray, such as housewives use for containing soap to be agitated in a dish washing bowl. Into the tray went the dough. The wire tray was fixed that it might be left and so in the course of a quarter of an hour we saw the bread start to bake. Very good bread it was, too. We tasted it afterwards and ate it, sultanas and raisins and all, with relish.

"That's the foundation of my domestic economy."

"And your principle meal?"

"Oh, that's dinner in the evening. Wholemeal bread again, but, either I bake potatoes, or I boil them, together with carrots and other vegetables I may have been able to get. I am pretty expert at dinner meals. You see, when I camp in a tent and cook for a party that I have been taking in the hills, I have been in the habit of making four, five, or six courses. Simple dishes, if you like. Give me wholemeal bread, porridge, coffee and cigarettes and I am quite happy. I buy very good coffee at 2s. 2d. a pound. It's as nice as any coffee you may pay a lot more for."

You may have gathered now some insight into the life of Millican Dalton. Do not imagine, however, that he is a recluse. He goes down to the Post Office every day for his letters and a newspaper and he does his shopping in Keswick. Frequently he is visited by people who know him or of him. He is a busy man. He makes divers sorts of camp equipment. Tents are his speciality. Quite pardonably, he believes that a tent of his making takes a lot of beating.

He is full of ideas about clothes. He claims to have been the inventor of shorts and his followers, he says, are to be numbered by the million including Boy Scouts. To sail to the sea from Borrowdale is one of his ambitions. We shall not be surprised if he designs a raft to take him to the Solway this summer. At the age of 73½ years he climbs as well as ever, though he says that he is more cautious than he used to be. When the days grow longer and warmer he will be called upon to act as a guide to visitors and he will conduct adventure parties, the adventures being entirely of his own creation. Even in wartime he will have plenty of scope for his energy among young outdoor folk.

Then, further fuelling the media frenzy, which for many brought a touch of the lighter side of life bearing in mind the ongoing atrocities across Europe, was a solo appearance in a British Paramount newsreel after cameraman, Douglas H. J. Hardy, had descended on the Cave Hotel. The fleeting 34 second black and white clip, titled 'Britain's Cavemen at Home,' was released on 3 March 1941 and shown at cinemas across the country accompanied by the soundtrack Death of a Champion, and a sprinkling of one-liners delivered in an archetypal plummy tone by commentator, John Stagg.

Soon after Dalton's appearance in the British Paramount newsreel he was confronted by P. H. D. and his wife in May 1941, they wrote:

We spent a week at Grange-in-Borrowdale, memorable for our meeting with a quaint old character in shorts and a slouch hat we saw one day on Grange bridge looking over the upstream parapet. On impulse I went over to him and asked:

"Excuse me, could you be Millican Dalton?"

"Yes," he replied.

"Do you perhaps remember my father H. G. D.?"

"Of course, we climbed together. We carried our bikes over Sty Head—it would be about 1911."

H. G. D. worked as a chemist in London, his brother-in-law, G. P. A. Richards, worked (with Millican) in insurance—hence the connection. "We had a long, quiet walk with him next day," continued J. H. D., "Up on the fells around Watendlath via Lodore Falls, accessing the falls along Dalton's own 'personal' path, to avoid the hotel charge of 2d, making tea besides the brook running out of the little lake. Tea making kit produced by Dalton, with a wood fire, of course. We returned to Grange via Rosthwaite. Dalton was very tired at the end. Later, a pencilled note from Dalton awaited us at the Post Office above Grange bridge and that evening we went to his cave. We found the cave in Castle Crag with some difficulty, rather a damp spot at the top of a great slate rubble heap. Millican Dalton has a semicircular wall of slate about 2 feet high adjoining one side, the space enclosed being perhaps 6' by 2'6". Here he has his fire, bed and seats and numerous little shelves for papers, books, etcetera. All a bit dirty.

We sat down by the fire and he pulled a sort of sacking roof over our heads to keep out the draughts. The fire was soon kindled to a cheerful crackling glow and we sat talking for a good while. He talked of life and politics (he thought we were at war with the wrong enemy—it should be Russia not Germany). He is a great talker and though 74 does not repeat himself, though rather liable to be sidetracked. Dalton told us that he climbed Napes Needle solo, every spring, and if this ever became too much for him he would give up rock climbing. His old wrinkled face under the green velour hat looked magnificent in the firelight, with the paling sky behind him at the mouth of the cave.

At nine-thirty we got up to go and Millican accompanied us down to the track running into Grange. It was almost dark and he turned back. It was just possible to find our way down to Grange in the velvet night when some few minutes later his fierce battle cry rang out from above us, echoing from side to side of the valley and J. H. D. answered with her own. Next day, Millican talked of health doctors and inoculation, he advised J. H. D. not to have our baby vaccinated.

We avoided the subject of war, which had caused some heated discussion the night before. Millican always has some interesting topic ready to hand when necessary. He rode up to our lodgings on an incredibly old bicycle and we started along the Keswick road under his guidance for a round of Watendlath. After tea we visited Castle Crag but found Millican out. We broke up a pile of sticks for him and just as we were leaving we were hailed from below by the old man who had a good bundle of sticks on his shoulder. We said our goodbyes and after we had left gave him our call until the cliffs echoed but he cannot have heard for there was no reply.

For those lucky enough to have avoided conscription, a degree of normality was still possible, and outdoor enthusiasts looking for an escape from the incessant talk of war continued to venture on expeditions to the Lake District—and Millican, forever a social creature, continued to make friendships with many of the young folk who pitched their tents near him.

Morris Watkins, a regular visitor to the Lake District during the war, crossed paths with the valley's resident caveman during a week's holiday. He described his encounters with Millican:

One night I was camped in the Jaws of Borrowdale by the Derwent, upstream from the village of Grange. It was ten o'clock at night, fire burning and coffee on the boil, when in the darkness I noticed an old man wearing a strange hat, shorts and a pack on his back pushing a blue Raleigh bicycle and trying to get by without being seen. "Good evening! Hello!" I called him over to share the coffee, which he did. He introduced himself "I'm Millican Dalton, I have cycled up from Epping Forest" and I told him "I am Morris Watkins." A rapport developed between us and on leaving he said he lived in a cave on the side of the mountain and invited me to visit him.

The following evening I found the cave with a little difficulty, a huge cave with a high roof and, inside, a structure about five feet high, eleven feet in diameter and twelve inches thick. There was Millican, sitting cross-legged on the floor, a cigarette between his toes, a frying pan in his hand over a nice fire and cooking rolled oats that he ate sweetened with syrup. This seemed to be his staple diet. It was a wild stormy night and I took my quarters at the cave from the inclemency of the weather and furious storm that raged through the valley, and joined him by the fire to dry off and get warm. There was something particularly wild and awful about the night. Nothing could be more spectral; great flashes of lightning now and then made the hills look like giant phantoms, while the intervening hail showers had cloaked them in a shroud, the trees of the valley stood like huge skeletons, raising their twisted limbs towards the trooping clouds that hurried swiftly across the heavens, like the Witches of Pendle flocking to an unearthly feast.

The orange glow of the fire danced across the walls of the cave, the howling wind swirled around us, and a waterfall from the ceiling played a concerto of notes on the broken slate beneath. Sensing fear in my expression, he offered coffee and porridge, and then, stroking his pointy beard between his thumb and index finger, began to spook me further with a series of ghost stories. An almighty thunderclap boomed directly above, bringing me hastily back to the land of the living. The night progressed and the conversation flowed along with the coffee, both of which became increasing flavoursome.

I started spending my weekends and holidays with him. I then bought a new, maroon, 500 BSA motorcycle and one day he asked me to go rock climbing. I was very proficient having climbed on Dow Crag and Great Gable many times. We ripped along the Borrowdale Road just after daybreak and the passage all clear to Seathwaite. I twisted the throttle with intent as I knew he liked to take risks, he thoroughly enjoyed the ride, but I think it was his first trip on a motorcycle as he held onto my waist with the grip of a bear. We left the motorcycle at Stockley Bridge, and walked up Sty Head and the Napes, passing Napes Needle and then on to Arrowhead Ridge. Millican had a 120ft hemp rope and I led. Afterwards we went to the summit of Great Gable and ran down the scree-chute of Great Hell Gate, and back to the cave. Not bad for a man of seventy-three! I later stayed at the cave with friends Baron Williams, Frank Sharples, Leonard Dodds, Thirza Anderson and Bunny Frazer and we left our names beside the entrance to the lower chamber.

Clearly Millican was far from alone in evacuating to the Keswick area. World War II had brought hundreds of children from around the country, especially from the towns and cities of North East England where the shipyards and steel production facilities, designated as German military targets, put them at a high risk of attack. Keswick was a recognised 'reception area' for evacuees with children billeted in hotels or lodged with local families who were more than happy to help protect the youngsters safety. More children arrived from the docklands of London, but they were more intimidated by the mountains of Lakeland than bombs, and soon returned home.

Local resident Sam Hicks also happened upon the caveman evacuee. He was but a boy, but clearly remembered Millican's pale blue bicycle and its rough finish that led him to believe it had been hand painted. Playing around the Borrowdale Valley, he recognised when Millican was at 'home' as the bicycle would be left wedged between the hazel trees that grace the verges of the lane running between Holy Trinity Church and the River Derwent at Hollows Farm. One day in 1942 Sam was stood outside Grange Post Office with a small group of children who had been evacuated from South Shields when Millican pulled alongside on his bicycle, and then reached into his rucksack to share some of his homemade bread with them; a kind gesture so they thought, but all were left a little disappointed with their surprise snack—it was hard as rock and completely inedible!

As would be expected, family time was also a regular feature at the Cave Hotel with Henry Dalton, along with his wife and children, Nick and Nancy, bunking down on many occasions after making the journey up from Buckinghamshire. Nick, who worshipped his Uncle Millican wrote: 'By the time I was old enough to spend my summer holidays with Uncle Millican he was doing less climbing. After walking down to the Post Office at Grange to pick up his *Daily Herald*, chatting with his many friends en route, he was content to return to the cave to smoke his Woodbines and read his paper. I, being young and full of energy, had to exert all my powers of persuasion to get him to gather up his tackle and take me climbing. I fancy that the days on which a curtain of rain fell in front of the entrance of the cave, and we had nothing more strenuous to do than lie on our beds of bracken, with an occasional sortie out to gather wood for the fire, gave him a certain amount of satisfaction! His equipment was used by my family, and enabled us to enjoy camping holidays through such places as the New Forest in 1924, and later in 1926 in the Lake District. He never married although rumour had it that: "under his plaid he'd had a few." Knowing the man and the times in which he lived, I think this highly improbable.'

Regardless, rock climber and smallholder Paul Orkney Work, contradicting Nick somewhat, once said: "My mother, Alice Constance Viggars, had a short lived engagement with Millican Dalton, the Lake District "Professor of Adventure" who made his home in the quarry caves opposite the Bowder Stone in Borrowdale. He made his own clothes and equipment and never washed. My mother broke off the engagement eventually. She said that he had a rather strong goaty aroma. But he took no offence and when she married my father, George, he made them a tent for their honeymoon, in the gipsy style, with hoops rather than poles. Later he made me a rucksack, which I used until well on into the 1930s. In the winter he used to organise what now would be called instructional weekends in survival techniques. They took place in Epping Forest. My father was an artist and painted a water colour portrait of him. So from my mother I had a good grounding in the outdoors."

The onslaught of World War II dragged on, and whilst there were no air raids on Keswick, the enemies planes could be frequently heard rumbling overhead in the dark skies of the Lake District tracking the eleven lakes to the industrial heartlands of Manchester, Liverpool and Glasgow. Although there is no evidence to show whether Millican continued to stay year round at the Cave Hotel until the end of the war, the Allied victory on 2 September 1945 meant he had managed to survive a second war and live another day.

H. G. Dalton

MILLICAN & NICK MESMERISED BY THE FIRE

H. G. Dalton

NICK & NANCY DALTON OUTSIDE THE LOWER CAVE

H. G. Dalton

NICK SKETCHES UNCLE MILLICAN

H. G. Dalton

RIPPING YARNS RING AROUND THE CAMPFIRE

H. G. Dalton

HENRY & MILLICAN REUNITE

Whitehaven News

"ONE OF THE CREATURES OF THE WILD"

H. G. Dalton

BORROWDALE'S CAVEMAN WRITES A LETTER

M. D. Entwistle

DON'T WASTE WORRDS, JUMP TO CONCLUSIONS!

M. D. Entwistle

F. M. - A GOOD COMRADE

Daily Mirror

THE BEST AIR RAID SHELTER IN BRITAIN

Aladdin's Cave
Friday morning
2/5/41

Postal Address
P.O. Grange
Keswick

Dear Friends

I'm off shopping to
to Keswick — but shall
be back 'home' about
5.30 & shall be glad
to see you later, when
it suits you —

If you have an
electric torch, you
will be able to stay later
at the cave — I have an
acetylene bike lamp anyhow
& can take you down
as far as necessary —
if it is dark —

I have of course coffee
& tea here — but may have
no milk — (I haven't

Millican Dalton

"AN INVITATION TO TEA" - LETTER FROM MILLICAN TO P. H. D.

brought any milk since
I arrived here last July —
(I prefer my drinks without).
— Swiss milk is now rare
in the shops — I did
buy some last year for
stray visitors here —

Do if you like milk
in your drinks perhaps
you can bring along
some this evening —

Yrs

Millican Dalton

Robinson Crusoe
Robin Hood
Rob Roy
Sinbad
& Co

Lieut. Dale

A Modern Cave Man
Millican Dalton
———————————— (1941)

The cave is an old deserted slate quarry amongst the wild crags & woods of the Jaws of Borrowdale, in the English Lake District

He discovered it ~~35~~ 40 years ago, and has often bivouacked in it with his camping parties for ~~the~~ their experience.

Last summer he went as usual to the district for a climbing & camping holiday. As the place is the safest spot in England from the kind

MILLICAN'S POTTED-BIO WRITTEN FOR BRITISH PARAMOUNT NEWS

2

attentions of Hitler, & the cave
is a most excellent dugout,
he decided to spend the
winter, for a fresh experience.

For comfort ~~in the cave~~ a
good fire is a necessity. Any
amount of dead timber can
be picked up in the surrounding
woods which are, in the
narrow valley, subject to
tremendous gales.
In severest winter weather
the temperature has descended to
zero & the cave becomes festooned
with icicles 10 ft. long.

The sleeping accommodation
is a bed of bracken, with a
down quilt & one blanket —

3.

quite enough for warmth.

From the titles given him
by the general public —
~~Millican Dalton~~
Robinson Crusoe, Robin
Hood, Rob Roy &c &c
he appears to be looked on
as a sort of reincarnation
of all the romantic adventurers.

Up to 40 years ago he was
an ordinary City clerk, but
as he decided that wasn't a
man's job he gave that up,
and became a guide for the
Cooperative Holidays Association
in the Lake District.

4

He also ~~provided~~ started camping
holidays, for both sexes, with
deliberately planned real
adventures — rock climbing, rapid
shooting, rafting &c.

He has mountaineered in the
Swiss Alps, having done most
of the biggest peaks, and has
also climbed in the Austrian
Tyrol & the Dolomites.

He is the oldest rock climbing
guide in Britain, being
73 years of age & still climbing
as well as ever.
Vegetarian & simple lifer.
Dress Reformer — originator of
the Shorts fashion, and
of breeks for women
tourists &c.

5/

Socialist, philosopher, &
pioneer in life &c.

He says – "This cave in the
wilderness is a fine retreat
for thinking out the problems
of life."
"Life – simple but complete
is the ideal, with the
object of self developement
& the developement of others"
"The 2 greatest problems of
life are War & Love.
"A sufficiently satisfactory
peace can be obtained –
the only alternative being
a 5 years world war, including
a risky gamble with the
British Empire."

6

"The simplest & best cure
for disappointed love is
another attack of the same
disease, with a fresh object!

CHAPTER TWENTY-TWO

FAREWELL MILLICAN DALTON

As your journey through this book draws to a close, you may wonder what eventually happened to Millican Dalton? Well, the seasons came and went, but nothing else changed for Millican, who invariably lived a simple outdoor life, continuing to alternate between his Buckinghamshire hut and Borrowdale cave throughout the gloaming of his years.

Towards the end of World War II Dalton considered his future as a guide and, after half century of guiding, eventually decided to retire—at around 75 years old! In the meantime, Henry Dalton had died several years prior in May 1940 and was buried in the grounds of Jordans Meeting House. Millican, never one for mourning suits, as will have now been gathered, attended the funeral dressed in his usual 'Robinson Crusoe' attire. Although the only remaining sibling, he was seen by many folk all through his seventies, who commented on his lively and sprightly nature whether walking, cycling or climbing. Though well past middle age, he was as full of vigour as any young man, and more physically fit than the great majority.

In 1945 he chose to spend Christmas with Henry's widow, his niece and nephew, and to celebrate with a traditional Christmas tree and yuletide trimmings. However, he was uncomfortable with the festivities and, regardless of much persuasion to stay, he left on Boxing Day and made his way up Oxford Road in the direction of Maidenhead.

Irrespective of retirement the Professor of Adventure continued with his annual summer visits to the Lake District, even as a late septuagenarian, with the Cave Hotel remaining his chief residence. It was from his cave on Castle Crag that Mabel M. Barker received an amusing letter posted without an envelope in 1946. It concerned a difference of opinion with Harold Spencer Jones, the Astronomer Royal: ("He said I was wrong, but I have reason to believe that he was") "I should have liked to have you dropping stones on them (his opinions on the universe!), and trying to dodge them." Millican, as energetic as ever, disclosed his immediate plans for the summers climbing.

Commendably the veteran cragsman never regarded himself as past climbing even in his 80th year! Regardless of his hearty lifelong appetite for tobacco Dalton remained fit, strong and agile.

On cue, summer in Borrowdale came to a close and in the autumn of 1946 he packed his meagre belongings into his rucksack and leaving the gaping mouth of his Cave Hotel checked-out for what would prove to be the last time. Shunting towards a ninth decade, he committed himself to yet another winter in the open at High Heavens Camp.

Of course, winter waits for no one, although on this occasion it was to arrive with a difference, and whilst Dalton may have been content to camp out in his hut at High Heavens Camp, he was not prepared for what Mother Nature had in mind.

The stark reality of his stoic situation became chillingly apparent during the severest, coldest winter of the twentieth century; the worst since 1740. The Arctic conditions of January 1947 laid an icy hand over the entire country, including Dalton's domain in which the nearby River Thames froze over. Many parts of the nation ground to a halt with schools and bus services being severely affected with problems exacerbated due to fuel shortages. With no respite, almost constant northerly winds kept average temperatures hovering around freezing point.

Millican was coping fine albeit aided by a well-stoked fire, until, one night, sometime at the beginning of January, the hut met the same disastrous fate as its predecessors and was accidentally burnt to the ground. With no specific explanation for the blaze it was assumed his cat had knocked over a candle—though the fact that he lit large fires in the hut would be a more probable reason for its demise. Despite the dreadful weather conditions, and perhaps stubborn or confident of his abilities, he was adamant to remain at High Heavens Camp and immediately moved into one of his gipsy tents. Serious kudos to Millican Dalton!

He then swiftly wrote to his young friend, Ken Way, explaining his predicament which, bearing in mind his age, was undeniably a perilous position to face. Indeed, the move into a tent was Millican's swan song, as, unfortunately, the glacial conditions made life under canvas hard to bide, and proved far too much for both his resolve and ageing frame.

He consequently became ill, and after a number of weeks of illness he was admitted to Amersham Hospital where he remained an in-patient for several weeks. After failing to respond to treatment Millican Dalton died alone, far from his beloved hills, on a hospital ward 5 February 1947 at the age of 79. As a result of the inclement weather he died due to a combination of acute heart failure, pulmonary bronchitis and bronchopneumonia.

271

Lying uncompleted by his bedside was his life's work, *Philosophy of Life*, which had been started many years earlier. As would be expected for a man of his character he left no Will and Testament or Letters of Administration. The whereabouts of his lifework is uncertain—presumed lost. According to his niece, Nancy, he now rests in an unmarked grave in either Chalfont St. Giles or Chalfont St. Peter, both in Buckinghamshire (crucial gaps in the church burial records prevent the exact location from being confirmed).

In hindsight Millican Dalton clearly discovered the romance and freedom he was searching for, as a return to conventional living was never made. Freedom was his life, which he found having announced, "Free I am as the buzzard mewing by day or the owl hooting by night. Freedom is everything." Summarising his life, pictured in the press under the headline, *A Happy Lifer*, a photograph showed Dalton sat on the step to his hut with the remarkable quote:

"I have treated life as a chemical experiment to see what is really necessary for existence, and I have found that life which is the simplest is the happiest."

Millican's mission was accomplished in an outstanding fashion!

An obituary appeared in the *Keswick Reminder* on Friday 14 March 1947: 'All those people who knew Millican Dalton, better known as the Borrowdale Hermit, will learn with great sorrow of his passing last week. At the age of 79 years he died at Marlow, Buckinghamshire, in a hospital after weeks of illness. Millican Dalton turned his back on society and came to Borrowdale to lead the Simple Life. His home was a craggy cave on Castle Crag where he made his headquarters for his Spartan life on the fells he loved so well. Millican spent all his summers here where he was well known for the homely way he dressed and went about among folk of all grades and calibre. His tattered shorts, mountaineering sports coat and his Tyrolean hat complete with feather will always linger in the memory of those who knew him best. The world is much poorer for the loss of such men.'

After reading this article in the *Keswick Reminder*, his good friend Mabel M. Barker wrote an obituary for the *FRCC Journal* 1947: 'His picturesque figure and loveable personality have surely become part of the heritage of Lakeland so long as the hills endure and men love them. It is difficult to strike a fair balance between his firm belief in his own opinions and his innate modesty; to assess his curious self-assertiveness, and the absence of any self-seeking. He had, I think, early worked out a theory of life for himself and if ever anyone did so, he lived up to it consistently and completely. He had found something, and was well content with it. Into this unison of theory and practice of life, climbing fitted as a natural part. He did things on the rocks, as everywhere else, to please himself, but not for self-seeking; to fit in with his theory of life and of earth and his relation to it. He believed that people (astronomers included) were "shutting their eyes to the foundations of the universe." Perhaps he was wiser than most of us, and his long and happy life indeed trod a pathway to the stars. I wonder how many owed to him their first thrills on rock and rope; in camp and caves in all weathers; in forest and on water, and in the cunning management of wood fires. Personally I owe him much.'

In the same Journal, Ralph H. Mayson added: 'He was a well known figure throughout Lakeland in his picturesque garb, respected by all who knew him. A man of simple pleasures and tastes, conductive to a mind at peace with the world, whose knowledge of things in general was very sound. After a day on the hills with him, or just pottering about, one had a feeling of contented happiness and peace of mind, proving the simple pleasures of life to be most lasting. He will be greatly missed as a companion and guide, made lasting by the Valley of Borrowdale and its hills, with Castle Crag, the guardian fortress of them all.'

R. E. Williams said: "His resources for adventure were never ending."

Many people became acquaintances with Dalton through contact with him in Borrowdale. One such person was A. Harry Griffin, climber and journalist, who said: "He was just a 'character'—an unusual man who was only happy when he was in the hills, climbing, or in the woods and the rivers."

L. M. W. wrote in the Essex Review 1948: 'It is not all of us who can follow our dreams as wholeheartedly as Millican Dalton; indeed if any appreciable percentage of the community did so it would play havoc with the tidy plans of our administrators; but characters such as he are an admirable leaven and at his passing we can truly mourn the extinction of "a candle which lights others while consuming itself." '

A tribute, overheard on the typically overcrowded Borrowdale bus not long after his death, was as follows: "Now a man like that has learned the great secret, the secret of going without so many things that we feel essential. He knows the comradeship of the fells and of all those who love them. He was a great gentleman and will be missed in the mountains."

The summer of 1948 arrived, but the cave lay silent. A cracked cup, rusty teapot, cracked mirror and a cushion the only signs of previous habitation.

Mother Nature stepped in to fill the void and to this day the cave lies empty—the two chambers still exist, the fresh water supply still flows—but the only remaining signs of Millican's existence are a few epitaphs carved into the cave walls. Nonetheless his spirit lives on through legend and in the cave which he made his castle.

Today the sun has long since set on those distant halcyon days of the Borrowdale Valley, no longer is it a place sympathetic of people wishing to live rent free, rate free, tax free—hermit or not. Visitors are welcomed, but they must obey the strict rules and stay at one of the numerous campsites, hostels, B&Bs or hotels in the valley. Which leaves the question: Where will the next Borrowdale Hermit live now?

Millican Dalton

1867 - 1947

EPILOGUE

Millican Dalton lived a remarkable life, as most readers by now must surely agree, and it is easy to see why he caused such a stir. For his name to remembered to this day he obviously left behind a significant impact. However, despite his lifetime achievements, whether it be dismissing Victorian protocol with the groundbreaking guiding of mixed-sex groups or his experiments with lightweight camping equipment, he is primarily revered for his aesthetic appearance and spirit of adventure which saw him roam the globe for over fifty years searching relentlessly for thrills and danger—his caveman lifestyle and outdoor escapades have become something of a sideshow overshadowing his contribution towards progressive movements in an era of colossal change. As a result Millican is often mentioned, but never given the credit he justly deserves as one of the greatest characters to grace Lakeland, Essex, and Buckinghamshire.

Although much information remains unearthed, hopefully, with what facts are known, he will now be elevated from relative obscurity to his rightful position in England's heritage and the annals of history alongside the likes of Near Sawrey's Beatrix Potter, Loughton's Sir Jacob Epstein and Marlow's T. S. Eliot. Though, unlike these characters, Dalton stands distinct. Quitting work to pursue his dreams; choosing home be it tent, hut or cave; his promotion of social justice; his strange lifestyle and unorthodox philosophical approach to life in general all distinguish him as a true quintessential English character outlying his contemporaries in the nineteenth and twentieth centuries. He deserves permanent recognition.

Especially apparent was a complete lack of greed. Success in commerce would simply have been a matter of course and a more than comfortable lifestyle achievable. In preference to a life of comfort and ease he opted for extreme simplicity. Dalton unequivocally possessed a genuine adoration of simple living, accepting that material items did not bring happiness or real satisfaction. With the oppression of ostentation and fashion discarded, and free from the meretricious inventions of modern times he was liberated from the fake perceptions of comfort. Certainly no champagne socialist, his only want was romance and freedom—hardly a shameful ambition.

Conventional life verses untamed pleasure, deemed as a suitable basis for a "chemical experiment," was it seems worth a gamble. To this basis he added a philosophy which, with the addition of simplicity and romance, created a unique identity. The discovery of this self-shaped, idealistic, dreamy world was the perfect answer to his quest and proved the theory behind his "chemical experiment" correct. His genius and courage to experiment with life must be applauded. Here was a deep thinking philosopher who appeared to be more than satisfied with his paramount enjoyment of life, well aware that there would be no compromises.

Millican Dalton was totally dedicated. He made no show of it, simply did it, and then stayed with it. Whether he ever considered his break from civilisation a mistake, we will never know. But, however we may view it, life is no walk in the park; it prises a call for fighting; for endurance and for grit; for rugged disposition. Remarkably resilient and evidently totally comfortable and at peace with his off-grid way of life he coped with the loneliness of isolation, especially through the long, dark winter months, transcending decades of what most would consider unnecessary self-inflicted hardship; the solitude and discomfort of which would break the average person. Picture the scene for yourself: spending the better part of a lifetime alone, night after night with no family or companionship; no creature comforts save a campfire, an eiderdown quilt and some salvaged junk; surviving off only the most basic foodstuffs. How many would live like that through their own choice? A few at best. Testament to his indomitable spirit, his outstanding staying power can summed up nicely in the wise words of Thomas Carlyle: "Endurance is patience concentrated."

Upon deserting his desk in the City he engineered the opportunity to forge his own destiny. He woke each and every morning to a day that he could call his own. Each day was enjoyed hour by hour and the most was made of any situation. Happiness was achievable through freedom. Life in the outdoors was his symbol of freedom, made more significant with the associated proximity to Nature and wildlife he so much adored. A lifetime's contentment in the open allowed for a union with Nature, his companion with whom he never felt lonely. To enjoy Nature to its full extent he chose to live amongst it, study it; watch its varying moods and changing features. He made friends with the weather; the rocks and peaks; lakes and rivers and they never proved false. Mother Nature taught him well; he followed her ethical code—comprehending fully the fragile link between Nature and mankind—and became one of the few people who never lost those primeval connections. It is almost certain something was found in

276

the wilds as he upheld his alternative lifestyle right up to his final days without wearying, leading one to believe he reached self-actualisation.

Do not be mistaken though, this cannot have been a panacea to all of life's problems, and one can be assured he still encountered his own woes—we are all human after all—though his strength of mind and ability to deal with these issues was the deciding factor in achieving longterm inner peace. Such was his determination he refused to settle down and marry. Intimate relationships, yet to be disproved, are unlikely to have existed, but an open-minded view should be adopted. Charisma, warmth of personality, an acceptance of women as equals and his localised fame would have definitely been an attraction, leaving the point open to speculation. Mabel M. Barker though not romantically linked with Dalton shared something with him—there was an obvious connection and a degree of chemistry between the two. Did their relationship ever go further? The fiery relationship enjoyed with Pixy Poole was also, supposedly, of an innocent nature. She chased him, having fallen in love, but he never entertained her romantically. What was the full extent of their relationship? Who knows what would have happened if he had married Alice Viggars. Would the arrival children have carried on his legacy and provided an accurate insight into his way of thinking—or would his life journey have changed completely leaving no story to tell?

It was his resolute, non-compliant, freethinking approach towards social injustices that formed a paradox with his laid-back, stress free outlook on life. Despite the laid-back approach and self-funding existence, he always upheld an agenda and a smart outward appearance irrespective of his homemade clothes. His homely appearance and life as a solitaire resulted in him commonly being perceived as a hermit, earning him the title "Borrowdale Hermit."

Although he did live something of an eremitic existence, he was not a hermit in the true sense of the word. Whilst he had an argument with the confinements of the City he chose to quit employment not to hide from society but to escape the rush and stress of convention and follow his true calling in life. Yet far from a recluse, he maintained a busy calendar with his involvement in a variety of pioneering organisations, and throughout life he was socially active with friends, family, prominent individuals and even strangers. Dalton was regarded as a true gentleman, universally liked by all who knew him because of his down-to-earth attitude and ability to accept and relate to all people regardless of their gender or social status. It is possible that he was something of a self-publicist, but commendably, self-fulfilment was achievable without selfishness.

Considering his long, active and healthy life and, as importantly, his feisty appetite for tobacco, it is highly unlikely he suffered from rheumatism, consumption or neurosis —unless the open-air life was indeed a cure.

Sadly, the exact basis of his philosophy may never be fully understood. If only a *Philosophy of Life* had survived, what enlightenment would be available to all? Without this explanation maybe some consideration should be given as to whether lessons could be learnt from his search for romance and freedom and attention paid to the conclusion of his "chemical experiment."

In the current age of social reform and political correctness Millican Dalton's lifestyle and accomplishments become increasingly relevant. If he was to be singled out for one achievement, his greatest legacy must be his radical subcultural approach to gender equality gaining him mutual respect from women far and wide—but no matter how hard he tried to make positive changes the barriers in society which he tried to break down are still prevalent, and ones which cannot, apparently, be overcome even in this modern era. They remain a shameful memento from our collective past.

It may never be fully admitted, but Keswick, now promoted as the "Adventure Capital of England," has Millican Dalton to thank. A new generation of admirers, or modern day 'Daltonites,' who travel to the Lake District in search of their own romance and freedom will ensure his name becomes part of England's heritage and his memory exists for years to come.

M. Watkins

MILLICAN WANDERS THROUGH BORROWDALE

278

R. H. Mayson

M. D. STANDS IN "FOOT CLOTHS" BESIDE THE RIVER DERWENT

279

"Peter the Hermit's" task was unfinished

"SUNDAY EMPIRE NEWS" REPORTER

"PETER THE HERMIT" has just died down at Marlow, Buckinghamshire—not beneath the stars he loved so well, but in a hospital bed after weeks of illness.

His life's work, a "Philosophy of Life," which he first wrote years ago and lost in a fire, lay uncompleted by his bedside.

Forty-seven years ago a promising young architect named Millican Dalton put away his drawing-board for the last time, turned his back on society, and disappeared in search of the simple life.

London knew him no more, but to a craggy cave high above Borrowdale, in the Lake District, came a bronzed six-foot figure to live in Spartan simplicity, with no creature comforts.

Contemplation

It was here, during the summer months, that Millican spent hours in contemplation.

In the winter his tattered corduroy shorts, mountaineer's jacket, and feathered Tyrolean hat became familiar to Marlow people. It was there he spent the winters. There he built himself a cottage—but continued to sleep in a tent under a hedge.

It was there, too, that the results of his simple living and deep contemplation high up in the hills, where the silence is so tangible that it assails the ears, were recorded in his "Philosophy of Life." But cottage and manuscript both disappeared in flames while he was away in the mountains.

Though now an old man, Millican set himself the prodigious task of rewriting it all. But age defeated him. He was 79 when he died.

Sunday Empire News

MILLICAN'S LIFE WORK - "PHILOSOPHY OF LIFE"
(WHILST NO ARCHITECT, A USEFUL INSIGHT)

ACKNOWLEDGEMENTS

All the material (defined as photographs and published articles) used in this publication is either out of copyright or relevant permissions have been obtained from the copyright holders. Where any uncertainty arose regarding copyright ownership during the research process, every effort was made to ensure the material was usable and therefore deemed to be out of copyright. Importantly, all material used in this publication has been reproduced in good faith. However, if you believe that any infringements have been made please contact Mountainmere Research using the email address on the copyright page located at the front of this book, and the material will be removed from subsequent prints.

Many thanks to all of the following who assisted with my research. Without their help this book would not have been possible:

My parents, Helen and David, who have helped in every aspect.

Family and friends who assisted in collating information.

Mr. and Mrs. L. Barker for their extremely warm welcome, trusting nature, photographs and help.

Mr. J. A. and Mrs. E. C. Potts, always pleasant and helpful, who supplied photos and diaries.

Librarians at Keswick, Billericay, Loughton and High Wycombe Libraries who helped even in my absence.

Staff and Archivists at Cumbria, Buckinghamshire and Essex County Records Offices, always helpful.

The volunteers at Preston Temple of the Latter Day Saints Family History Centre who explained all.

Friends of the Society of Friends, who were quick in their responses.

Members of Billericay Archaeological & Historical Society and Loughton & District Historical Society.

Judge Smith and the Kibbo Kift Foundation.

Dalton family members Nancy Sogge (nee Dalton) and Ann Yould (nee Dalton), Sheena Downie (nee Dalton) and Mrs. Norah Dalton who supplied photos and vital answers to questions.

Residents of Keswick, Marlow Bottom and High Wycombe for their anecdotes who responded to my public requests for information.

The Fell & Rock Climbing Club of the English Lake District for their photographs and articles.

The *Daily Mirror*, *Keswick Reminder* and the *Whitehaven News* for use of their articles.

Reach Publishing PLC
   [1, 2, 3, 4] *The Essex Chronicle* 10 September 1920 - Mirrorpix

Aviva Group Archive (Aviva PLC)

Also many thanks to those not named who helped in one capacity or another with the compilation of this book.

ABOUT THE AUTHOR

M. D. Entwistle

After being introduced to the high peaks of the English Lake District at the age of eleven by his dad, M. D. Entwistle has been a regular amongst its mountains and lakes ever since. There he developed his love affair with outdoor adventure and he now spends his spare time seeking expeditions with a difference. He is a regular wild camper, mountain biker, skier, canoeist, and ghyll scrambler and has taken his passion far and wide, from the thermal springs of Iceland to the dense man fern glades of South West Tasmania.

In addition to writing Entwistle has featured on radio and TV talking about his specialist subject Millican Dalton; the pinnacles being appearances on BBC1 Countryfile, BBC2 The Lakes with Paul Rose and ITV1 The Lakes: Series 2 with Rory McGrath.

If you were to ask Entwistle what was his biggest claim to fame, he would say his 2006 book launch of *Scratch & Co: The Great Cat Expedition* (Molly Lefebure and A. Wainwright) on the summit of Scafell Pike, which took the credential of England's highest book launch—an unsurpassable event—complete with a cheese board and wine selection, which left inadvertent attendees speechless. He is currently creating a series of travel guides and outlining biographies of other Lake District legends, all of which will be released in due course.

OTHER BOOKS AVAILABLE

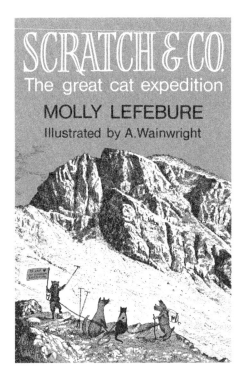

SCRATCH & CO.
The Great Cat Expedition

Molly Lefebure
Illustrated by A. Wainwright

New Edition - September 2006
ISBN-13:   978-0-9547213-1-2

This unique and intriguing account of the first ascent of the H. K. P., the Highest Known Peak in the Kingdom of Catland, originally published in 1968 with illustrations by the well-known Lakeland guide book author, artist and topographer, Alfred Wainwright, is seriously in the tradition of classic mountaineering stories and over the years since its first appearance it has built-up an enthusiastic readership amongst the mountaineering fraternity.

As well as being a most exciting adventure story, this is a witty send-up of a mountaineering book—complete with 'Alpine Club' type characters, hairbreadth rescues and all the tensions of a Himalayan expedition. Climbers, dedicated fell walkers, Wainwright fans and Lakeland devotees of all ages and persuasions have followed the adventures of Scratch and his fellow climbing-cats, his high-altitude terrier sherpas, his twitchy low-level rabbit porters and his free spirited adversaries, the foxes, emerging from their borrans amongst the crags to waylay these expeditionary offcomers.

Such are the colourful and keenly observed characters, making this book witty and gripping reading; not to mention Manx Scoop and Whiskey Bylines, ace reporters for the *Cat Times* and *Cat's Courier* and Manx Scoop's fighting mad mongoose ever keen to sink his teeth into anything that vaguely resembled a snake.

The choice of illustrator was an easy one. A. W. was, of course, good friends with Molly Lefebure for many years, a friendship originally started by post after she wrote to him regarding an error in one of his guides. They shared a lot in common, not only their love of the countryside and the Lake District—but also for cats. When asked to illustrate *Scratch & Co.* he was all enthusiasm until he met the mongoose, "The cats I can draw with my eyes shut. But a mongoose? I've never as much glimpsed one!" he said. Fortunately a stuffed mongoose was discovered in Kendal Museum, where he worked as Curator. When reporting the good news A. W. confirmed "I've spent a couple of days with the little chap and I think I've got him!"

The letters accompanying the illustrations were written in typical Wainwright humour. Within these typed letters were several of his concerns, primarily for "prostituting his talents." He jested that he may have to walk the streets holding his head in shame for drawing a scruffy little dog having a piddle and confessed "I have sunk very low indeed!" The original copy of the frontispiece showing 'The route of the expedition' also carried signs of Wainwright's character. A small patch near Stockley Bridge covered a burn mark which occurred when he experienced "a moment of tense excitement" when his pipe spilled onto the paper.

The Great Cat Expedition was ready to start. Readers have been joining it ever since.

REVIEWS

SUNDAY TIMES: A super-ingenious and most diverting book.

THE KESWICK REMINDER: A very quirky read.

HUNTER DAVIES: All A. W. fans should have a copy in their collections.

CUMBRIA MAGAZINE: An engaging mixture of parody and Ripping Yarn…it deserves a new generation of fans.

TIMES EDUCATIONAL SUPPLEMENT: The cat's whiskers.

SKIDDAW HERMIT
The Struggles of George Smith

M. D. Entwistle

First Edition - May 2021
ISBN-13: 978-0-9547213-3-6

After a relatively conventional upbringing and a liberal education in North East Scotland, George Smith (1827-1876) voluntarily became a vagabond and took to the road plying his trade as a wandering artist, living wherever he saw fit to lay his head. He quickly learned that the vile hand of tyranny had a different idea, and he was repeatedly run out of town.

Eventually arriving in the English Lake District, he settled on Dodd Fell, a protuberance on the mountain of Skiddaw, where his unorthodox choice of home—a 'nest' between forest and crag—earned him the soubriquet of "Skiddaw Hermit."

Dressed only in a shabby wincey shirt and trousers cut off at the knee, he eschewed all other raiment including shoes, nonchalantly travelling through the various districts barefoot and half-clad whatever the weather. Throughout his travels he was persecuted for his unique appearance and wild antics, and once again found himself moved on from place to place.

Receiving a vast amount of publicity for his eccentricities and strange way of life, notoriety led him to be cruelly misjudged as a troublesome and truculent character. Thereafter deemed a terror to the Lake District, he was arrested numerous times for apparent drunken and violent behaviour, and was frequently incarcerated in the gaols of Cumberland and Westmorland.

What the authorities failed to recognise was the fact that Smith suffered from mental health issues, and his imprisonment was therefore unjust—a crucial point which makes his story far more poignant.

The vicious circle continued, but, eventually, at Bowness Bay on the shores of Windermere he was converted after hearing a preacher of the Gospel, and persuaded to reject his demi-savage life before making a return to conventional society.

However, this did not last long and his nomadic existence prevailed; he subsequently wandered home to Scotland where he was committed to an asylum on the recommendation of his sister. From hereon in Smith's life took a grave turn for the worse when, in time, he was detained for the term of his natural life, never to walk through the Highland glens or smell the mountain heather again.

The tragic clash between his quest for a free life among the beauties of Nature and the strict confinement of his involuntary detention within the granite walls of an asylum makes for grim reading, yet highlights the antiquated perceptions of Victorian Britain towards the eternal problems endured by mankind.

M. D. Entwistle's *Skiddaw Hermit: The Struggles of George Smith* is a gritty, heart-wrenching story packed with blunt, archaic terminology referencing mental health issues and therefore reader discretion is advised.

Mark Richards - www.markrichardswalking.co.uk

MILLICAN'S CAVE - THE HOME OF ADVENTURE

INDEX

Printed in Great Britain
by Amazon